# Cuba in Transition

# Latin American Perspectives Series

Ronald H. Chilcote, Series Editor

† Available in hardcover and paperback.

# Cuba in Transition
## Crisis and Transformation

*edited by*
*Sandor Halebsky, John M. Kirk,*
*Carollee Bengelsdorf, Richard L. Harris,*
*Jean Stubbs, and Andrew Zimbalist*

**Westview Press**
*Boulder • San Francisco • Oxford*

*Latin American Perspectives Series, Number 9*

Copyright © 1992 by Westview Press, Inc.

Published in 1992 in the United States of America by Westview Press, Inc., 5500 Central Avenue, Boulder, Colorado 80301-2847, and in the United Kingdom by Westview Press, 36 Lonsdale Road, Summertown, Oxford OX2 7EW

Library of Congress Cataloging-in-Publication Data
Cuba in transition : crisis and transformation / edited by Sandor
   Halebsky, John M. Kirk, Carollee Bengelsdorf ... [et al.].
     p.   cm. — (Latin American perspectives series ; no. 9)
   Includes bibliographical references (p.   ) and index.
   ISBN 0-8133-8094-4 — ISBN 0-8133-8095-2 (pbk.)
   1. Cuba—Politics and government—1959–     . 2. Communism—Cuba—
History.  3. Cuba—Economic conditions—1959–     . 4. Cuba—Social
conditions—1959–     . I. Halebsky, Sandor. II. Kirk, John M., 1951–     .
III. Bengelsdorf, Carollee.  IV. Series.
F1788.C816  1992
320.97291—dc20
                                                                    91-41764
                                                                       CIP

Printed and bound in the United States of America

The paper used in this publication meets the requirements
of the American National Standard for Permanence of Paper
for Printed Library Materials Z39.48-1984.

10    9    8    7    6    5    4    3    2

# Contents

# Foreword

The collapse of the socialist economies of Eastern Europe and the retreat of the Soviet Union from central planning and its drift toward a market economy have led many observers to predict the demise of Cuban socialism. Cuba's socialism has evolved in a different form, however, and although changes can be anticipated, the revolution probably will not only remain intact but will also continue to evolve in unique and imaginative ways. Even a conservative critic, Sergio Roca, has affirmed that the revolution "is long consolidated and unquestionably strong . . . firmly entrenched and well defended" (see his contribution to this volume). Other contributors agree with this assessment.

The recent unification of Germany has deprived Cuba of a reliable trading partner, and under its trade agreement with Moscow, Cuba will pay more for Soviet petroleum and receive less for its sugar. Thirty years ago the Cuban revolution came to power in the face of official U.S. opposition, an abortive Bay of Pigs invasion, and an economic embargo. Cuba adjusted by transferring most of its commerce and financial flows to the Soviet Union and Eastern Europe. The adjustment underway in the early 1990s must confront both the U.S. embargo and changing Soviet-Cuban relations, and Cuba has implemented an emergency program of energy reduction and food rationing. Although Cubans long ago learned to deal with shortages and to make sacrifices no matter what the difficulties of the revolution, the current crisis necessitates new thinking, the raising of new questions, and the reworking of old ideas in creative and refreshing ways. The issues at hand include not only economic adjustments but the search for political space and the enhancement of the notable social advances of the revolution.

The scholars whose work makes up this volume have observed Cuba for many years, some having followed the revolution since it came to power in 1959. They have visited Cuba and carried out careful research there. Some of them bring new findings based on recent visits—for example, Gayle McGarrity on the question of race and Sheryl Lutjens on democracy and bureaucracy—whereas others such as Richard Harris, Nelson Valdés, and Andrew Zimbalist offer retrospective views of the revolution, its origins, and the difficulties in its evolution to the present day. Although these chapters emphasize the accomplishments of the past generation—especially in health care, education, and social service—they also anticipate questions related to the difficult path ahead as Cuba prepares to confront changing trade relations, a large external debt, and domestic shortages in material goods.

Intellectuals and academicians within Cuba are also involved in assessing these issues, and the academic quality of their work has gradually improved over the years. Yet Cuban scholars necessarily focus on policy questions as they debate the past successes and failures and search for a better society in the face of the seemingly insurmountable demands of the international capitalist order. A forthcoming companion volume in the Latin American Perspectives Series of Westview Press, *The Cuban Revolution into the 1990s*, edited by Juan Antonio Blanco, will bring together some Cuban perspectives on these questions.

The organization of this book involved substantial effort. Sandor Halebsky and John M. Kirk compiled the present volume, and the editors of the journal *Latin American Perspectives* organized, translated, and edited the companion volume. The result is a remarkable collection of scholarly, easily accessible, and up-to-date analyses based on close observation of and research on rapidly changing developments in contemporary Cuba.

*Ronald H. Chilcote*

# Acknowledgments

The chapters of this book are based on papers that were delivered at a conference on Cuba, "Thirty Years of the Cuban Revolution: An Assessment," held in Halifax, Nova Scotia, in November 1989. Without the generous assistance of a variety of institutions, this assessment of three decades of the Cuban revolutionary process would clearly have been impossible. Of particular importance was the generous assistance provided by the Ford and MacArthur foundations. Significant support was also provided by Saint Mary's University and its International Education Centre, Dalhousie University and its Lester Pearson Institute, Mount St. Vincent University, and the Department of External Affairs of the Government of Canada. The conference was organized under the umbrella of the Canadian Association of Latin American and Caribbean Studies.

On an individual level, thanks are due to the Conference Advisory Committee, whose members provided much-needed advice and words of encouragement: Max Azicri, Claes Brundenius, Jorge I. Domínguez, Saul Landau, Louis A. Pérez, Archibald R.M. Ritter, Rebecca Scott, Marifeli Pérez-Stable, Wayne S. Smith, Nelson P. Valdés, and Andrew Zimbalist. Earlier useful assistance was provided by Carmelo Mesa-Lago. Just as important was the army of unnamed volunteers who performed a myriad of tasks to make the conference a success.

The preparation of the actual manuscript was more difficult than it should have been, in part because of changing events in Cuba—not to mention difficulties inherent in translating the variety of word-processing systems used. Our sincere thanks in this regard are due to Anne Creaser, Wanda Hebb, Marie Richard, and John Barnstead.

Finally we would like to thank Ron Chilcote of the University of California–Riverside and Barbara Ellington of Westview Press for having had faith in this project at a time when changes in other socialist systems must have made it appear a somewhat whimsical idea.

*Sandor Halebsky*
*John M. Kirk*

# Introduction

## Sandor Halebsky and John M. Kirk

To all who have followed recent developments in Cuba it is clear that the country is in crisis—to no small extent because of eventful changes in Eastern Europe and, more significantly, within the Soviet Union. Some 70–75 percent of Cuba's trade was tied to the Soviet Union, but the Union's dissolution into its separate republics has created uncertainty about how much trade will continue. The impact of these changes will be serious. Indeed, Cuba received only one-third of promised oil shipments for 1991. The withdrawal of Soviet military aid in September 1991 further underlined the need for Cuba to rapidly enact contingency plans if the revolutionary process is to survive.

Cuba in the early 1990s is facing the most serious of challenges to its revolutionary trajectory. It has passed from its much-vaunted rectification process to what the Cuban government has referred to as the "special period," and the country is now on the verge of another phase known as "option zero"—in which zero assistance and zero trade will become the norm. Understandably, "option zero" will mean economic hardship for all Cubans; already many items not previously rationed have been placed on the *libreta*, while further reductions in rations have been made. Moreover, it will undoubtedly lead to the greatest internal political challenge, as the revolutionary government seeks to learn from the demise of socialist governments elsewhere.

The thesis of this collection is that Cuba is—of necessity—in a state of transition. The Soviet model of development, on which Cuba has depended to an unhealthy degree for nearly three decades, is widely discredited (indeed, since 1986 the Cubans have been seeking to "rectify" its influence), and Cuba now finds itself in a state of crisis-management.

As Fidel Castro himself has noted, the political model also needs to be made more responsive to the Cuban masses, in essence to reflect better their aspirations (and political maturity) after thirty-two years of the revolutionary process.

The question remains, however, as to how this necessary transformation is to occur—or which areas in fact need significant change or improvement. This volume seeks to provide an answer to this question, suggesting facets of Cuba's development model that need to be transformed. The collective opinion would appear to be that significant improvement has occurred over the last three decades but that clearly visible and serious problems still remain to be addressed. At a time when the model of the erstwhile "Soviet bloc" has been cast to one side, and the socialist model is being questioned throughout the world, this collection seeks to analyze the Cuban version and assess its strengths and weaknesses.

The chapters presented here are significantly updated versions of papers that were presented at an international conference on Cuba, "Thirty Years of the Cuban Revolution: An Assessment," held in November 1989 in Halifax, Nova Scotia, Canada. Approximately four hundred scholars—including most of the leading students of Cuban affairs—principally from North America but also from Europe, Latin America, Australia, and Africa, participated in the conference, with about 170 active presenters in some forty sessions. The considerable number of participants and sessions, the frank and wide-ranging discussion (which included the contribution of a goodly number of Cuban exiles sharply critical of the revolutionary experience), and the spirit of Nova Scotia glasnost all contributed to making this a historic event in the field of Cuban studies.

The conference provided a unique opportunity in the thirtieth year of the Cuban revolution to assess the revolution's efforts at societal transformation as well as the growing number of dilemmas it faced. Occurring at a time of severe stress and change, the conference was both an occasion for taking stock of past strategies and accomplishments as well as a time for a searching examination of the contemporary Cuban reality—in its political, economic, social, cultural, and international dimensions. For all who gathered in those intense days of discussion and debate (complete with cultural performances and video festival, bomb scares and death threats), it proved a memorable experience.

This volume owes its development to that conference and to the considerable changes and debate that have been taking place within Cuba in the early 1990s. Because the developments in Cuba are too recent to have as yet received any substantial analysis, there is a pressing need to make clear a number of the important problems and issues that Cuba faces today, as well as something of their character and origin, and the difficulties that remain even in areas of substantial accomplishment. This volume addresses these concerns, thereby seeking to provide a wide-ranging review and analysis crucial to understanding Cuba today—and the policies and changes that will take shape in the mid-1990s.

All of the chapters in this book reflect three of the four Halifax conference dimensions: the political, the economic, and the social. Essays in the fourth area, international relations, have been published as a separate volume,[1] and conference contributions by scholars from Cuba were published in the Spring 1991 issue of *Latin American Perspectives* and will also appear in book form.[2] All chapters have been substantially revised and updated in order to better reflect the significant debate and change that have been and are being enacted in Cuba.

The focus of the chapters that follow is directed toward providing a scholarly account of the reality of some key current dilemmas in Cuba and furthering an understanding of the processes and struggles for socialist transformation. By focusing on these dilemmas, however, we appear to leave untreated the vast steps taken over more than three decades to transform and improve the quality of life for the large majority of Cubans. The achievements of the revolution are many, and they are substantial—as can be seen by any comparative analysis of basic socioeconomic indices. Cuba's achievements are not confined to the well-being of its own people; Cuba has generously extended assistance to other less fortunate Third World nations. To a large extent, however, these matters have been considered elsewhere, and a number of the contributors to the present volume have contributed to recent works that considers this aspect of the Cuban revolutionary experience.[3]

The revolutionary government is at its most critical point since the October 1962 Missile Crisis, and this book addresses the dilemmas and problems faced by Cuba at this particular historical juncture and as the country seeks to resolve these problems in ways true to its socialist vision. The contributions, although diverse in their concerns, share a sense of the interplay of external economic and political forces with internal policies. They reflect the ways in which the predominance of a world capitalist economy, the decline of the socialist bloc, and Cuba's historical economic and political dependence have all contributed to the current circumstances and constrain strategic policy choices. At the same time, the authors recognize how Cuba's efforts at radical transformation—shaped by its response to external forces, its distinctive political culture, and its commitment to Marxist-Leninism—have created political, organizational, and economic structures that currently impede the nation's development. The decade of the 1990s will witness Cuba's massive and resolute effort to adjust to these circumstances and in important ways to attempt to overcome them. The extent to which this attempt will free the country from the constraints of the structures and practices created by the revolution while allowing it to retain its socialist commitment is still to be determined.

In Part 1, The Search for Political and Organizational Forms, the contributors discuss fundamental political and organizational issues in Cuba's effort to create a socialist society and to respond to current difficulties. The overarching concerns of the contributors are the relationship between democracy and socialism, excessive bureaucratization and centralization, and the retention and expansion of socialist principles and advances. These issues are considered within the context of the current period of economic constraint and rectification.

The relationship between Cuba's current economic development policies and the rectification process is at the crux of the opening and provocative chapter by James F. Petras and Morris H. Morley. The authors critique Cuba's effort to succeed in the global economy and interpret the rectification campaign negatively in that context. Max Azicri provides a discursive treatment of the rectification process, Sheryl L. Lutjens discusses socialist democracy and its development, and Richard Harris focuses on the problems of bureaucratic centralism. To varying degrees, all these interlinked issues and processes receive some consideration in each of the chapters.

Questions of economic policy and functioning have always been nettlesome issues for Cuban decision makers. Although a number of notable achievements have occurred within the Cuban economy—especially in regard to securing growth with equity, providing social services, modernizing sugar production and developing by-products, creating a capitalist goods industry, and producing a highly educated professional and labor sector, among other accomplishments—ongoing shortcomings and recent developments have created severe economic problems for the nation. Cuba faces the sharp disruption of economic relations with the socialist bloc and decreasing assistance from the Soviet Union which compound the difficulties caused by problems in productivity and economic management, low sugar prices, deteriorating terms of exchange, a growing debt, and the inability to develop a sizable competitive export sector.

The changes and difficulties in Cuba's economic circumstances provide the context for the contributions to the second section of the volume, Whither the Cuban Economy? These chapters reflect the disparate assessments that have characterized scholarship on the Cuban economy over the years. They all highlight how changes in the "international environment within which Cuba must exist" (Archibald R.M. Ritter) have increased Cuba's economic difficulties and necessitated adjustments. Sergio G. Roca notes the weaknesses that have been exhibited by the

Cuban economy and the current absence of an overall strategy or model for the economy and its management. He stresses the importance of moving from charismatic to more routinized or rational forms of planning and economic organization. In a searching review, Archibald R.M. Ritter outlines the shortcomings of the Cuban economy and the forces that are pushing it toward fundamental change. He concludes with a series of recommended institutional and policy changes involving, among others, expansion of the private sector, greater decentralization in decision making, and expansion of market mechanisms and reliance on market forces. Among other benefits, these changes will help to reinstate Cuba in the global economy. Gareth Jenkins's summary overview of the Cuban economy and its successes and weaknesses concludes this section. The most distinctive feature of his chapter is its account of the Cuban effort to greatly expand its tourist industry, given its potential for foreign exchange earnings. This plus efforts at expanding the biotechnology sector and basic food production are the principle areas of current Cuban economic concentration.

Although political and economic structures and policies are of vital importance in the life of a nation and its people, analysis of these structures and policies sheds little direct light on the personal world and everyday life of the individual. The usual treatment of the social and cultural properties of contemporary Cuban society—the attention to health care, education, nutrition, and the like—provides a somewhat clearer sense of personal circumstances and experiences. Yet even such a treatment is somewhat removed from the more intimate and personal aspects of individual life. Accounts of Cuba's social policies and achievements are now readily available.[4] Little attention has been given, however, to the more intimate arenas of personal life in which dilemmas or shortcomings are still present—the focus of the last section of this volume.

The chapters in this section also make clear the link between social policy and personal experience, as well as the disparities between policy and outcome and between reality and a socialist vision. They thus raise questions concerning the insufficiently revolutionary—or too traditional—orientation in the Cuban approach to matters of family, sexuality, and race.

Carollee Bengelsdorf and Jean Stubbs open the section with a thoughtful introduction that urges us to recognize both the complexity and the multifaceted character of each dimension of Cuban social life and experience, as well as of political and economic reality. The authors emphasize the impossibility of one summary judgment or assessment covering each of these spheres. They also point to the social advances as well as traditional continuities that arise at times in Cuban social policy.

Marguerite G. Rosenthal analyzes the high incidence and the circumstances of single mothers and presents actual or possible social and economic policies to ameliorate their plight. Lois M. Smith describes sexual policy and codes and the gaps between knowledge and behavior and policy and between male and female orientations. Gayle L. McGarrity focuses on evidence that racism persists, although individual attitudes and policy generally deny or ignore this reality.

The section and the volume concludes with Nelson P. Valdés's penetrating analysis of Cuban political culture. He describes the underlying fundamental "codes" that he suggests have characterized Cuban political culture and personality and hence have shaped orientations and behavior both before and after the revolution. He thus shows the common element in otherwise sharply divergent views and illuminates the details of action and belief in light of a much more general and fundamental reality.

The Cuban effort at revolutionary transformation is clearly at a crucial juncture. It is evident to most scholars, however, that the nation seeks to respond to its current problems in ways that are consistent with the values, goals, and socialist vision that have characterized the last three decades. Cuba disavows the competitive, individualistic, profit-driven, ruthless, materialist, and amoral society that is at the heart of capitalism. It believes that high levels of performance, commitment, and development are achievable in a society structured and guided in significantly different ways from those that characterize the Western industrial nations. Cuba seeks, as it has for more than thirty years, a humane society in which all of its members may live lives of dignity and be assured of place, respect, security, and efficacy. The value of the present volume, as of the conference on which it is based, is that it forces us to recognize and ponder an alternate route to such ends.

Cuba's attempt to come to terms with a troubling set of dilemmas is thus at odds with the wholesale jettisoning of basic principles, as has happened in Eastern Europe. We urge caution upon those who would see Cuba as "another Poland," Fidel Castro as "another Ceausescu," or the country as another debt-ridden Latin American nation. Cuba is too complex, its historical roots too singular, and its geopolitical situation too unique for one-dimensional analyses to apply.

Critics of the Cuban revolutionary process have understandably been overjoyed as dictators such as Ceausescu and Honecker were replaced in Eastern Europe, and some predicted that exiles would be eating *lechón asado* (roast pork) in Havana by Christmas of 1990. They pointed out that the socialist system is essentially flawed (conveniently overlooking the lack of success of capitalism in most of the developing world) and that Cuba's own brand of socialism was doomed to fall under the weight of its own errors. Although many problems result from Cuba's brand of socialism (as can be seen in this volume), such a facile analysis ignores the impact of U.S. enmity on Cuba—as well as the strength of Cuba's socialist society.

The blind spot toward Cuba that permeates U.S. thinking results in ignorance about this small (population of under 11 million people) island. A fitting epitaph for the Halifax conference—but also, more important, as a commentary on the U.S. response to Cuba—was the comment of an exiled scholar who said to a colleague from Cuba, "How stupid it all is. . . . We're only ninety miles apart, and yet we have to come two thousand miles north in order to engage in a civilized discussion." He was, sadly, correct.

With the goal of disseminating challenging and thought-provoking insights into the dilemmas and problems facing revolutionary Cuba, we hope that in some small way this collection will help to promote a more balanced analysis on the part of Cuba-watchers and possibly allow political leaders to move from rhetoric to dialogue.

## Notes

1. H. Michael Erisman and John M. Kirk, eds., *Cuban Foreign Policy Confronts a New International Order* (Boulder, Colo.: Lynne Rienner, 1991).

2. Juan Antonio Blanco, ed., *The Cuban Revolution into the 1990s* (Boulder, Colo.: Westview, forthcoming).

3. See, for example, Philip Brenner et al., eds., *The Cuba Reader: The Making of a Revolution* (New York: Grove Press, 1989); William A. Chaffee, Jr., and Gary Prevost, eds., *Cuba: A Different America* (Totowa, N.J.: Rowman and Littlefield, 1989); Sandor Halebsky and John M. Kirk, eds., *Cuba: Twenty-Five Years of Revolution, 1959–1984* (New York: Praeger, 1985), and *Transformation and Struggle: Cuba Faces the 1990s* (New York: Praeger, 1990); and Andrew Zimbalist, ed., *Cuba's Socialist Economy: Toward the 1990s* (Boulder, Colo.: Lynne Rienner, 1987).

4. See citations in note 3.

# PART 1
# The Search for Political and Organizational Forms

# Introduction to Part 1

*Richard L. Harris*

Cuba's political development has been and continues to be unique. It is the first nation to have undergone a socialist revolution in the Western Hemisphere, and it is the only country in the region with a socialist regime today. In contrast to existing socialist and former socialist regimes that have embarked on a course of development that involves the widespread introduction of capitalist relations of production and liberal democratic forms of government, Cuba's socialist regime has reaffirmed its commitment to socialism and has made it clear that it will not adopt the kind of economic and political reforms that have been introduced in the Soviet Union and Eastern Europe. Cuba also has the distinction of being the only country in the hemisphere that has been led by the same political leader for the last three decades, which helps to explain why the Cuban revolution, more than any other revolution in the twentieth century, tends to be identified with one man—Fidel Castro.

Cuba's uniqueness and exceptionalism have been the subjects of considerable analysis and debate, and the chapters in this volume provide further evidence of this. Yet Cuba's political development since the triumph of the revolutionary insurrection in 1959 has also been shaped, as has the development of many Third World countries, by both international and internal conditions that are linked to its past history of capitalist underdevelopment. Therefore, many of the unique and exceptional characteristics of its socialist regime are in fact Cuba's particular responses to the kinds of problems confronted by many Third World countries.

Cuba's political development since 1959 reflects the regime's response to a series of problems and opportunities associated with the country's insertion in the larger international order. The two chapters that follow by James F. Petras and Morris H. Morley (Chapter 1) and Maz Azicri (Chapter 2), focus on this relationship. They examine the extent to which the regime's current and past policies have been shaped by the changing international context. Petras and Morley analyze the impact of changes in the socialist community and the international economy on Cuba's foreign and domestic policies. They argue that Cuba's political leadership is trying to restructure the economy and curb domestic consumption so the country can survive the dismantling of the international socialist community and the reorientation of the Soviet Union's economic relations with Cuba. In the same vein, Max Azicri examines the regime's ongoing rectification campaign in relation to recent external developments that have affected Cuba's economic and political security, particularly the recent transformations in Eastern Europe and the increasing efforts of the U.S. government to isolate Cuba internationally and destabilize its economy. Azicri sees the rectification campaign as both a response to the country's economic crisis and a defense of traditional Marxism-Leninism on the part of the Cuban leadership, whereas Petras and Morley see it as part of a larger strategy to create a new accumulation model and restructure the country's economy so it can survive the disintegration of the socialist economic community and compete in the international market.

The adjustments being made by the regime in response to the country's changing international environment and economic difficulties have produced tensions and pressures at various levels of both the state and the economy. Petras and Morley argue that the current efforts of the regime to restructure the economy involve forging an alliance between the "top" and "bottom" strata of Cuban society against the incipient petty bourgeois elements in the "middle" stratum. The regime seeks to forge this alliance, they argue, in order to impose austerity measures on the population, curb the growth of corruption and bureaucratic abuses, increase labor productivity and discipline, and reorient the economy away from production for internal consumption toward the production of exports capable of bringing in badly needed hard currency. Petras and Morley link the current campaign against managerial abuses, corruption, and bourgeois tendencies to the political leadership's efforts to forestall large-scale popular discontent stemming from the imposition of austerity measures and the reduction of consumption. Azicri also contends that as goods have become more scarce and the need for increased productivity has grown, the regime has been faced with no alternative other than to return to a reliance on moral incentives and *conciencia comunista* (Communist consciousness) to motivate the work force and offset discontent over the decline in consumption.

All the chapters in Part 1 address the problems resulting from the excessive bureaucratization of Cuban society. Azicri notes that the state bureaucracy in Cuba grew two-and-a-half times between 1973 and 1984, despite a continuing effort on the part of the regime to curb the bureaucratization of Cuban society and increase popular participation in planning and administration. Sheryl L. Lutjens' focuses on the relationship between popular participation and the state bureaucracy in Cuba and examines the efforts that have been undertaken since the 1970s to democratize the political system through the institutionalization of elections and various forms of popular participation at the local government level. Lutjens argues that the structures of *Poder Popular* (People's Power) were introduced largely to counterbalance the bureaucratization of the governmental system rather than to open up the political process and increase popular participation in the formulation of state policies and the selection of the country's political leadership. This use of popular participation as an antidote to bureaucratic centralism rather than as a means for empowering the people calls into question the democratizing potential of the regime. In fact, the regime's commitment to maintaining the present single-party system, restrictions on political opposition, and the predominant role played by Castro all appear to preclude a more fundamental democratization of the political system in the near future.

Nevertheless, as Lutjens notes, democracy has become an important issue in contemporary Marxist theory and socialist political thought. The collapse of the state socialist regimes in Eastern Europe and the democratic reforms that have been introduced in the Soviet Union have provoked a reconsideration of the relationship between democracy and socialism. Cuba has not escaped this reconsideration of the democratic potential of socialism, even though the political leadership has asserted that there is no need for Cuba to follow the course of development being pursued by the Soviet Union. Thus, political debate has begun to surface over the need to increase popular participation, strengthen the organs of People's Power, and democratize the internal structure of the party. In this regard, Azicri's chapter reveals that the preparations for the Fourth Congress of the Communist party of Cuba in 1991 opened the doors to public criticism of the regime's deficiencies and discussion of changes in the political system. Two major themes, however, were excluded from the public debate: the socialist nature of the regime, and the single-party system.

All the authors suggest that the verticalism, bureaucratism, and vanguardism that characterize Cuba's single-party–dominated political system pose serious obstacles to the democratization of the country's centralized state apparatus and the efficient performance of its centrally planned economy. The development of effective forms of democratic organization and participation have been blocked by over three decades of reliance on a top-down approach to decisionmaking and personnel selection, the substitution of bureaucratic methods and procedures in place of democratic processes, and the continued use of authoritarian capitalist forms of organization and management in the state enterprises.

Although the regime has encouraged limited forms of worker participation in the management and planning of Cuba's state enterprises and limited forms of popular participation in Cuba's governmental institutions at the local level, the development of democratic forms of organization in both the economic and political spheres is still at an embryonic stage in contemporary Cuba. The chapter by Richard Harris on Cuba's organizational development arrives at this conclusion. Harris also suggests that the elimination of private property in Cuba has not guaranteed the development of socialism because capitalist forms of organization and management continue to be used by the new regime and the development of genuine (democratic) socialist forms of organization and management has been hindered by the continued reliance on capitalist relations of production and bureaucratic centralism. Harris contends that the regime has neglected to develop socialist forms of organization, which entail worker self-management and democratic forms of planning. Unless this type of organizational transformation takes place, Harris argues that increasing bureaucratization or the restoration of capitalist relations of production will occur in Cuba.

In sum, Part 1 addresses fundamental questions about the development of revolutionary Cuba's political system. For more than three decades, Cuba has served as a model for progressive forces around the world. Today the democratic potential of the regime is being questioned, as is its ability to survive in the face of increasing economic difficulties and the collapse of the socialist economic community. In other words, the very survival of the regime is in doubt due to the international crisis of socialism, Cuba's relative isolation in the face of increasing U.S. hostility, and the internal problems that plague its political system and economy. It remains an open question as to whether Cuba's socialist regime will overcome its present difficulties and continue to develop in a socialist direction. The authors in Part 1 provide tentative answers to this question based on their analyses of the last three decades of Cuba's political development and the current political and economic conditions. However, the questions now being asked about Cuba's future course of development can only be answered definitively by the Cuban people and their leaders as they respond to the challenges and problems facing their country in the decade of the 1990s.

# 1

# Cuban Socialism: Rectification and the New Model of Accumulation

*James F. Petras and Morris H. Morley*

The setting for an understanding of Cuban development in the 1990s is the basic shift from dynamic growth to economic stagnation and austerity. The decade-and-a-half between 1970 and 1985 was a period of economic growth, expanding consumption, liberalized markets, consumer spending, and generous Soviet aid. But the structure of the Cuban economy remained basically unchanged: In the absence of new export industries, excessive dependence on volatile primary commodity exports to finance imports necessary for producing goods for domestic consumption continued unabated; market diversification was not possible because of dependence on fulfilling commitments to the USSR and Eastern Europe, and efforts made were thus unsuccessful; and sugar sales and oil re-exports to the Soviet Union continued to predominate in the external sector.

Beginning in the mid-1980s, these persistent structural vulnerabilities converged with shifts in the international environment to produce a marked downturn in the Cuban economy, generating a number of political, economic, and social changes by the revolutionary leadership: Centralized political control at the top was matched by widespread criticism from the lowest-ranking middle-level bureaucrats, a more centralized direction of the macroeconomy and increasingly decentralized management at the microeconomic level, moralization campaigns attacking inequality and corruption, and the initiation of a new period of austerity.

Preceding and paralleling these changes was a major internal policy debate over how best to confront Cuba's economic stagnation and its hard currency balance-of-payments problem. On the one side were those who argued for greater integration into COMECON and for the need to more closely approximate the new Soviet model (economic liberalism and political openness) unfolding under Mikhail Gorbachev. On the other side were those, including Fidel Castro, who countered that combining political openness with economic austerity could provoke serious political polarization and the consequent weakening of the revolutionary leadership. This latter argument carried the day. Castro's decision to tighten up the pre-1985 "openings" while Gorbachev moved in the opposite direction reflects the Cuban leadership's different evaluation of the international political-economic setting (continued U.S. hostility) and the impact of the post-1985 economic crisis. For the Cubans, the declining external sector is not a propitious conjuncture for internal liberalization because the latter may upset the existing social equilibrium. Nonetheless, whereas restrictions on domestic market activity may have political payoffs and provide symbolic social gratification, they still do not address the unfilled economic needs resulting from the incapacity of the state distribution system to provide goods and services the private sector supplied—even if at a certain political cost.

Against the background of this economic crunch—the need to export and become more globally competitive—Castro presented a major critique of the functioning of the party and the state institutions in early December 1986. In the course of the speech, he attacked the key problems of labor indiscipline, low productivity, and high costs (over-inflated payrolls and resource squandering).[1] But he neglected to explore perhaps the most critical source of the absence of motivation: the political structures that centralize power and decisionmaking at the top and alienate workers who thus lack the power to implant their own decisions and set their own levels of work and rewards.

In late December 1986, the revolutionary regime established the context for political rectification and recentralization-decentralization with the announcement of an austerity program that involved cuts in consumer goods, price increases, and the elimination of automatic wage bonuses and bureaucratic perks.[2] The new economic sacrifices were not to be accompanied by greater political openness in order to avoid the likelihood of public protest and a weakening of regime authority. To counteract internal pressures for greater centralized planning and economic market mechanisms, Castro responded with an egalitarian moralistic approach; to compensate for external weaknesses and possible declining Soviet subsidies, he emphasized the necessity of labor discipline. By balancing consumer cutbacks with the elimination of some bureaucratic and managerial perks, the government hoped to forge a new internal consensus.[3]

Early in June 1987, Castro replaced the editor of *Granma*, and the press began to attack state managers. Popular forums to express mass discontent with corruption were encouraged, and reports on inadequate services were publicly aired. Anticorruption campaigns against high officials were launched. Castro returned to a kind of selective glasnost, an alliance of the top and bottom against the middle. Even the top elite was not immune, although the elite structure remained intact. Mass populace mobilization to attack middle levels of power became the basis for relegitimizing the leadership. This policy weakened the intermediary sectors, strengthened the political elite, and defused popular discontent. Openness was directed toward strengthening state policy by producing focused objects of criticism. But although black marketeers, currency speculators, and self-aggrandizing bureaucrats were all worthy targets of opprobrium,[4] the government again refused to confront the deeper structural issues to explain why long-standing, senior officials such as General Arnaldo Ochoa resorted to counterrevolutionary or corrupt activities. The leadership has failed to present systematic explanations for such extravagances and "lack of revolutionary education." Yet if these officials were appointed or approved by Castro, their actions are his responsibility, or at least that of the system by which they are selected, promoted, and protected.

Meanwhile, according to Castro, the shortage of hard currency, decreasing imports from market economies, foreign debt payments, and the absence of major new sources of funding dictate the continuation of the austerity program in the 1990s. At the same time, liberalization has not been totally eliminated. Rectification did not mark the end of the private sector in Cuba. As many as fifty thousand workers are employed in the private sector despite the prohibition on unlicensed individuals that has led to an erosion of services to the public, causing widespread shortages and discontent.[5] Although the regime has eliminated the 250 private markets that were opened in 1980, it has also promoted private farms in the form of incentives (improved water supplies, access to machinery, and similar enticements), in order to increase food production for the domestic market.[6] Finally, accompanying the regime's centralization of the economy in order to limit imports and impose austerity so as to save hard currency has been its tendency to liberalize the export tourist sector in the search for such currency.

In his speech to the Cuban people on July 26, 1988 (the thirty-fifth anniversary of the Moncada uprising), Castro articulated two major themes: The need to accumulate hard currency earnings constitutes the instrumental and practical basis for the shift from material to "moral" incentives; and work is part of an individual's collective responsibility to society and the means for increasing collective rather than individual welfare, blending pragmatic short-term economic interests with long-term ideological concerns.[7]

## Prelude to Rectification

In the late 1970s to mid-1980s, as Latin America's market economies sank in a deepening crisis of negative growth and triple-digit inflation and incomes plummeted, Cuba's noninflationary growth was an island of sanity and stability. Industrial, agricultural, and material products continued to experience impressive annual growth rates. Between 1980 and 1985, real Gross Social Product (GSP) increased at an average annual rate of approximately 7 percent, in striking contrast to a 1.7 percent yearly decline in the rest of the hemisphere's real per capita Gross Domestic Product (GDP). In post-1970s Cuba, a large number of new industries emerged, exports diversified, and expanded health and educational services lowered infant mortality rates, increased life expectancy, and created a more skilled labor force.[8]

Since the end of the era of rapid expansion, however, real economic growth rates have been either minimal or negative—a decline that cannot be understood without reference to the liberalization policies of the pre-1985 period. The dynamic growth decade of 1976 to 1985 was based on Cuba's deepening external dependence on the global economy. Consequently, shifts in the behavior of international economic forces after 1985 adversely affected Cuba as well as (albeit to a much greater extent) the rest of Latin America. Andrew Zimbalist details these factors and their impact on the Cuban economy.

Low sugar prices, plummeting petroleum prices, devastation from Hurricane Kate, several consecutive years of intensifying drought, drastic dollar devaluation, the tightening U.S. blockade, growing protectionism in Western markets—all combined in 1986 to reduce Cuba's hard currency earnings by nearly 50 percent or $600 million. Cuba's failure at the summer 1986 Paris Club negotiations to obtain a new $300 million loan led to severe shortages of needed imported inputs. The ensuing shortages of outputs greatly diminished the possibilities for material incentives to function properly. This fact provides the objective backdrop to the subjective re-examination of the use of material and moral incentives.[9]

Although external factors provoked the "subjective re-examination," the internal sociopolitical configuration of power was also deeply implicated, not only in the policy changes but also in developing the overall orientation of the regime in the period preceding rectification; thus, it also figures in the reformulation of policy. Moreover, the issues raised went far beyond problems of incentives—as important as they are—and touched on the style of life, institutions, and behavior of the social structure from top to bottom. This suggests that the economic policies pursued in Cuba between 1975 and 1985 had a profound impact in transforming Cuban structures and its value system and that these transformations, at both the internal and external levels, created a series of contradictions that the 1986 Party Communist Congress began to confront.

In the 1970s Cuba initiated an economic liberalization program based on market mechanisms, material incentives, financial accountability, private consumer markets, and greater managerial-ministerial autonomy within the overall pattern of central planning. These internal changes were accompanied by increasing ties to external financial trade markets, which secured greater material rewards but within a framework of weak or nonexistent democratic worker accountability—thus giving license to the emergence of a new class of privileged managers, party functionaries, and globe-trotting technocrats on expense accounts and with access to hard currency. These social strata were willing and able to secure high-priced consumer goods in the free market and hard currency stores. Although the economy was expanding, the political and social conse-quences of these inequalities were mitigated by general increases in incomes across the class spectrum. Worker salaries and consumption levels increased—although at a more modest rate—along with those of the new class of entrepreneurs, technocrats, and managers.

However, the economic crunch of the mid-1980s rendered this situation intolerable—the conditions and lifestyles of the organizers and principal beneficiaries of economic liberalization stood in stark contrast to the austerity demands imposed on the majority of the labor force. Moreover, the negative impact of this crunch extended to the most productive sectors of the economy. Within the top echelons of the Cuban social structure, one can identify two groups: (1) those tied to domestic production who derive their income from increasing productivity, eliciting worker-management cooperation, and securing inputs and markets—in other words, those able to function within the discipline of the productive process; and (2) those tied to the re-export of imported commodities (mainly sugar and petroleum) who are engaged in the "buying and selling" process and act as intermediaries among different producers. This latter group thrives on market speculation and, in time of windfall profits, finances and stimulates greater levels of imports and consumption. During the 1970s and early 1980s, the two groups functioned in tandem, with the incomes of one source financing the other. Nevertheless, the easy sources of income generated by buying and selling weakened market discipline and postponed needed structural reforms while simultaneously intensifying Cuba's dependence on overseas suppliers and financiers. The post-1985 economic crisis initially affected the comprador sector but soon reverberated throughout the economy, also affecting the productive sectors.

It was within this context of a shift in the balance of socioeconomic forces—between compradores and producers—that Castro launched his rectification program. It essentially reflected an effort to strengthen the productive classes in the face of a faltering performance by the compradores. Unregulated compradorism is incompatible with the social relations of industrial production, most of all in the context of austerity and a class-conscious working class. At the social-psychological level, the uneven gains undermine social solidarity and the notion of common sacrifice; at the structural level, they undermine and distort resource flows from public to private sectors, weakening the calculations of investment decision makers and disrupting the productive process.

The regime targeted the free-wheeling style associated with the compradores for a concentrated attack: Not only the farmers' markets and private home builders but also the high-spending consumers, many of whom were able to accumulate small fortunes through their unrestricted external ties, were targeted. The July 1989 trial of the narco-General Arnaldo Ochoa publicly exposed the self-aggrandizing behavior emblematic of an entire stratum of ministerial compradores who linked "legitimate" comprador activity to illicit profiteering.

The rectification process launched by Castro was based on his effort to mobilize the productive classes against the compradores: to subordinate the latter to the former while mobilizing both for a relaunching into the world market. Rectification involved "reforms" because although the farmers' free markets were abolished, the state-controlled parallel market was left untouched.[10] The reforms led to personnel changes in some cases, but the vertical control structure was retained; reforms increased the technocratic presence but tightened the central allocation of hard currency. The process of change is not a generalized shift toward some abstract notion of "centralization" but is a complex process of centralization and decentralization that focuses on strengthening the productive sector at the expense of the compradores.[11]

Although the above discussion describes one tendency in the rectification process, there is a second tendency that in many ways goes in a different direction. It explicitly takes its cues from the capitalist marketplace and conforms much more closely to the export market strategy that increasingly defines the Cuban political economy. The export sector of the Cuban economy generated a series of *corporaciones* (corporations), each with its specific economic functions. These in turn were divided into "real" and "fictitious" entities. The former included a number of mixed enterprises—joint ventures in which foreign capital predominates. The latter were dummy corporations managed by individuals who were closely linked with the principal nucleus of power in the government—the Politburo and the Ministries of Defense and Interior. These corporations were set up to evade the U.S. economic blockade and to import scarce and strategic products. (It was these fictitious corporations—out of public scrutiny—that fostered the corruption and illicit speculative activity of the Ochoa group.) Parallel to the emergence of corporate structures in the export sector is the widespread presence of highly specialized military officials in key sectors of the economy, giving the impression of a militarization of civil society. The Ochoa trial was less an effort to revert back to civil power than an attempt to rein in the absolutist power tendencies military officials tend to transfer from one sphere to the other and to affirm the principle of political party supremacy.[12]

The third feature of this tendency has been the basic shift in Cuban policymakers' views of the labor process, with increasing emphasis on learning from Japanese and U.S. managerial and organizational experiences. The Cuban approach is to retain public property ownership and introduce profit-maximizing and capitalist organizational principles. Carlos Aldana, head of the Cuban Communist party's Revolutionary Orientation Bureau, highlights the new directions in Cuban economic policy.

> We are applying Soviet economic calculation [enterprise profitability]; but within much more precise limits than in the USSR. In the basic system that will follow this sometime in the future, the Japanese and North American experience should be contemplated. Experts from the Rockefeller Group are already advising us on enterprise management. We think we should incorporate capitalist experience in the organization of production, in work payment, and in quality control. We are not going to change the system of collective property, but we will apply scientific methods in the global organization of work. We have a great deal to learn from capitalism in this sense.[13]

Thus, the shift in the Cuban model in the late 1980s represents a deepening of the liberalization process and, in the context of scarcity and austerity, an increase in technocratic and managerial power (scientific methods) over the working class. There is an explicit rejection of the populism (increases in general income and consumer goods) and job protection (paternalism) that accompanied the earlier variant of liberalization during the previous expansive decade in favor of cost efficiency and a flexible labor force (unemployment). According to Aldana,

> we have had to rectify previous lines. More than 70 decrees and decree-laws have been eliminated. The old permanent employment of workers in an enterprise is incompatible with our own modern model of economic calculation. We do not think that in production the collective will should have primacy; the work post belongs to the most qualified worker. Of course, the Cuban road to labor force efficiency does not pass through automatic unemployment as under capitalism. . . . Here we will adopt . . . gradual approaches. . . . We think there are democratic formulas in the relation between the firm and worker, as in Japan [sic], but we have already learned the error of a forced march toward socialism.

Cuban income policies, however, are to be oriented toward favoring the lower class at the expense of the new middle class.

> Our priority is to raise the welfare of these [low-income sectors]. Not as before, by raising the average level. Here there is a "middle class" that already has satisfied its necessities, including in excess, while others are confined to urban slums. It is a "middle class" that says that the revolution is going badly when it cannot conserve its level of life. They are bothered now because the priority is the popular strata, the workers who are quite below their status.[14]

It appears that the Cubans are trying to combine a progressive income policy, a strengthening of management prerogatives, and an increased emphasis on enterprise cost accounting while holding down the incomes of the middle class. Given the qualifications in the application of the reforms (on employment, for instance) and the split between increasing management authority and restricting middle-class income levels, it remains to be seen how effective the implementation will be.

### The Rectification Campaign and Cuban Development

In analyzing Cuban policy since the mid-1980s, in particular the rectification campaign launched by Fidel Castro, it is important to sort out what is ideological from what is expedient or pragmatic: which measures reflect underlying principles and methods of socialist development and which reflect adaptations to externally or internally imposed exigencies. It is necessary to examine the rectification policy in terms of whether it reflects a major historical turn involving a decision shift in the internal structure of society or is simply a product of conjunctural circumstance, subject to modification with changes in the external environment.

Several questions emerge regarding these alternative hypotheses. Did the rectification campaign result from internal struggles from below—confrontations among contending social forces over the direction of Cuban development? Or was it a product of an internal faction fight among contending elites over how to respond to economic problems in which issues of personal power and authority were mixed with or cloaked in ideological issues? Was the rectification campaign part of an effort by Castro to go back to the original roots of the revolution in the 1960s—to renew the spirit of egalitarianism, voluntarism, and idealism—or was the rectification a product of an economic crisis in which the government, left with few material resources, fell back on the moral and symbolic strengths of the revolution to implement unpopular economic measures?

To what extent has the population responded favorably to the rectification campaign? Which changes have evoked support, and which have provoked opposition? Has the Castro leadership been successful in re-creating the revolutionary mobilization of the earlier period? Or conversely, without much mobilization has the regime been able to carry out unpopular austerity programs without evoking countermobilizations?

By launching a campaign from above against some of the commonly disliked features of Cuban socialism—corruption, managerial abuses, private appropriations of public transport, and the like—the government preempted any campaign from below against the restrictive economic measures imposed by the regime (such as increases in prices, reductions in salaries, and increased costs for utilities and transport). By simultaneously attacking the profiteering of the market and the work rules and salary-bonus structure of labor, the regime neutralized the potential for large-scale discontent.

The radicalism of the rectification was localized in time and place, adding substance to the notion that it reflected the convergence of a specific set of forces. The rectification campaign was launched as the economic constraints (particularly balance of payments in convertible currency) began to fully emerge in 1985, and it intensified as the crisis continued toward the end of the 1980s. The radical measures, ostensibly based on a renewal of socialist egalitarianism, were accompanied by an aggressive effort to expand and deepen ties with capitalist regimes, especially in Latin America and Western Europe. The appeal to socialism internally was matched by the deliberate policy of relegating socialism in foreign relations to the back burner and adopting a "broad-front" strategy in Latin America that at least raised the possibility of forming an alliance with any civilian democratic regime in the region—no matter how reactionary—that had diplomatic and commercial relations with Cuba.

This apparent paradox of Cuban policy—a radical Guevarist rectification campaign at home and a broad-front hemispheric policy that surpassed the blandest formulations of local Communist parties—reflects the dual effort of the Castro leadership to lessen domestic consumption while creating a competitive export sector based on a disciplined labor force and opening markets externally. Unlike the 1960s, when radical egalitarianism was linked to an alliance with international revolutionary movements, the current campaign of sacrifice and moralization is directed toward dissimilar goals—the reduction of labor costs, the creation of nontraditional export sectors, the search for new markets to compensate for declining hard currency income, the effort to compensate for reductions in Soviet subsidies, and the development of a means of responding to increasing pressure from Western and Japanese banks to keep up debt payments. In the present conjuncture, the world market—not revolutionary politics—is in command, even as the peasant market has been abolished and socialist exhortations abound.

Unlike his Soviet and Eastern European counterparts who are also pursuing economic restructuring in order to compete in the world market, Castro has chosen the strategy of recentralization rather than decentralization, of selective criticism of middle functionaries rather than wholesale attacks on the top leadership, of cloaking the entire endeavor in the symbols of the national revolutionary past rather than in the contemporary modernist liberal rhetoric of the West. Perhaps more than the other Communist leaders—probably because of his proximity to the United States—Castro is keenly aware of the destructive and uncontrollable centrifugal forces that could be unleashed by discarding existing political structures and authority without having an alternative political base. The foreign exchange crunch provides few possibilities for sustaining private consumption, particularly of imported items. The problem involves cutting back on individual consumption and imports and increasing exports and production while retaining basic collective welfare services. Free-market rhetoric and glasnost are perceived by Castro as ideologies and practices compatible with a period of expanding consumption and social consensus, which is why they were tolerated and promoted to some extent during the decade preceding 1985. The present period of austerity and increasing demands on labor calls for an ideology and the practice of centralized socialism—strong state control to mobilize resources for the external market. For that policy to be effective, public authority must be sustained. Hence, in order to secure popular respect a powerful moralization campaign was launched to ensure state legitimacy while pursuing unpopular economic policies. In other words, the rectification campaign focuses on the personal, moral attributes of the policymakers rather than on the overall socioeconomic policies being pursued. Personal enrichment and individual profiteering are condemned, and the economic system extracts and transfers income to the international bankers and finances investment in market-competitive enterprises.

Cuba's attempt to find a middle road between bureaucratic isolationism and indiscriminate liberalization combines the introduction of market techniques with central planning. It is the Cuban way of promoting political openings and the continuity of political authority, the selective retention of the revolutionary past rather than wholesale debunking in order to avoid the disarticulation of the structure of power and the collapse of the social structure. This account fits in with our analysis of the Cuban perspective—a prudent transition toward an export-oriented, welfare-based model rather than following a radical liberalization with no solid basis of political support, a formula more likely to lead to the Latin Americanization of the Eastern countries than to their Western Europeanization.

Cuban economic restructuring still faces several key obstacles: the entrenched bureaucratic party political machinery resists efforts to reorient from the existing patterns, and the mutual support system extends this behavior across enterprises. Workers are likely to object to harder work for less wages, scarcer consumer goods, and fewer opportunities to earn extra income through sideline employment. Finally, there are indications of divisions within the regime between those who support the opening toward the Western markets and those who favor a policy of deeper ties with the Soviet Union—a policy that was given a certain credibility by the recent demotion of several prominent pro-Moscow policymakers and party officials.

It seems clear that Cuba's labor-oriented productive system and its new export-oriented development system are in conflict. The attempt to mesh the two seems to lead to the worst of both worlds: declining incomes and productivity at home and no major expansion in overseas markets. The export strategy seems to require a wholesale restructuring of at least the leading economic sectors and the resocialization of labor along the lines of long-term delayed gratification, a restratified salary and wage system, and heightened managerial prerogatives. It combines efforts to implement a program of consumer austerity and the ratio-nalization of wage-productivity norms in the context of a political campaign against managerial incompetence and leadership corruption.

The key to any successful conversion to an export strategy is the emergence of a managerial elite capable of organizing the factors of production and penetrating overseas markets. It is not clear how the economic changes at the bottom will translate into efficient use of resources at the top if the current managers and officials are denounced, replaced, or demoted. Will a new group of entrepreneurial technocrats emerge from the current campaign primed to pursue the new strategy and mindful of the recent trade union accusation of managerial abuses? Will the weakening of the consumer power of the workers be amply compensated by the symbolic gratifications emanating from the anti-corruption moralization campaign? And, finally, when will Cuban managers have the resources to compete internationally if the government continues to pay out much of its hard currency earnings to service its foreign debt?

The Cuban effort to contain and limit the negative consequences of the economic restructuring accompanies the turn toward the export market that is evident in Castro's constant denunciation of corruption as well as his recognition that the unregulated market dissolves the elementary social bonds that tie state and society in a workable relation. The pursuit of an export market strategy and regulation of internal market differentiation may seem a contradictory halfway house approach, and it may even be creating bottlenecks in the effective pursuit of the overseas markets, but it also reflects the prudence of a political leader who is deeply aware of the corrosive effects the market has on social solidarity sustaining state power. The tensions and the ebb and flow of Cuban policy in the coming years will reflect the pressures emanating from the contradictory demands flowing from the collectivist-worker traditions and the exigencies of market competition.

## The New Model of Accumulation and Cuba's Foreign Policy

The rectification campaign is not simply a series of discreet policy measures but is part and parcel of a larger effort to create a new accumulation model—and is thus part of the restructuring and adjustments inherent in the transition. The model ascendant in the 1970s and the first half of the 1980s—specialization in primary goods exports and imported finished and capital goods in order to build, diversify, and meet the consumer needs of the domestic market—was largely financed by deficits and by subsidies from the Soviet Union. In a period of expansiveness in the socialist bloc as well as in the West, this model functioned quite successfully: Cuban GSP grew at a rate far above the average for Latin America, consumer incomes improved substantially, and industrial growth rates were acceptable.

By the mid-1980s, however, this model of accumulation based on external financing for internal growth began to exhaust its historical possibilities. The prices of sugar and oil declined precipitously; the socialist bloc countries began to reallocate their external financial resources toward internal modernization and to look toward greater integration with Western markets; Cuba's hard currency balance-of-payments accounts deficits widened; and debt payments to Japanese and Western bankers increased pressure on hard currency reserves and export earnings.[15] Cuban economic policy began to shift from an internal market, import-substitution strategy to an export strategy—combined with an intensified effort to create the internal structural conditions necessary to compete successfully in the world market. In entering the world market and adopting the export strategy, labor was seen increasingly as a factor of production—a cost—and salary and labor relations were geared accordingly.

The transition from an inward-oriented consumer economy to an outward-looking export economy implied a number of internal socioeconomic dislocations as well as shifts in Cuba's foreign policies. The first basic structural shift was increased investment in means of production and increased charges for public services: Economic resources were reallocated away from consumption toward production and, it was hoped, export production. Second, efforts were directed toward lowering labor costs through readjusting wage-salary-bonus payments and linking them to actual increases in production. Third, efforts were made to separate party control from day-to-day management of economic enterprises: Professional managers and technocrats increasingly replaced older political party stalwarts. Fourth, efforts were intensified to promote new lines of foreign exchange earnings—principally through tourism and through efforts to forge new links with market economies in Europe, Latin America, and elsewhere.[16]

This effort to promote a new model of accumulation took place within the shell of a centrally planned economy and was accompanied by constant reaffirmations of Marxist-Leninist principles.[17] The regime placed a premium on sustaining ideological-organizational continuities in order to cushion the inevitable shocks and discontent accompanying the transitional period. Castro purposely sought to avoid the problems of simultaneously weakening ideological and political control while implementing deep structural changes that were likely to have adverse effects on the population.

The change in the accumulation model led to a series of socioeconomic dislocations: Salary-bonus payments declined while public service costs increased, engendering some discontent and real declines in income; the abolition of the private markets and the promotion of state-regulated parallel markets provoked protests from those who benefitted from the private markets; and the elimination of unlicensed service workers produced widespread protests over the loss of services and income.

Consumer goods shortages, tighter work norms, and increasing disguised or real unemployment are all part of the dislocations accompanying the transition period.[18] The changes instituted, however, are not temporary but are in the process of being routinized if Cuba is going to make an effective transition to an export-oriented economy: It cannot return to the relaxed and excessive absenteeism atmosphere and high consumption period of the early 1980s.

Internally, the regime's ability to successfully consummate the transition to a new development model faces a number of potential political and economic problems. Castro depends heavily on popular support to sustain the regime, particularly in the face of continued U.S. belligerence. The austerity and readjustment measures have provoked some discontent. Castro has responded by taking certain populist measures to alleviate disaffection, including punishing corrupt officials, attacking profiteers, and canvasing neighborhoods to discuss the measures. He has evoked the revolutionary symbols and reaffirmed basic social gains to mitigate against the application of the new economic rationalization of work and rewards. The opening of the press to critical debate within political-party guidelines and the liberalization of migration are two areas that could also serve to ease the pressure on the domestic front. The regime hopes that by increasing production for domestic consumption through private farms it can compensate for increased exports. Whether high enough levels of production can be attained in a reasonably short time to serve both increased export targets and domestic consumption is debatable. In any case, the centralized political and economic structures are effective levers in neutralizing autonomous bases of opposition. At the same time, the success of the export model depends to a considerable degree on Cuba's capacity to produce quality products on demand at competitive prices, which depends sooner or later on unleashing technical and skilled labor from the bureaucratic fetters of the authoritarian personalist regime.

The new export model has also had a profound impact on the broad thrust of Cuba's international relations. Above all, it has meant that foreign relations are now determined increasingly by market possibilities, not revolutionary politics. Cuba is pursuing economic and political ties with existing regimes without regard for their domestic or foreign policies—provided the minimum condition of diplomatic recognition is accepted. Cuba seeks to play an important role in Latin American economic organizations, promoting common commercial and investment policies while intensifying its efforts to increase financial and economic ties with the European Economic Community (EEC) and Japan. To the extent that Cuba's debt position has weakened its import capacity, its actual trade relations with the advanced capitalist countries have declined, and Cuba has turned to South-South trade talks—mostly with the more dynamic regional countries such as Brazil and Argentina.[19] Castro's advocacy of the doctrine of ideological pluralism in Latin America and of a collective front against the foreign debt and his efforts to avoid any socioeconomic criticism of the internal policies of what he describes as democratic regimes in the hemisphere are also indicative of his efforts not only to break Cuba's isolation but also to promote Cuba's new export accumulation model.

Externally, this attempt to shift to a new model of accumulation faces several formidable challenges: increasing competition from all Third World countries that adopt export strategies; growing protectionism in the Western capitalist countries, which limits market access; problems presented by the EEC, particularly the privileged access granted to former colonies; the probable downturn in the world economy in the early 1990s; the increasing linkage between Eastern Europe and the advanced capitalist countries; and last but by no means least, foreign debt payments and restrictions on fresh financing.

Nevertheless, there are also positive signs. Cuba has built bridges to the EEC;[20] it is promoting closer links with Latin American producers and markets; it has an abundance of skilled professionals who are competitive with those of other nations, particularly in servicing less-developed countries; the tourist industry can be expected to expand several-fold; and major high-tech, biotechnical laboratories are being developed. In a broader context, the decline of U.S. hegemony and the pressures of a diversified competitive world economy should further weaken the U.S. blockade. Finally, the demise of the current liberal electoral regimes in Latin America may produce more progressive governments that maybe interested in furthering Cuban trade and investment.

## The Foreign Debt Dilemma

Cuba has fallen into the same Latin American debt trap that Castro so eloquently denounced in recent years: borrowing at exorbitant interest rates, pursuing the risky commodity export-based development game, rescheduling and capitalizing an increasingly insurmountable debt, imposing austerity programs to continue the flow of foreign funding, and trying to increase exports in a period of declining prices and restricted markets. Efforts to promulgate the notion of Cuban *exceptionalism* cannot be sustained: The terms of payment, interest rates, rescheduling costs, and time frames established by Japanese and European creditor banks were no different from those demanded of other regional governments by private U.S. multinational banks.[21]

Although Cuba invested its loans in productive activity, this does not change the global relations—shaped by creditor classes and nations—

that affect the terms and consequences of payment. Moreover, Cuba did not invest sufficiently in productive activity with a hard currency export component to enable it to pay back the loans in kind. Like other Third World debtors, it gambled on high commodity prices to sustain its interest payments, underestimating the instability of the market and the market's historical tendency to work against primary producers. All of this has occurred despite Castro's long and detailed discourses on the subject of unequal exchange. Since 1985, the prices of Cuban sugar and oil exports have declined significantly at a time when exports were pegged to the falling U.S. dollar and imports and debt payments to the appreciating Japanese yen and the West German mark—thus increasing trade deficits; "moving" interest rates simultaneously pushed up interest obligations to foreign creditors.[22] In the absence of sufficient sources of long-term, low-cost financing, the revolutionary regime faces more austerity and declining economic growth as it pursues domestic policies and an export development-accumulation model resembling those of the rest of Latin America.

This domestic austerity–export strategy logic the Castro leadership has embraced raises a difficult question that needs to be addressed: As debt payments to the West mount and trade opportunities decline,[23] is the solution to be found in deepening market ties, increasing dependence on external funding, and making more market adjustments to increase exports at the cost of declining local consumption and greater subordination to foreign capital? Decentralizing decisionmaking to enterprise managers will likely increase the debt and trade imbalances while absorbing more foreign currency. Devaluations will not necessarily increase exports (given the constraints on access to overseas markets) while increasing the price of the imports and the cost of financing the debt. Decentralization and marketization could imply a worsening of the debt while decreasing the central government's capacity to control the variables affecting world trade.

To answer the previous question, a further set of questions emerges. First, should Cuba consider reducing its convertible currency needs instead of mapping strategies to increase them under conditions that are unfavorable? Second, is it time that Cuba started to lessen its dependence on its mid-person role reselling sugar and oil for foreign currency and began to produce its own competitive commodities? Third, should Cuba repudiate its foreign debt and reorient its economy away from the market?

Growing indebtedness is only the first step toward greater integration into the market on the market's own terms: eroding domestic consumption, increasing labor discontent, deepening inequalities, and promoting foreign control of the economy through debt swaps, joint ventures, and the like are also likely to follow further integration into the market. The greater the debt, the greater the need to find new sources of hard currency and to make concessional agreements; this in turn leads to a spiraling debt and a greater need to sell off resources, cheapens labor power, and sacrifices consumer living standards—until nothing is left of socialism. In other words, socialist relations of production and worker-oriented welfarism increasingly come into conflict with the exigencies of an export-oriented development strategy that primarily benefits overseas lenders. Instead of a decentralized market economy, the end result of this scenario is a foreign-controlled, polarized society vulnerable to the decisions and cycles of the capitalist marketplace.

Paradoxically, as Cuba attempts to broaden its market ties, commercial trading opportunities are diminishing: Trade with capitalist countries declined from 22–25 percent of total trade in 1980–1981 to less than 14 percent in 1986. Between 1986 and 1987, the total value of this trade decreased from $1.6 billion to $1.25 billion.[24] As Cuba struggles to find new sources of external financing, what it generally receives is old debt refinancing. With declining market and financial opportunities in the capitalist world and few medium-term prospects for any dramatic shift in either area, it seems unrealistic for Cuba to squander its economic resources in plying uncooperative market players. A new direction might involve deepening its import-substitution policies, diversifying its processing of sugar into local sources of energy and other uses, and bringing its investment rates down to levels that can balance with consumer needs.

## Cuban-Soviet Relations

The shift to the new export accumulation model as well as internal economic restructuring has not been intended as distancing from the Soviet Union. These changes are building on the foundations of the existing bilateral relationship, at least for the foreseeable future. If the Cubans are successful in developing new markets and new sources of foreign exchange (from, say, Western tourism) and in building up their export capacity, they could redefine their relations with the Soviet economy—but these are big "ifs." In the areas of trade, aid, security, and defense assistance, however, the Cubans have been major beneficiaries of Soviet largesse, and the Cuban economy's linkages to the socialist bloc have been instrumental to its sustained economic growth since 1970. Diversification in the manufacturing and service sectors was built on the foundations of economic gains based on stable purchases of Cuban exports at relatively favorable prices by the Soviet Union and other Eastern European countries.

Today the crisis in socialism, not only in Eastern Europe but also in the Soviet Union, has understandably placed this model in some jeopardy. As a result, in the future we should expect to see relations between Moscow and Havana develop increasingly on a commercial basis, with decreasing aid and international solidarity from the Soviet Union. (Indeed, the greatest obstacle to a growth in bilateral trade—much less in Soviet aid—will likely prove to be political uncertainty in Moscow.) That said, however, the provision of a semblance of stability is important in internal Soviet politics, and the long-term picture for the Havana-Moscow linkage remains positive.

One of the peculiarities of current Cuban-Soviet relations is that the "center" wants to end the "periphery's" dependence—to diminish the historic process of large-scale, long-term net transfers from East to South. The shift in Cuban policy toward an export strategy, particularly its effort to penetrate market economies, is supported by the resource-depleted Soviets who would like to redeploy as much of their Cuban transfers as possible to bolster their own economy and finance their own restructuring. The inward turn of the Soviets under Gorbachev has been accompanied by Moscow's encouragement of Cuba's outward turn. The convergence of Soviet and Cuban policy on the new directions in Cuban economic strategy is indisputable. No doubt there are areas of disagreement about the right mix of political change and economic restructuring; there are differences over Gorbachev's disarmament initiatives and the continuities in Cuba's security policy in the face of continuing and unremitting U.S. hostility; there are also rather substantial political differences about the nature of the foreign debt problem and somewhat lesser conflicts over U.S.–Latin American relations.

Regarding the new era of superpower détente, Castro has repeatedly expressed concern about any supposed benefits for Cuba given the continuing imperialist threat: "The news that there may be peace, that there may be détente between the United States and the Soviet Union, does not necessarily mean that there is going to be peace for us." He has also directed criticism at Gorbachev for his willingness to engage in discussions with the Reagan and Bush administrations about Central America, the Caribbean, southern Africa, and other issues of critical concern to Cuba without prior consultation with his Latin American ally.[25] Indeed, in the wave of momentous—and unexpected—events in the Soviet Union in August 1991, the decision in September by Moscow to withdraw 11,000 Soviets from Cuba (a decision that was taken unilaterally without consulting the Cuban government), Fidel Castro must be increasingly concerned over Moscow's Cuban policy.

However, there are basic similarities that seem to overshadow these differences. First, in dealing with its debt problem, Cuba has moved in the same direction as Eastern Europe—trying to increase its foreign exchange earnings rather than repudiate its debt. Second, Castro is working toward closer relations with Latin American governments in much the same way as Gorbachev has done in Western Europe. Regarding the Soviet and Cuban positions on Latin America, the differences have become less and less significant. For both Castro and Gorbachev, open trade and diplomatic ties are more important than the class composition of the regimes. Third, Castro has offered to mediate regional civil wars and accept nonrevolutionary outcomes in a pattern not dissimilar from that of Gorbachev. Fourth, Castro has moved toward accommodating religious and other historically antagonistic forces in a fashion parallel to the Soviets.

The signing of the strategic 1989 Soviet-Cuban Friendship Pact was an expression of this convergence of policies and institutional developments and not the result of any victory or defeat of one or the other side. It would take a much more decisive shift toward Western liberalism by the Soviet Union or a major upheaval in Cuba resulting from the new development strategy to undermine the relationship between the two countries. Although there are probably forces within the Soviet Union that are interested in pursuing deep structural links with the West at the expense of the Cuba relationship (selling out Cuba for high-technology agreements with the United States), they remain isolated and lack political clout. If some degree of political stability remains in Moscow, Soviet policy toward Cuba probably will not diverge drastically from its course since the late 1980s; it will gradually reduce subsidies, encourage the growth of bilateral trade, and deepen the process of export growth based on increasing productivity, diversified products, and expanded markets. Trade and not aid thus will increasingly become the key to bilateral relations.

## Conclusion

Cuba's foreign policy has become increasingly oriented toward establishing greater links with the capitalist marketplace. But what needs to be recognized is that this policy orientation is not a linear process; nor is there a single, specific marketplace to which the Cubans are tied. Moreover, the openings to overseas markets have in many cases been preceded by diplomatic-political linkages that, in turn, clearly indicate the basic shift in Cuban economic strategy. Essentially, Cuba's push to deepen the role of the world market in its accumulation process has been accomplished by the increasing role given to establishing or cultivating state-to-state relations. International cooperation and pragmatic ties with existing regimes on global economic issues such as the debt and economic integration, not class struggle and revolution, are Castro's current priorities.

If Castro and Gorbachev have any conflicts in their relations, it is not because they have differences but rather is due to common policies. Both are focusing on opening new export markets, deepening ties with incumbent regimes (no matter how politically and socially reactionary), and distancing themselves from revolutionary movements in favor of state-to-state relations. The differences are over the methods of carrying out their policies.[26] Castro's concern is that in Gorbachev's wholesale pursuit of Western markets, Cuba might get frozen out. Furthermore, Castro wishes to retain ideological continuities (the new accumulation model is accompanied by constant reaffirmation of Marxist-Leninist principles), whereas Gorbachev wants to combine economic restructuring with an ideological rupture. Yet, Cuba's liberalization strategy—the pursuit of Western markets, the debt ties with capitalist creditors, the promotion of foreign investment and tourism, and the broad-front policy— belies those who see a return to a socialist vision in Castro's attack on peasant markets and material incentives.

The internal difficulties provoked by the debt payment policy and the ineffectiveness of the broad-front strategy due to the interlock among local regimes and classes and international finance capital suggest that Castro's liberalization politics will need heavy doses of populist rhetoric to forestall discontent. The fact that Castro relies on the Ministry of Interior to mobilize against "liberal bourgeois tendencies" suggests that he wants to control the site and source of any attack on liberalism. The placement of a new generation of technocrats in power may increase efficiency and lessen corruption, but it will not necessarily strengthen socialist tendencies from below. On the contrary, the new managers and technocrats can become prime supporters of the new liberal shift toward market integration. Although Castro may continue to direct public wrath against the emergence of the "new millionaires" and the mentality of the "small entrepreneur,"[27] his international economic policy is forcefully directed at promoting new ties with foreign investors and maintaining existing relations with overseas bankers.

Castro is a shrewd analyst who knows that his moves toward international liberalization must be legitimated by a resort to populist measures and moral exhortations at home. He walks a middle course between raising the question of debt repudiation and practical accommodation with Cuba's foreign bankers, between reaching out to the market externally but cracking down internally, between cutbacks domestically but spreading the burden equally. This is a difficult course to carry out, but it would be a mistake to underestimate Castro's political skills in attempting it.

## Notes

1. "PCC Told to Deal with Criticisms," *Latin American Weekly Report*, December 11, 1986, p. 3.

2. Archibald R.M. Ritter, "Cuba's Convertible Currency Debt Problem," *Latin American Weekly Report*, January 15, 1987, pp. 10–11.

3. "Liberal Reforms Are Outdated," *Latin American Regional Reports: Caribbean*, July 24, 1986, p. 2.

4. "Police Crack Down on Speculators," *Latin American Monitor: Caribbean*, December 1988, p. 613; "Black Market Crackdown," *Latin American Monitor: Caribbean*, April 1989, p. 709; "Crackdown on Black Market," *Latin American Regional Reports: Caribbean*, November 2, 1989, p. 2.

5. "Ideologue Hits at 'Private Sector,'" *Latin American Weekly Report*, November 12, 1987, p. 9.

6. "Private Farms to Play Bigger Role," *Latin American Regional Reports: Caribbean*, March 31, 1988, p. 6.

7. "Cuba Shuns Gorbachev's Reform Policies," *Latin American Regional Reports: Caribbean*, August 25, 1988, pp. 4–5; Frank T. Fitzgerald, "The Reform of the Cuban Economy, 1976–1986: Organization, Incentives and Patterns of Behavior," *Journal of Latin American Studies*, vol. 21, part 2 (May 1989), pp. 304–307.

8. Andrew Zimbalist and Susan Eckstein, "Patterns of Cuban Development: The First Twenty-Five Years," *World Development*, vol. 15, no. 1 (January 1987), pp. 10–17; Andrew Zimbalist, "Cuban Industrial Growth, 1965–84," ibid., pp. 83–93; Morris H. Morley, *Imperial State and Revolution: The United States and Cuba, 1952–1986* (New York: Cambridge University Press, 1987), pp. 345–346; Susan Eckstein, "The Impact of the Cuban Revolution: A Comparative Perspective," *Comparative Studies in Society and History*, vol. 28, no. 3 (July 1986), pp. 502–534; Claes Brundenius, *Revolutionary Cuba: The Challenge of Economic Growth with Equity* (Boulder: Westview Press, 1984).

9. Andrew Zimbalist, "Cuban Political Economy and Cubanology: An Overview," in Andrew Zimbalist, ed., *Cuban Political Economy* (Boulder: Westview Press, 1988), p. 11. Also see "Smile Off the Faces of Policy-Makers," *Latin American Regional Reports: Caribbean*, January 22, 1987, p. 3; "A Negative Balance for 1986," *Latin American Regional Reports: Caribbean*, October 1, 1987, p. 2.

10. "Castro Shuts Down Peasants' Markets," *Latin American Weekly Report*, May 30, 1986, p. 2.

11. Zimbalist, "Cuban Political Economy and Cubanology," pp. 12–13.

12. "Purge Continues After Executions," *Latin American Regional Reports: Caribbean*, August 24, 1989, p. 2.

13. Quoted in *Brecha* (Montevideo), June 23, 1989, p. 4.

14. Ibid.

15. Ritter, "Cuba's Convertible Currency Debt Problem," especially pp. 127–132; "Cuba Warns Creditors on Loans and Trade Squeeze," *Latin American Regional Reports: Caribbean*, May 9, 1986, p. 1.

16. Tourist sector earnings in 1988 ($125 million) made it the island's fourth-largest hard currency earner. Economist Intelligence Unit, *Quarterly Economic*

*Review of Cuba*, no. 2 (May 1989), p. 17. Also see Canute James, "Castro Cashes in on Caribbean's Tourists," *Financial Times*, August 26, 1988, p. 4.

17. See, for example, "Revolution's 'Marxist-Leninist' Principles Will Not be Abandoned, Says Castro," *Latin American Regional Reports: Caribbean*, January 19, 1989, p. 1.

18. The unemployment rate, for instance, was 6 percent in 1988 compared with 3.4 percent in 1981. Economist Intelligence Unit, *Quarterly Economic Review of Cuba*, no. 2, May 1989, p. 12.

19. Ritter, "Cuba's Convertible Currency Debt Problem," pp. 117–125.

20. Cuba is the first non-European member of COMECON to have diplomatic ties with the European Community. On Cuba's links with the EEC, see *Latin American Regional Reports: Caribbean*, July 21, 1988, p. 8, and November 3, 1988, p. 8.

21. Ritter, "Cuba's Convertible Currency Debt Problem," p. 119.

22. Ibid., p. 134; "Cuba's Debt Rises as US Dollar Weakens," *Latin American Regional Reports: Caribbean*, November 2, 1987, pp. 4–5.

23. Between September 1987 and the first quarter of 1989, Cuba's hard currency debt increased by over $1 billion. See Robert Graham, "Austerity . . . and Experiment," *Financial Times*, section 111, February 17, 1989, p. 3; "Rise in Cuba's Hard Currency Debt," *Latin American Regional Reports: Caribbean*, November 2, 1989, p. 5.

24. Ritter, "Cuba's Convertible Currency Debt Problem," p. 121; The Johns Hopkins School of Advanced International Studies, Cuban Studies Program, *Opportunities for U.S.-Cuban Trade*, June 1988, p. 11. Also see "Castro Warns of Further Belt-Tightening," *Latin American Regional Reports: Caribbean*, February 25, 1988, pp. 4–5; Economist Intelligence Unit, *Quarterly Economic Review of Cuba*, no. 4, November 1988, p. 13.

25. Quoted in Joseph B. Treaster, "Castro Scorning Gorbachev Model," *New York Times*, January 11, 1989, p. 10. Also see "'Stormy' Talks with Gorbachev Delayed," *Latin American Regional Reports: Caribbean*, January 19, 1988, p. 2.

26. "Our methods cannot be similar," declared Castro in his July 26, 1988, address to the nation. "It would be erroneous to copy other countries." Quoted in "Cuba Shuns Gorbachev's Reform Policies," *Latin American Regional Reports: Caribbean*, August 25, 1988, p. 4.

27. Quoted in "CDRs Urged: Stamp Out Corruption," *Latin American Weekly Report*, October 9, 1986, p. 5.

# 2

# The Rectification Process Revisited: Cuba's Defense of Traditional Marxism-Leninism

*Max Azicri*

Halifax, Washington, London, Stockholm, and other major cities on both sides of the Atlantic held international conferences in 1989 evaluating thirty years of revolutionary government in Cuba. These were mostly academic meetings convened to study a Latin American political phenomenon with unquestionable world significance. There was much to examine—good and bad, depending on the analyst's professional viewpoint and ideological persuasion. After three history-making and rather successful decades, Cuba is facing one of the most difficult periods of the revolution. The 1990s remind some Cuba-watchers of the 1960s: The survivability of the revolution again seems at stake, an outcome not seriously considered possible in the 1970s and 1980s. Although Cuba has been attempting a rectification of its errors and negative tendencies since 1986, the rest of the world has been watching and wondering whether Havana will survive the international crisis among socialist regimes.

## Rectification's External Environment

A backdrop to the events in the island and the demise of Central and Eastern European socialism was the renewed activism among anti-Castro Cuban exiles that was visible throughout Miami. Southern Florida Cuban-Americans' behavior in 1990 amounted to quasi–mass hysteria.

Suddenly, they were making plans to return home, many rushing to sell their homes and other properties. Illustrative of the people's happiness about the demise of regional political enemies, cars carried bumper stickers with the slogan: "First Manuel [Noriega], second Daniel [Ortega], and next Fidel [Castro]." In anticipation of the myriad of problems that might occur, the governor of Florida appointed a special commission charged with planning emergency measures for southern Florida once the Castro regime ends. Suspecting that Cuban exiles might rush to bring to Florida relatives left behind when they emigrated to the United States, the Immigration and Naturalization Service (INS) has made plans to stop them before they reach U.S. soil, so there would be no repetition of the 1980 Mariel boatlift.[1]

Sponsored by the Cuban-American National Foundation, an organization of wealthy conservative Cuban exiles, Ronald Reagan traveled to Miami in April 1990 to "speak" to Cuba through Radio Martí from a largely empty Orange Bowl, to the organizers' chagrin. The head of the foundation, Jorge Más Canosa—whose dream is to become Cuba's next president—used the event to propagandize himself to a Cuban audience (possibly in violation of the rules governing Radio Martí).[2] Reportedly, a new Cuban constitution has been drafted by the foundation, and Más Canosa requested a capitalist economic recovery plan for Cuba from Nobel laureate economist Milton Friedman, who turned down the assignment. From an undisclosed point south of Key West, Florida, Cuban exiles launched "aerial attacks" against their native country with helium balloons, each measuring twenty-three feet across. Under the name Operation Command L ("L" for liberation), the balloon lifts began in November 1989; 1,500 balloons were launched in February and 200 in March 1990. The balloons carried political messages, coffee, and razors: "In each package, we gave them several times the monthly quota of coffee per person," stated the head of the operation.[3]

Under President George Bush, TV Martí went on the air in March 1990, expanding Reagan's objective of destabilizing the Castro regime with Radio Martí, which went on the air in 1985. Havana denounced the forceful intrusion of U.S.-made television programming into its own airwaves as another policy of aggression and made plans to stop it— even to retaliate in kind. However, the transmissions did not reach their audiences as they were intended. Cuba's jamming of the television signal was prompt and effective—a technique Castro is now planning to use against Radio Martí. Cubans refer to the successful jamming of TV Martí as their "electronic Bay of Pigs" (*Girón Electrónico*), in reference to their April 1961 victory over the CIA-sponsored and -directed invasion by a brigade of Cuban exiles.

When President Bush used a request to Congress for financial aid to Panama and Nicaragua (once Noriega and Ortega were no longer in office) to remind the legislators that this was "a way of raising the pressure on President Fidel Castro to let 'democracy have a chance' in Cuba," the White House stated that his remarks could be taken *"as a preview of tough administration policy on an increasingly isolated Castro government"*[4] (emphasis added). In the U.S. Senate, a Republican senator from Florida, Connie Mack, organized a congressional Cuban Freedom Caucus to step up pressure for political change in Cuba.[5]

If the Berlin Wall and the European socialist regimes allied to the Soviet Union suddenly collapsed, why could not the Castro regime, was the question repeated by Miami's Spanish radio stations. Parallels were drawn in Florida and elsewhere between the fates of Nicolae Ceausescu and Castro. The prevailing view in Miami was that the bloodbath in Rumania would be repeated sooner or later in Cuba. Was this merely wishful thinking among the enemies of Cuban socialism, or was it more than just anti-Castro political rhetoric, now more believable after what had happened in Europe?

These are relevant questions. The inner logic of the events discussed above is based on the generalized assumption that the West, specifically the United States, has "won" the cold war. (Poignantly, however, the chairman of the political science department at the Chicago University, John J. Mearsheimer, in "Why We Will Soon Miss the Cold War" [*The Atlantic*, August 1990], displayed a point of view that differs from Washington's triumphant euphoria and that points somberly to the problems ahead in a multipolar Europe.) The setbacks in the Soviet Union and the collapse of Central and Eastern European socialism underscore the current Western perception that the domino theory seems to be working in reverse this time against socialist regimes. They also acknowledge that Cuba's economic status, which is dependent on Soviet economic support, might worsen as future Soviet trade and aid dwindle given the growing problems affecting Moscow.

## Rectification's Internal Environment

Cuba's rectification of errors and negative tendencies campaign departs markedly from the Soviet Union's perestroika and glasnost policies and stands contrary to the 1989–1990 Central and Eastern European rejection of socialism. "Socialism or death" is the cry heard in Cuba today. Rather than signifying a collective death wish, this sentiment is meant as a reaffirmation of the country's socialist system. Viewed in the light of Cuba's effective exercise of its sovereign rights and national traditions and as a defense of the socialist system, rectification is a lawful, independently agreed-upon course of action. Alluding partly to the Central and Eastern European upheaval, a Cuban social scientist adds a nationalist light to the analysis of the rectification policy:

> The socialist transformation of contemporary societies is not a permanent fact, nor [is] what has been attained guaranteed forever, nor do the existing realities correspond to the right decisions to make the project a reality. In Cuba, as a result, an analytical process is in motion; a process of rectification and change which, even though [it] is not alien to what is happening in the world, stems from our problems and from the forces at our disposal for our progress, and that is essential.[6]

Rectification, however, has received mostly negative reviews in the West, among former European socialist nations, and even in some quarters in the Soviet Union. In August 1987, after over two years of practicing glasnost, Moscow's *New Times* published several articles critical of the Cuban economy and the direction it is taking. Among the issues discussed were food rationing, lower labor productivity, shortages of housing and electricity, and the foreign debt. Vice President Carlos Rafael Rodríguez was forced to write an article in the same publication disputing the facts supporting the reports.[7] In March 1990, after five years of glasnost, *Moscow News* published a more critical portrait of Cuba as "repressed, destitute and politically antiquated."[8] Havana responded by banning the sale of two Soviet publications—*Moscow News* and *Sputnik*.

Whether from the West or the East, such a negative analysis does not evaluate rectification's potential to save Cuba from its current predicament. The main concern of such analysis is to condemn Castro for his refusal to open the island to a market economy and liberal democratic modalities, as in other socialist countries.

Cuba's severe problems and its chosen way of taking care of them— the rectification process—should be examined according to the country's needs, shortcomings, and general experience. Havana has had over three decades of building a socialist system under rather adverse geographical and political conditions—given its proximity to the United States, the principal enemy of Castro's revolution. No matter how unfair, rectification's fate is closely intertwined with events in present and former socialist nations. In addition to its potential for improving present conditions, rectification could also be a liberating experience for Cuba. The island was freed from capitalism when U.S. economic and political control ended in 1959. This time, Cuba might liberate itself from the dominating influence that European socialism, with all its historic contradictions and ideological deviations, has exerted over the country for more than three decades. (In retrospect, Cubans now bitterly lament how easily they accepted European socialist models and practices.)

The problems facing Cuba are complex. They have to do with the limited options available for developing nations to escape from their present conditions and build new, egalitarian societies. Could contemporary nations today, especially those with an economy as open and dependent as Cuba's, abandon capitalism altogether and adopt a socialist system entirely free of any capitalist form of economic production and incentives, particularly when socialism has abruptly diminished as an international force? On the other hand, is Gorbachev's retreat from pre-1985 Soviet socialism a road to incremental capitalism and the eventual demise of socialism, as viewed by Cuba?[9]

After a history of mistakes in following European socialist models, the prevailing view in Havana is that it is time for Cuba to experiment with its own approach and even to make its own mistakes based on its own models, not those of Europe—to use Cuban solutions to Cuban problems. This is seen abroad, however, as destructive obstinacy, as a collective blindness that misses what could be the last opportunity to put Cuban socialism back on the right track. Nevertheless, Cuba's role as a champion of traditional Marxism-Leninism appeals to committed revolutionaries in the island and elsewhere. In a cynical and materialistic world, it seems highly idealistic—even romantic—to see a nation commit its scarce resources to save a political and socioeconomic system and to make a historic promise to create a fairer society than those of its enemies.

Seemingly, the idea behind Cuba's stance is that what happened to European socialism is not an inherent systemic Marxist-Leninist failure. Historical and contextual conditions created Central and Eastern European socialism's structural performance failure, which was compounded by a serious leadership failure. Therefore, under the right leadership and structural performance conditions, Havana's argument goes, the system will rectify its shortcomings. It could then perform satisfactorily and render the egalitarian socioeconomic benefits expected from socialism.

But despite Havana's commitment to independent socialist thinking and systemic corrective actions, limited choices are available. Although it retains major structural features of the more pragmatic 1976–1985 period, rectification entails a partial retreat to some 1960s politics with its emphasis on service, denial, and popular mobilization. This gives pause to many analysts who examine this political phenomenon closely. Thus, some questions are in order: Is it possible to save Cuba's Marxist-Leninist system at this time of profound international socialist crisis? Also, is the rectification process the proper way to go about saving it?

In spite of the problems besieging their country, most Cubans would answer yes to both questions. Moreover, many Cuba-watchers would agree that both Castro and the socialist regime are very popular and are widely supported. The fact that Cuban socialism is the product of a genuine domestic revolution makes a difference in the comparison with the former Central and Eastern European socialist regimes. Most of the latter were set up forcefully and reinforced by the Soviet army under Stalin's orders, but Cuba's socialist regime's legitimacy is home-grown and deeply rooted.

In commenting in 1990 on Cuba's social and economic shortcomings and achievements, Castro stated that "Cuba has solved in thirty years [of socialism] what Latin America hasn't solved in 200 years."[10] Castro's statement is highly nationalistic if not simply hyperbolic, but the truth remains that Cuba's major social indicators have no equal among Third World nations and even sometimes match highly industrialized Western countries. Cuba's public health system is high-quality, readily available, and free. The country enjoys one of the lowest infant mortality rates and longest life expectancy rates in the world, with the highest doctor-patient ratio among Third World nations. Its comprehensive social programs, including a free education system that runs from the elementary to the university level, did not suffer substantially under the rather difficult economic conditions of the 1980s. Cuba's social services record has been evaluated favorably.

> There is widespread agreement, even among Cuba's critics, that in the areas of collective and substantive rights, Cuba has made enormous progress in meeting the population's needs regarding employment, education, health care and social services. . . . When measured against other countries in the region, Cuba's accomplishments stand in marked contrast to the massive unemployment, high infant mortality rates and brutal impoverishment that typify Third World countries. Cuban doctors working in Angola, for example, treat illnesses associated with underdevelopment—tuberculosis, meningitis, malaria, cholera and severe malnutrition—which do not even exist in their own country.[11]

However, if, as expected, the Cuban economy continues to decline further in the 1990s (among other reasons, because of the apparent collapse of the credit and commodity exchange trading system with former socialist allies), the future growth of social programs could be impaired, one hopes without suffering a major decline from their current level.[12] Cuba is actively looking for new trade partners in a move to expand its commerce with Western and Eastern countries. It has increased trade relations with the People's Republic of China and a few Latin

American countries, compensating somewhat for the vanishing Central and Eastern European trade. In 1990 Cuba and China signed a half-billion-dollar trade agreement. Also, sales to Brazil of a new meningitis vaccine developed in Cuban laboratories increased trade between the two countries in 1990 by $100 million in hard currency. (Reportedly, Brazil has had problems making the payments as planned; Cuba suspects a pressure campaign by the United States as part of an overall effort to thwart Havana's attempt to expand its trade with Latin American and other Western countries.)

## The Revival and Decline of Ideological Commitment

Rectification has created a new activism in Cuba. Political participation, mass mobilization, and the exercise of revolutionary *conciencia* (political awareness) are fashionable again. They mirror deeply felt sentiments, and rightly so: Rectification works as long as the populace remains fully integrated into the political process. The regime needs a level of support as high as or even higher than what it has had since 1959. Castro's challenge, however, is not to generate such support by motivating the population to back up his policies—he has accomplished that many times—but to be sure that the present enthusiasm will survive the routine of daily life, that it will continue in the future, and that the precious energies and time used on rectification are being invested in the right policy. In spite of the advances made under rectification since 1986, particularly in the economy, there is no guarantee that the policy will cure the present ills, including economic problems.

Analysts of Cuban politics fear that the ideological mind-set of the past will reestablish itself under rectification at the expense of the more decentralized modalities applied from the mid-1970s to 1986. On this subject, I have stated elsewhere, however, that

> there is logic in President Castro's position. His approach seems more ideological on the surface than it may really be. For a small developing country, such as Cuba, consumerism as the West practices it is an untenable goal in the short run, and most likely in the long run as well. . . . The collective and egalitarian approach toward consumption followed after the initial consumerist stage of the early 1960s is realistic and in keeping with the limited resources of a country that is planning its development toward the future and not simply satisfying today's needs.[13]

With the consumer facing increased shortages, the need to deemphasize material consumption and to entice the population effectively to embrace revolutionary *conciencia* remains as strong as ever. Realistically, however, Castro could not rely on moral incentives alone to increase productivity substantively in both quantity and quality. But with material goods becoming increasingly scarce in the second half of the 1980s and the early 1990s, a large dose of *conciencia* to make moral incentives more palatable has been necessary to mollify frustrated consumers. This approach offers a solution—even if temporary—to the regime, which can then begin to work its way out of its current predicament.

The problem tends to repeat itself, however, with a vicious cycle developing and being perpetuated by economic scarcity. Even if the economic problems suffered today were not as acute as they are, the larger problem would probably exist: What kind of people should socialists be? Should they be motivated by material incentives with a desire for consumerism as it exists in the West (a desire four decades of socialism were not able to erase among Central and Eastern European consumers), or should higher, loftier ideals of socialist morality motivate them? Given Castro's long-standing preoccupation with the centrality of socialist values in a socialist society, if the latter prevailed it seems clear that the issue of *conciencia* would then be as real as it appears to be now.

## Background and Rationale
## of the Rectification Campaign

Despite the controversy among Cuba-watchers regarding the true meaning, extent, and possible outcome of the rectification process, one thing is certain: Rectifying mistakes is not new to the Cuban revolution. George Black poignantly characterized the rectification policy as "a rectification of the rectification."[14] He based his observation on Castro's condemnation of the policy carried out until 1975 and his defense at the time of the policy that replaced it. In 1986 Castro criticized the latter policy (which was a rectification in meaning if not by name, according to Black) and defended its replacement, the actual rectification process.

With the suspicion that rectification was Castro's personal decision, with little if any input from the party and political apparatus, another analyst took issue with the decisionmaking process followed in reaching agreement on this policy.

Indeed, present directions were the initiative of Fidel Castro, not the Communist Party. The February 1986 party congress was certainly critical of the economic management and planning system, but it would be difficult to extract the full extent of rectification from its documents. Charismatic leadership—not institutional politics—was the catalyst for current politics. . . . That it came through Fidel Castro's initiative, however, is somewhat worrisome, for it does not provide a precedent for governing Cuba after he is gone.[15]

These are conjectural conclusions based on factual but mostly circumstantial evidence. They could be correct or far-fetched deductions, but the analyst cannot always be blamed for arriving at such conclusions. Normally, outsiders do not have access to the actual decisionmaking processes. Also, the field of Cuban studies has been rooted in Castro's central role in over thirty years of revolutionary rule, and the general perception is that the island is Fidel's Cuba and Castro is Cuba's Fidel. Major national policy decisions and changes usually appear to outsiders as personal decisions made by Castro alone. Hence, according to the prevailing notion of revolutionary decisionmaking, Castro's leadership style would allow him to take advantage of his well-known communication skills to defend the policy of choice at the time, later attacking the same policy once he has decided against it. Moreover, analysts opposing the revolution have charged Castro with intentionally glossing over the real issues behind the regime's decisions and policy shifts.

Notwithstanding Castro's charismatic leadership in the revolution's course, major objective facts decisively influence policymaking—even when the policies agreed upon seem at times erratic and unwise. Although personality traits and individualized decisions might carry more weight in Cuba than elsewhere (a problem that the institutionalization process of the 1970s did not remedy and that rectification may also prove unable to correct), these are not the only components of the policymaking process. The extant domestic and international forces affecting the process of building a socialist system in an underdeveloped country such as Cuba play a major role in limiting policy choices. Although some of these forces remain under Cuban control, many lie beyond its reach. And yet, underscoring the centrality of Castro's leadership in socialist Cuba (which raises the specter of succession awaiting the country down the road), the main objective of his recent speeches was to raise the people's consciousness (indoctrinating them to the regime's critics) and to make them aware of the seriousness of the reality facing Cuba and its possible consequences. Castro has also insisted on his early request for a massive rectification effort. The people's response has been positive, as Cubans basically support rectification as a way out of their present predicament.

The state of the Cuban economy—which includes production, distribution, trade, financing, marketing, management, labor, and most other activities related to the economy—is the main reason for rectification. Castro's harsh criticism in 1986 of the country's economic performance revealed the true dimensions of the problem. Even before the international socialist crisis of 1989–1990, the economic perspective in 1986 was grim.

> Cuba's Third Five Year Plan, for 1986–90 (which includes a projected 5 percent annual growth), was born under rather difficult auspices. Achieving such a goal depended on correcting past mistakes and improving economic performance. It included increasing efficiency in the use of resources; reducing material consumption (including fuels and their byproducts); servicing the foreign debt with Western (and socialist) creditors; meeting export commitments to [present and past] socialist countries; curbing consumption without reducing the population's standard of living; and adjusting investment in development programs to assure the external trade sector of the economy.[16]

In order to understand what has happened in Cuba since the mid-1980s, it is necessary to visualize rectification's scope. It is also important to realize the degree to which the population has been energized by the regime so that it would involve itself effectively in the campaign. Closely related to the national economy, most social and political agencies and activities have been closely examined, as they fall to some degree under the rectification process.

In a 1988 publication, Martínez Heredia, former editor of *Pensamiento Crítico*, an important ideological journal, listed a significant number of national problems under the heading "What Do We Want to Rectify?" These included stopping (1) the unlimited appeal to individual material interests; (2) the uncontrolled growth of the bureaucracy (it grew 2.5 times between 1973 and 1984) and bureaucratism as a system; (3) the technocratic approach to the direction of the economy (a controversial issue); (4) the costly waste in the utilization of the country's resources; (5) the different forms of corruption; (6) the practice of misinformation; (7) the payment of bonuses to which workers were not entitled; (8) the use of materials and services for private ends; (9) the way in which enterprises circumvented legal norms and economic rules for self-aggrandizement; and (10) the advantages derived from one's official position to gain privileges and material goods.[17]

To this list could be added a growing trend toward social differentiation (a pernicious practice in a society committed to social equality) and a weak rapport between the party and the populace. (This is the root of the political problems confronted by Poland and other former European socialist regimes in 1989–1991 and by the Soviet Union. It surfaced most dramatically in the events and transformations that occurred in the Soviet Union in the summer of 1991). Other problems include an increasing formalism in the ideological field, unwelcome rigidity in the state power structures, and a general trend in the social sciences to conform to orthodoxy and rigid ideological reasoning.[18]

Rectification is not new to the Cuban revolution, but no past experience matches today's campaign and agenda. Today's intense sense of urgency has not been felt to this degree. According to Castro, Cuba could no longer continue along the road it had been following since the 1970s, which paradoxically had led to the highest level of institutionalization and decentralization achieved by the regime since 1959. As part of the current practice of critically examining three decades of revolutionary policymaking, the institutionalization of the revolution in the 1970s, when the regime was acting under European socialist influence rather than on its own initiative, is seen by some as having been improperly carried out.

In reality, however, the 1980s were a period of rectifications. The changes started early in the decade, grew into the 1986 rectification campaign, and have continued ever since. The country's military preparedness was the first major change. Fearing an attack by President Ronald Reagan, the defense system became organized as a people's army under the so-called territorial militias. This was followed by a renewed emphasis on ideological issues, with the promotion of new cadres, and the experimentation with new ideological approaches. The 1986 Congress report to the Communist party plenum reflected such changes.

Economic-administrative changes started with the appointment of a Central Group (no longer in operation) under the direction of Osmani Cienfuegos, minister-secretary of the Council of Ministers and member of the party's Central Committee. Cienfuegos and the Central Group took over some of the responsibilities assigned to the Central Planning Board (JUCEPLAN), including the revision of the 1985 economic plan and the development of the 1986–1990 economic plan and later plans. Another blow to JUCEPLAN was the dismissal of Humberto Pérez in 1984. In addition to heading JUCEPLAN, Pérez was an alternate member of the party's Politburo and a member of its Central Committee. Finally, at the 1986 Third Party Congress, the rectification policy was inaugurated by Castro in his report to the Congress. The unsettling effect of the adopted changes has been rather mild in comparison with the shock felt by the Central and Eastern European upheaval and the transformation of the Soviet system.

## If the Worst Scenario Becomes Reality

Rectification was born out of Cuba's internal problems. It is a reactive policy aimed at solving the country's deficiencies and correcting its errors. The demands of having an open economy (one that depends primarily on exports) force Cuba to keep monitoring the effect of its economic performance on its external commerce. As Cuba enters the 1990s, its uphill struggle to improve its economic performance is being fought on the national and international fronts. This makes one wonder to what extent recent international developments, primarily the political and economic changes in the former socialist bloc, will render rectification irrelevant or whether they will make a difference. Could the efforts of a small country be enough to stop what seems to be an irreversible tide against socialism in the world today? Cubans answer this question affirmatively, convinced that their efforts will make a difference and that they have over three decades of socialism to prove it. As it was initially, the present struggle is still focused on whether subjective commitment can overcome whatever objective obstacles exist. The revolution was fought on the firm belief that commitment will always prevail over obstacles.

Countries that only yesterday were Cuba's partners and friends have become political antagonists. Hungary, Bulgaria, Poland, and Czechoslovakia have openly taken positions against Havana. They have supported U.S. anti-Cuba diplomatic initiatives. The island has lost valuable friends and has gained new, unexpected adversaries. Taking advantage of their economic vulnerability, Washington pressured Hungary and Bulgaria to vote in Geneva in support of a resolution asking for continued scrutiny of alleged human rights abuses in Cuba. As nonvoting members of the United Nations Human Rights Commission, Poland and Czechoslovakia publicly affirmed their support for the U.S.-sponsored resolution, which was approved by the Human Rights Commission. A frustrated Raúl Roa Kouri, Cuban deputy foreign minister, asked, "What has happened to the socialist world?"[19] Just before the U.S. invasion on December 20, 1989, Panama also voted for the resolution.

Rectification's external and internal environments are interacting closely with one another. The question as to what the state of Cuba's external commerce will be one, two, or three years from now is almost impossible to answer today. How can a planned economy operate under present conditions? Yesterday's friends are not friends anymore. Socialist internationalism in Europe, which was never that strong, has become increasingly a relic of the recent past.

How are the changes in the Soviet Union affecting Cuba? Most of Cuba's socialist trade, which amounts to 86 percent of its total trade, is with the Soviet Union. This has shielded Cuba somewhat, so it has not yet been seriously affected by the radical changes in European socialist nations. Also, most of the trade agreements with former socialist European countries were extended for an additional year in 1990; however, new agreements will be needed after 1991, probably under very different trade conditions.

The mounting difficulties in the Soviet Union (in addition to Washington's pressure on Gorbachev to stop aiding Cuba) are more pressing to Havana. Moscow's growing problems with the economy, the nationalities, and the succession of some of the republics, to mention just a few, are also Cuba's problems—because they might determine the state of Cuban-Soviet relations.

Soviet delays in the delivery of supplies in December 1989 and January–February 1990 caused serious dislocations in the production and distribution of essential staples to consumers as well as an oil shortage. This was not a deliberate action based on a new policy toward Cuba but was the product of Moscow's internal problems. Castro has confronted and discussed these issues publicly. His recent speeches have covered some of the rather extreme measures Cuba might have to take if the socialist trade breaks down entirely.

## Living Under War Conditions in Peacetime

In the closing session of the 16th Congress of Cuban Trade Unions (CTC) on January 28, 1990, Castro explained how the changes in European socialism had affected Cuba and how they could affect it even more in the future.

For decades, our plans and yearly and five-year programs were based on the existence of numerous socialist countries in Eastern Europe with which we worked out agreements and had close economic ties, in addition to the Soviet Union. We had reliable markets for our products and supply sources for important equipment and merchandise. We made efforts in these fields, an effort to implement and complement our economy, *and now in political terms that socialist camp no longer exists.*

The Council for Mutual Economic Assistance [COMECON] [still] exists . . . but you can just imagine what sort of changes there have been in the organization when people used to call each other comrades and now that word has been ruled out by some who now call each other Mr., Mrs., Miss—if there are any there. The vocabulary is changing.

Our economic relations with the Soviet Union have not been very [much] affected by these processes, up to now. On the contrary, I must say it in all honesty, the Soviets have expressed throughout all these times and continue to express their greatest willingness to maintain economic relations with us and continue the trade between our two countries under the same or similar principles. . . . But it may also happen that problems may occur for the Soviet Union from the situation currently prevailing in the countries that were part of the socialist community. . . . Any difficulty that the

Soviet Union may have . . . must inevitably affect the supplies earmarked for our country. *And so, we must understand that the stability of the Soviet Union is of the utmost importance for our country. . . . [And] currents are now developing inside the Soviet Union that are opposed to the type of economic relations currently existing between the Soviet Union and Cuba. . . . Profoundly unjust articles [in the Soviet media] are undertaking an opinion campaign against the economic relations between the Soviet Union and Cuba.*[20] (emphasis added)

Anticipating the worsening of current economic conditions, Cuba planned two different kinds of so-called special periods, that can be carried out whenever the need arises. The first is a special peacetime period, to come into effect under very adverse economic conditions. The second, which has been referenced only loosely, is a period of serious difficulties that requires great sacrifices if people are to survive.

If internal problems make it impossible for the Soviet Union to send supplies to Cuba, then the special peacetime period would be necessary. This would be a real nightmare for the consumer: Oil, food, and most essential products would be drastically rationed, rapidly reducing national consumption. As Castro stated to the delegates attending the Fifth Congress of the Federation of Cuban Women (FMC) in March 1990, "You watch closely events in the USSR and you will be able to judge whether or not a special period becomes more or less likely."[21]

Living conditions, social services, and economic production would be seriously affected during the special peacetime period. Social development programs carried out under normal conditions would come to a halt, but important economic sectors such as the biotechnological and pharmaceutical industries would continue, as would the food program. National cement consumption, presently at 4 million tons per year, would be reduced to 1.5 or 1.3 million, or maybe less. The 30,000 daily trips on public transportation in Havana would be cut to 10,000 or less, affecting the standard of living and working conditions in the capital (riding to work on bicycles and reducing working hours are possible alternatives).

Anticipating special peacetime shortages, some work centers have been operating without lights and without air conditioning or fans. Under the special peacetime period, the country's capacity to generate electricity would be reduced to one-third of its normal capacity.

The special peacetime period is a unique experience demanding strong support and commitment by the population—probably for a long time if it ever comes into effect. Although the rectification process is a domestic policy in response to internal problems, errors, and shortcomings, the special peacetime period is a response to unexpected external developments: the collapse of Central and Eastern European socialism, the radical changes in the Soviet Union, and the serious challenges faced by Moscow within the country's borders.

As Castro told the delegates, "We [have] spen[t] some time thinking about how to adapt the economy and the life of the country to whatever circumstances may arise during the special period in peacetime." If necessary, Cuba will resort to "oxen and mules" during the sugar harvest. For Castro, this and any other sacrifice is the price the country is willing to pay to save the revolution. But seeking to reassure the country, he also explained how far things will go: "Whatever we have we [will] distribute evenly among everyone. Not even during the special period will we have beggars here, because there won't be anybody without food."[22]

Although the rectification years have improved Cuba's ability to face these harsh times, these new developments will probably halt any future economic and social progress.[23] The fact that Cuba cannot be blamed for the turn of events in Europe makes no difference as far as its being affected negatively by such events. Hence, Cubans are preparing to live under rather adverse conditions and to salvage as much of their development programs as possible, struggling in the process for the survival of the revolution.

Equally important to the improvements in the economy under rectification and the advance preparations for the special periods are the proposed changes in the political system. The Communist party launched a campaign in March 1990 for open participation in the preparations for the October 1991 Fourth Party Congress.

Participating in the different plenums held across the country, the people raised significant issues, many of which will be included in the Congress agenda. The scope for public discussion is seemingly wide open with only two major issues excluded from the discussions: the socialist nature of the revolution and the regime, and the single-party system.[24]

The people have requested important changes in the political system, including improving the Organs of People's Power's (OPP) responsiveness to local and national needs and concerns, giving more authority to municipal and provincial delegates and to the national deputies, and extending the number and length of the National Assembly sessions. A rather incisive criticism of the OPP was made at a plenum of the Communist Youth Union (UJC) in Havana; this was published in the press and received wide attention. Rather than waiting until the Fourth Party Congress, the National Assembly decided to heed some of these complaints in its summer 1990 session. It approved allowing 100 of the 496 deputies to henceforth dedicate themselves full time to their National

Assembly responsibilities. The deputies had only been responsible for attending two short sessions of the National Assembly every year, working year-round in standing committees, and rendering accounts of their work as deputies to their constituency.

The deterioration of the economy has had a negative effect on the public image of the country's political institutions. In a recent public opinion poll, the weekly *Bohemia* reported that only 59.1 percent of those polled trusted the OPP delegates. Also, only 51.4 percent felt OPP delegates had the needed authority to take care of their circumscriptions' problems, and only 40.6 percent found the OPP useful politically. Fewer than two-thirds (60.7 percent) felt that as individuals they effectively participated in governing the country, but 70.5 percent supported making the OPP more effective and dynamic while preserving its present structure.[25]

Cuba today is at a crossroads. The political and economic changes that will be approved at the Fourth Party Congress should reinforce the improvements made under the rectification process. The Congress will chart the revolution's path for years to come, including the future of rectification. Cuba's self-appointed role championing revolutionary socialism and traditional Marxism-Leninism runs contrary to European changes that favor market economies. Paradoxically, this serious discrepancy gives a new dimension to a revolution that has maintained the world's attention for over three decades. As defiant as ever, Cuba seems confident that it will overcome the challenges of the 1990s and beyond.

## Notes

1. David E. Pitt, "Rising Hopes for Castro's Fall Have Cubans in Miami Abuzz," *New York Times*, February 10, 1991; Sandra Dibble, "Governor Forms Panel on Cuba," *Miami Herald*, February 6, 1990; Mirta Ojito, "Exiles Step up Plan for a New Cuba," *Miami Herald*, February 18, 1990; Pablo Alfonso, "Panel Offers a Plan for Governing New Cuba," *Miami Herald*, March 3, 1990; David Hancock, "INS Plans Ahead for Free Cuba," *Miami Herald*, March 29, 1990.

2. Georgie Anne Geyer, "Stop Más Canosa's Takeover Attempt," *Miami Herald*, March 17, 1990. In the middle of one of the controversies that have plagued Radio Martí and just a month before the Orange Bowl rally, Más Canosa stated: "Well-known critics of U.S. policy toward Cuba can enjoy Radio Martí as a forum for their views, while the foundation [Cuban-American National Foundation] frequently described as the most prominent Cuban-exile group, does not. That this is so is a result of our own prudence. For example, *I have spoken briefly on Radio Martí on only two occasions since 1985.* We are a serious organization whose goal is a free and democratic Cuba." Jorge Más Canosa, "Radio and TV

Martí—Betancourt's Power Grab Failed," *Miami Herald*, March 17, 1990 (emphasis added).

3. Karen Branch, "Exiles Send Hope and More to Cuba," *Miami Herald*, March 20, 1990.

4. Martin McReynolds, "Bush Urges Raising Ante Against Castro," *Miami Herald*, March 21, 1990.

5. Paul Anderson, "Mack Initiates Cuban Freedom Caucus in Congress," *Miami Herald*, March 2, 1990.

6. Fernando Martínez Heredia, *Desafíos del Socialismo Cubano* (La Habana: Centro de Estudios Sobre América, 1988), p. 13.

7. Reported in the *Miami Herald*, October 18, 1990.

8. Reported by Katherine Ellison, "Cuba: Succeeding Castro," *The Atlantic*, June 1990, p. 38. The quotation is Ellison's description of the characterization of Cuba by the *Moscow News*.

9. Cuba has given mixed signals regarding Gorbachev's glasnost and perestroika. Castro has publicly criticized current Soviet policies, even if rather obliquely and without giving names. Associated Press, "Magazine Airs Feud on Economy: Cubans, Soviets at Odds on Form," *Miami Herald*, October 18, 1987, as cited in Max Azicri, *Cuba—Politics, Economics and Society* (London: Pinter Publishers, 1988), p. 160. Other Cubans have been more outspoken in criticizing Gorbachev's policies, even on U.S. television. But Castro has also been conciliatory, recognizing the Soviet Union's right to pursue its own policies—just as Cuba does with rectification. Also, Castro stated that he should not interfere in internal Soviet affairs. Ted Turner, "A Conversation with Fidel Castro," CNN, June 25, 1990.

10. *Granma Weekly Review*, April 1, 1990.

11. Tony Platt and Ed McCaughan, "Human Rights in Cuba: Politics and Ideology," in Sandor Halebsky and John M. Kirk, eds., *Transformation and Struggle—Cuba Faces the 1990s* (New York: Praeger, 1990), p. 68.

12. "President Fidel Castro, worried about the aftershocks in Cuba from what he calls Eastern Europe's political 'catastrophe,' is warning the country that he is prepared to put the island's economy on a wartime footing and even halt key social development programs." Lee Hockstader, "Castro Says Cuba Faces Hard Times," *Washington Post*, April 7, 1990.

13. Azicri, *Cuba*, p. 125.

14. George Black, "Toward Victory Always, But When?" *The Nation* (October 24, 1988), p. 374.

15. Marifeli Pérez-Stable, "Socialism and Democracy: Some Thoughts After 30 Years of Revolution in Cuba," in Halebsky and Kirk, eds., *Transformation and Struggle*, p. 30.

16. Banco Nacional de Cuba, *Economic Report* (Havana: Comité Estatal de Estadísticas, 1985), pp. 3–5, 44–47.

17. Martínez Heredia, *Desafíos del Socialismo Cubano*, pp. 22–23.

18. Gerardo Timossi, "Cuba: Una Agenda Diferente Para los Cambios," *Pensamiento Crítico* (May 1990), pp. 22–23.

19. "U.S. Wins Vote to Press Cuba on Rights," and "Cuba Flays Third World for Backing U.S. on Rights Scrutiny," *Miami Herald*, March 7 and March 8, 1990.

20. *Granma Weekly Review,* February 11, 1990, pp. 2–3.

21. *Granma Weekly Review,* March 18, 1990, pp. 10–11.

22. Ibid., p. 11.

23. For a discussion of the impact rectification has had on the Cuban economy, see José Luis Rodríguez, "Aspectos Económicos del Proceso de Rectificación," and Silvia Domenech Gerardo Gómez, "Una Reflexión Crítica: ¿Cumple sus Objetivos la Economía Política del Socialismo que Hoy Tenemos en Cuba?" *Cuba Socialista,* vol. 40 (April–June 1990), pp. 86–101 and 45–69, respectively. For an opposite point of view, see Carmelo Mesa-Lago, "Cuba's Economic Counter-Reform (Rectification): Causes, Policies and Effects," in Richard Gillespie, ed., *Cuba After Thirty Years—Rectification in the Revolution* (London: Frank Cass, 1990). For an insightful analysis of the economic ideas of Ernesto Ché Guevara, now widely discussed and reexamined in Cuba, see Carlos Tablada, *Ché Guevara: Economics and Politics in the Transition to Socialism* (Sydney, Australia: Pathfinder/ Pacific and Asia, 1989).

24. Interviews with senior officials from the Revolutionary Guidance Department; José R. Vidal Valdés, editor of the daily *Juventud Rebelde*; Eugenio R. Balari, director of the Cuban Institute of Research and Direction of Internal Demand; José Luis Rodríguez, deputy director of the Center for the Study of the World Economy; Esteban Morales Domínguez, director of the Center for the Study of the United States; Mercedes Arce Rodríguez, director of the Center for the Study of Political Alternatives, Havana University; several researchers and academicians associated with the Center for the Study of the Americas; and economist Carlos Tablada, Havana, Cuba, July 1990. Also, see "Llamamiento al IV Congreso del PCC: El Futuro de Nuestra Patria Será un Eterno Baraguá," La Habana, Cuba, Editora Política del CC de PCC (March 15, 1990), pp. 1–21; "Acuerdo del Buró Político Sobre el Proceso de Discusión del Llamamiento al IV Congreso del Partido," *Granma,* June 23, 1990, pp. 4–5.

25. "Opinión Pública: ¿Qué Piensa el Pueblo de Su Poder?," and "La Democracia Cubana Frente al Espejo," *Bohemia,* July 6, 1990, pp. 4–9 and 10–11, respectively.

# 3

# Democracy and Socialist Cuba

*Sheryl L. Lutjens*

The ongoing debates about democracy and socialism have been invigorated, not resolved, by the tumult of change in Eastern Europe and the Soviet Union, by events in China, and by the Sandinistas' commitment during their tenure to a mixed economy and political pluralism in Nicaragua. Competing theories of democracy continue to set the terms and tone of political and academic discussions of reforms in socialist states. Liberal theories of procedural democracy and Marxist theories of socialist democracy justify different forms of political organization, reflecting different goals, different beliefs about human nature, and, ultimately, different standards for evaluating democracy in capitalist and postcapitalist societies. Within this traditional conceptual terrain, the puzzling sweep of reform as well as recent efforts to rethink both Marxist theory and democratic socialism challenges the prevailing models of democracy and the debate they have defined. The invitation to reexamine the democratic potential of socialist political organization is compelling because it offers the possibility of moving beyond dichotomous models to an explanation of the dynamics and likely future of democratic reform in both socialism and emerging postsocialism.

My purpose is to explore Cuba's postrevolutionary political experience in light of contemporary debates about democracy and socialism. Competing models of democracy have generated many of the controversies and contending conclusions in the literature on Cuban politics since 1959. The process of rectification of errors and negative tendencies launched officially in 1986 reasserts socialist democracy, distinguishing Cuban reforms from the democratic "revolutions" elsewhere. Although the issue of "Castroika" demands attention, Cuban exceptionalism cautions us to carefully inspect the logic and primacy of the liberal and the socialist models of democracy and to consider an alternative approach with equal care.

## Cuban Perspectives on Democracy

Cuba's vision of socialist democracy reflects the convergence of Marxist theory and Cuban history. Although Cuba adopted and maintains a Marxist-Leninist theory of the dictatorship of the proletariat, three phases in the development of political organization and goals after 1959 explain a combination of centralization and participation characteristic of the Cuban theory and practice of socialist democracy. As discussed below, these phases include the turbulent 1960s, the intitutionalization period (1970–1986), and the post-1986 era, which has been based on the rectification campaign.

Cuba had a republican political order from 1901 until the revolution in 1959. Although liberal democracy patterned after the U.S. system was constructed during the U.S. occupation of Cuba after the Spanish-Cuban-American War, liberal ideals had strong roots in Cuba's own struggle against Spanish domination. Cuba was a colony for a much longer period than other Latin American societies, and its democratic tradition emerged prominently through the constitutions of the nineteenth-century independence movements and such spokespersons as José Martí. This tradition was deflected by the occupation's disbanding of the revolutionary movement, by the Platt Amendment to the 1901 Cuban constitution and the direct U.S. intervention it permitted, and by the actual dynamics of Cuba's liberal democracy. Corruption, violent party competition, military coups, and attempts at reform and revolution characterized the republican politics. By the 1950s, demands for a meaningful liberal democracy reflected the political crisis of a neocolonial state that could offer neither genuine representation nor the economic sovereignty required in a liberal democracy.

The immediate postrevolutionary period was one of consolidation of power during which the option of liberal democracy was precluded. Although leadership statements before and after the revolution and the form of provisional government reflected respect for liberal political principles,[1] unfolding nationalist reforms raised conflicts and made political unity a necessity. In the face of domestic and international opposition to agrarian reform and nationalization, to the role of Cuban Communists, and to a suspected identification with the Soviet Union, the need for unity—among leadership, around national goals, and for survival—postponed and then foreclosed the possibility of liberal democracy. If the revolution hesitated in eliminating the private sector, after April

1961 revolutionary goals were identified as socialist. As Ché Guevara explained, "It is an agrarian, anti-feudal, and anti-imperialist revolution, transformed by its internal evolution and by external aggression into a socialist revolution, and it so proclaims itself before the Americas; it is a socialist revolution."[2] The transformation of the foundations of the economy and political needs together precluded a return to liberal democracy.

The political arrangements created in the consolidation period organized unity and direct, not liberal, democracy throughout the 1960s. The People's Militia, formed in 1959, and the Federation of Cuban Women, the Committees for the Defense of the Revolution, and the Association of Small Farmers, formed in 1960, are good examples of this phenomenon. With the labor unions, student organizations, and the attempt to build a single, unified party, which began in 1961, mass organizations became a central feature of a new political order. On May Day 1960, Fidel Castro publicly defined direct democracy.

> Democracy is where the majority governs. Democracy is that form of government in which the majority is taken into account. Democracy is that form of government in which the interests of the majority are defended. . . . Democracy guarantees not only the right to bread and the right to work but also the right to culture and the right to be taken into account within society. Therefore, *this* is democracy. The Cuban revolution is democracy.[3]

Two characteristics of direct democracy underpinned the emergent centralization of a new political order: Castro's leadership role and mass participation. Mass rallies, televised speeches, and visits by Castro and other leaders throughout the island were a means to maintain the unity of the Cuban people around the revolution's goals. Active participation through new organizations, not simply expressing loyalty or faith, was also required for two interrelated reasons. First, defense, development, and social change required the mobilization of the population. Mass organizations were thus used to direct the energy of the Cuban people toward collective goals. At the same time, participation was viewed as a means to the social, cultural, and political transformation of the Cuban people. Guevara's vision of the "new man," characterized by discipline, egalitarianism, and an ethic of sacrifice, was itself a goal. Castro's leadership and the instrumental and transformative logics of participation organized the unity of the Cuban people and expressed the union of economic and political strategies.

Also called the "Cuban model," the arrangements of direct democracy were considered necessary but not sufficient elements of the revolution's political vision. As Guevara explained in 1965, restraint in creating more political structures came from a desire to retain the direct bonds between leadership and the people.

> The institutionalization of the revolution has still not been achieved. We are searching for something new which will allow perfect identification between the government and the community as a whole, adjusted to the peculiar conditions of building socialism and avoiding the commonplaces of bourgeois democracy transplanted to the society in formation (such as legislative houses, for example). . . . Our greatest restraint has been the fear that any formal aspect might separate us from the masses and the individual, making us lose sight of the ultimate and most important revolutionary ambition: to see man liberated from his alienation.[4]

The idealism of direct democracy found expression in other unorthodox features of the centralization of the 1960s: an emphasis on moral rather than material incentives; experimentation with the organization of economic planning; the small and underdeveloped Partido Comunista de Cuba (PCC) developing *within* the revolution; and the multiyear push toward a 10 million ton sugar harvest in 1970, which revealed the Cuban belief that politics could overcome economic constraints.

The experimentation of the 1960s gave way to a more traditional definition of socialist democracy—the second phase of political development—after the shortfall of the 1970 sugar harvest. From 1970 until 1976, preparations were made for the formal institutions of a socialist state. Central planning was revamped along more orthodox lines for the pursuit of efficiency and a more pragmatic economic development—culminating in the System of Economic Management later in the decade; the adoption of a constitution in 1976 laid the legal foundations for stable decisionmaking structures; the role of the PCC was clarified, statutes and a program approved in its first congress in 1975, and membership doubled between 1970 and 1975; and political and economic relationships with the Soviet Union were strengthened. In 1976, a political-administrative system called *Poder Popular* emerged as the core of a socialist state system.

State-building, or institutionalization, did not abandon the idealism of the 1960s entirely, however. An emphasis on participation marked the preparations for and the design of the socialist state system. The critical assessment of the immediate past and preferred future that informed state-building counted on the successes of the 1960s. The Cuban people, said Castro, had demonstrated "will power, morale, intelligence and determination."[5] Mass organizations were revitalized through an expansion of membership, internal elections, and national congresses. Major legislation during the transition was discussed at the grass-roots level; for example, 6,216,981 Cubans discussed the constitution prior to its adoption in 1976.[6] The System of Economic Management included worker participation; the union structure had been revamped in the early 1970s; and the National Congress in 1973 discussed a new Cuban labor policy, including the use of incentives. New arrangements of centralization expanded participation, abandoning neither the instrumental nor the transformative logic of mobilized participation entirely.

State-building established the representative institutions of a socialist state. As Raúl Castro explained in 1974 at the beginning of a two-year trial run of *Poder Popular* in Matanzas province, representative participation had been constrained by "violent aggression on the part of imperialism and of the internal counter-revolution. . . . The tasks of the moment required an agile, operative state apparatus that would exercise the dictatorship in representation of the working people, that would concentrate legislative, executive, and administrative faculties simultaneously in a single organ, and that would be able to make decisions without much delay."[7] Established nationwide in 1976, the new system of *Poder Popular* was to be a "vehicle for the institutional and systematic participation of all the population in the affairs and decisions of the State."[8] Its installation required political and administrative reorganization.

Within the centralizing reform of planning and the strengthening of the PCC, the system of *Poder Popular* promised electoral representation and decentralization of decisionmaking. Formal representation involved the creation of local, provincial, and national assemblies of *Poder Popular*. Political and administrative jurisdictions were reorganized; the six provinces, 58 regions, and 407 municipalities became 14 provinces and 169 municipalities. In October 1976, 10,725 delegates were directly elected to assemblies in Cuba's 169 municipalities; the municipal assemblies subsequently indirectly elected 1,084 provincial delegates and 481 deputies to the National Assembly. A division of functions among the three political-administrative levels redistributed decisionmaking under the aegis of *Poder Popular*.

State-building acknowledged the problems of the 1960s. *Poder Popular*, according to Raúl Castro, was designed to eradicate the inefficiencies of excessive centralization, poor management, and the confusion in roles and functioning of the party, state, and mass organizations. Decentralization defined the local level of *Poder Popular* as "the highest authority for the exercise of state functions within respective territorial boundaries,"[9] relinquishing to the municipal assemblies control and management of specific economic and service units as well as the development of activities geared to fulfilling the needs of the community. Thus, 75 percent of commercial and public dining facilities, 86 percent of educational institutions and facilities, and 50 percent of health facilities passed to the municipal level of *Poder Popular* in 1976.[10] Normative and technical control and activities with a national scope remained central responsibilities.

The political and administrative reforms of the state-building period illustrated Cuba's interpretation of the Marxist theory of the state and socialist democracy. Cuba's perspective on the state institutions created in the 1970s explains what Cubans expected from their efforts. The ultimate purpose ascribed to political organization by Marxist-Leninist theory is the elimination of the state. "This state does not believe in supporting the division of classes, but in the disappearance of class distinctions," explained Fidel Castro in a 1974 interview; "When there are no exploiting classes nor [*sic*] exploited classes, the state as a coercive force will have no *raison d'être*."[11] The state will be eliminated, according to Olga Fernández Ríos and Gaspar J. García Galló, by the "material and spiritual emancipation" achieved by the people.[12] The ideal, then, is a "community of men"—achieved through the "transition of human society towards the future and full realization of man."[13]

Several key elements of the Marxist-Leninist theoretical tradition emerge in Cuba's explanation of its socialist state. First, the socialist state is identified as a class-based organization of political power characterized by the revolutionary seizure of power, collective ownership of the means of production, and the interests it serves. It is considered the dictatorship of the proletariat—an alliance of the Cuban proletariat with all the revolutionary masses, especially the peasantry.

Second, the existence of a state to exercise and defend the power of the working class is seen to provide for socialist democracy. In addition to representing the majority by ending the "exploitation of man by man" and "assuring the right to work, to education, to security in old age, to free medical and hospital care,"[14] socialist democracy permits a new type of participation. According to Fernández Ríos and García Galló,

[socialist democracy] is the last in the development of human society, and its establishment is a necessary step toward the withering away of the state and with it all forms of class democracy.

Proletarian democracy, through the different organizations that make it up, gives to the masses of people the most diverse tasks. This enables the masses to make a revolutionary break with the stagnation and unchangeability that are characteristic of democracy in capitalist society, which conceives of the masses as receivers of democratic concessions and not as active creators of that form of state.[15]

The socialist state, as with all states, is considered coercive: "The exercise of authority, no matter which way it is exercised, is the essence of the state."[16]

Third, the Cuban perspective on the socialist state accepts the leading role of the party within the dictatorship of the proletariat. A vanguard party is considered necessary because the working class as a whole does not emerge ready to exercise its own dictatorship; it "drags along defects and vices of the past which make it heterogeneous with regard to level of consciousness and social conduct."[17] The leadership of the party is not a "dictatorship of the Party," however; the state is the "ideal and direct institution for exercising power over society."[18] The party has moral power and an authority that is political and ideological, whereas the state has the capability to compel compliance and its decisions apply to all citizens. Mass organizations that group together social sectors according to their characteristics and interests are viewed, a la Lenin, as a vital link between party, state, and the people.

Fourth, democratic centralism is the organizational principle of the state. Based on the unity of power, democratic centralism governs the relations of higher- and lower-level bodies. Its expression includes reporting on activities to those above and below and the possibility of recalling elected officials; "liberty of discussion, exercise of criticism and self-criticism, and subordination of the minority to the majority govern all collective state bodies."[19]

By 1976, democracy meant something quite different from what it had meant in 1966 and 1956. The direct democracy of the 1960s is discussed by Cuban scholars as a first stage of socialist democracy with a provisional state apparatus, a stage characterized by the "active, not formal" participation of the Cuban people and the state's acceptance of its representative role. Institutionalization is seen as an advance in democracy that commenced when conditions were ripe for a formal state apparatus and direct, formal participation organized within it.

In 1986, what can be considered a third phase in the evolution of Cuban political organization began, although neither the theory of socialist democracy nor the institutional arrangements of the state system have been substantially altered. Characterized by the campaign for rectification of errors and negative tendencies launched in April 1986, this current phase of Cuban politics is one of correcting the mistakes of the recent past specifically and of the overall revolutionary effort generally. Much as the failed 10 million ton harvest focused criticisms of the first decade in which state-building was implemented, by the mid-1980s developmental difficulties prompted a critical reassessment.

The first indication of the onset of rectification was the creation of a Central Group for the emergency revision of the 1985 plan; at the February 1986 session of the Third Party Congress, Castro's criticisms outlined wide-ranging problems in virtually all areas of organized activity. A distinctly Cuban approach to cumulative difficulties, called by Castro a "new, qualitatively superior stage of the revolution," is attempting to correct mistakes that have affected Cuban socialism.[20]

Rectification represents changes within the existing arrangements of centralization and participation institutionalized in the state-building process. Acknowledging the constraints imposed by external factors, rectification focuses on domestic problems and Cuban solutions. Such errors as the insufficient adaptation of a planning system borrowed from the experience of others and excessive reliance on economic mechanisms, including material incentives, are seen to have contributed to inefficiency and poor economic performance.[21] Among the resulting problems— negative tendencies—are corruption, technocratic economic management, poor information, absenteeism, and the growth of the bureaucracy and *burocratismo*.[22] In attempting to resolve difficulties similar to those experienced by other socialist states, rectification relies on central planning, the vanguard role of the PCC, and the organized participation of the Cuban people.

As one example of worldwide reform in socialism, rectification has thus far rejected market reforms and political pluralism. Instead, the mobilization against errors and negative tendencies ended the free farmers markets created in 1980 and continues to count on the leadership of the PCC. Official explanations of rectification have defended Cuba's commitment to socialism, criticizing reforms elsewhere on that basis. The call for the Fourth Congress of the PCC declared that the revolution, socialism, Leninism, and internationalism will not be renounced; in a January 1990 speech, Castro pointed out that neither Marx, Engels, nor Lenin indicated "what day" the party would be finished or when the state would disappear.[23] Politics and ideology have been reasserted, however, as rectification emphasizes moral incentives, Ché Guevara's ideas, and voluntary labor and stresses improvements in the mass organizations, worker participation, and the party's work. Rectification, Max Azicri succinctly notes, has "a taste of déjà vu."[24]

The process of rectification remains unfinished and its results unclear. A closer look at the socialist state, participation, and the reforms initiated in the 1970s can shed some light on this third stage of democracy in socialist Cuba. An understanding of the dynamics of centralization and earlier decentralizing reforms is necessary for understanding the nature and likely results of rectification.

## Participation and the State:
## Decentralization and Democratization

In each phase in the development of Cuba's socialist democracy, political arrangements have been characterized by centralization and emphasis on popular participation. Although the power of the socialist state is generally attributed to the centralization of decisionmaking and the vast scope of state administration, it is ultimately the extent and nature of participation rather than formal structures that reveal the dynamics of power and the possibilities of democratization. Judgments about the success of past and current reforms must proceed from analysis of the participation that Cuban institutions facilitate as well as of the behavior of ordinary Cuban people.

General assessments of centralization in Cuba are intimately related to the approaches—or models—employed. Centralization of decision-making may be considered necessary, given the conditions of the socialist transition. The defense of the revolution, a scarcity of resources, the vagaries of world markets and fixities of world politics, or the weather are plausible explanations of the limits to decentralization. For others, centralization is not a practical necessity but a political choice. Thus, Castro's thirty-year watch over the state and the PCC reflects excessive centralization of representational opportunities at best and personal dictatorship at worst, and the refusal to choose market reforms is further evidence of an overextended state. Cuban standards for the state system created in 1976 acknowledge difficulties, including the threat of bureaucratic power created by socialist centralization. No general evaluation, including Cuba's, can be supported without a careful look at participation and its purposes.

*Poder Popular* was organized to provide new opportunities for popular inclusion in state activity and decisionmaking. Decentralization was to provide both representation and popular control over administrative functions, although *Poder Popular* did not supercede other forms of participation, including mass organizations and workplace participation. Although all forms of participation should be examined, my purpose permits only an introductory focus on *Poder Popular* and the results and nature of participation within existing centralization.

Elections are a key part of the representation offered in the new state system. Rates of participation in electoral processes have been high. The percentage of registered voters casting secret ballots was 93.6 percent in Matanzas in 1974, 95.2 percent in 1976, 96.9 percent in 1979, 97 percent in 1981, 98.7 percent in 1984, 97.7 percent in 1986, and 98.3 percent in 1989.[25] The electoral process also includes meetings for the nomination of candidates. Participation in these meetings increased from 72 percent to 75.4 percent of those eligible in 1976 and 1979, respectively, to 86 percent in 1981 and 91.2 percent in 1984; in 1989, 80.9 percent of registered voters attended.[26]

Elections are competitive, although competition differs in several ways from that in multiparty representative systems. Cuba is clearly a one-party system, yet the PCC is not an electoral organization. It cannot nominate a candidate, nor is campaigning by any entity or individual permitted. Electoral rules require that there be a minimum of two and a maximum of eight candidates from which to choose. The average has hovered somewhat above two in recent elections. Reelection is not guaranteed. After the Matanzas single-province experience (designed as a democratic prototype using Matanzas to measure public interest in local political reforms), 59.6 percent of incumbents were not renominated. In 1984 and 1989, 52.7 percent and 45.9 percent of delegates, respectively, were reelected.[27] Representatives at all levels of government are also subject to recall. In Matanzas, 14 delegates were replaced and 27 recalled. By 1979, 1,151 municipal delegates had been replaced, 114 of them recalled.[28] Although party competition is absent, elections do reflect choice and competitive movement.

The electoral process serves to organize representation of the community-electors rather than competition among parties, policy positions, or interests associated with race or gender. The distribution of municipal and provincial delegates and national deputies reveals that party members are numerically overrepresented, however. In 1976, 96.7 percent of the deputies belonged to the party or its youth branch (UJC). In 1979, 75.8 percent of municipal and 93.9 percent of provincial delegates were party or UJC members, and in 1984, 74 percent of municipal delegates were.[29] The party does preside over the commissions charged with developing slates of candidates for the indirect provincial and national elections and the executive committees of provincial and municipal assemblies, although slates may be challenged. As the party is to act in a vanguard role, successful fulfillment of that role might be expected to be demonstrated in elections.

On the other hand, women are underrepresented in the three levels of *Poder Popular*, a matter of concern since 1974. The percentage of women among local delegates has risen from 3 percent in 1974 to 8.7 percent in 1976, 7.2 percent in 1979, 7.8 percent in 1981, 11.5 percent in 1984, and 17.1 percent in 1986; it declined to 16.7 percent in 1989. At the provincial and national levels where election is indirect, the percentages are higher and have also risen over time. Women made up 17.2 percent of provincial delegates and 21.8 percent of national deputies in 1976; in 1989, the respective figures were 27.6 percent and 33.9 percent.[30] If the party dominates the process as directly as some believe, Cuba's official promotion of the election of women should be more effective.

Official concern about women in elected positions—and the analysis of electoral outcomes in terms of age, occupation, education, or more recently, race—is not reflected directly in the formal functions assigned to elected representatives. Postelection delegate activity is an important feature of the process of representation. Delegates must hold weekly office hours for constituent access, and the constitution requires that they report to their constituents in accountability sessions (*rendición de cuentas*) at twice-yearly meetings arranged by the mass organizations. The delegates provide a summary of municipal assembly activity and what they have accomplished, communicate assembly policy, and accept "opinions and complaints on any local or national activity of People's Power."[31] Rates of participation in these meetings have not been as high as those in voting, although they vary among electoral districts and municipalities. In the Matanzas experiment and the first few years of *Poder Popular*, attendance ranged from 50 to 70 percent of the registered voters.[32] In the March–April 1983 meetings, attendance was 86.3 percent; and in April 1987, 5,278,598 Cubans—78 percent of those eligible—attended 20,651 meetings.[33]

The delegate is an intermediary between citizens and the municipal assembly whose main duty is to represent the interests of the constituents. Community suggestions, demands, and complaints—*planteamientos*—are crucial in the representative process. By July 1978, some 300,000 proposals or criticisms had been made throughout the island.[34] Between 1981 and 1984, 522,051 *planteamientos* were recorded; from the start of the fifth electoral period in November 1986 through February 1988, 338,577 *planteamientos* were made.[35] Performance of delegates and assemblies is measured by the handling of *planteamientos*. Responses are required by law and are evaluated statistically. If problems cannot be solved, an explanation to the citizen is required. At the close of the November 1984 meetings, the national rate of solution of *planteamientos* was 64.6 percent. For the 338,577 *planteamientos* noted above, the rate of resolution was approximately 70 percent.[36]

What is the nature of these complaints and suggestions? Assessing media accounts in the early years, Jorge I. Domínguez concluded that "the scope of community problems is quite large, ranging from garbage collection and water supply to ice cream flavors and different prices for hair cuts."[37] Of the 522,051 *planteamientos* received between 1981 and 1984, 114,900 concerned communal services such as street repair, construction, and sidewalks, and another 88,661 dealt with commercial dining services. In the September 1984 meetings, for example, the most-often repeated issues nationally were repair and maintenance of grocery stores, milk distribution, electrification, and the quality of bread.[38] *Planteamientos* are not always about needs or problems within the jurisdiction of the municipality, although they usually are.

*Poder Popular* provides mechanisms for electoral participation and representation that have been used effectively. Cubans have noted the distinct features of this system, including the easy access to and accountability of nonprofessional "politicians," and they still defend the indirect rather than direct election of top leadership (quite strongly on the occasion of Castro's speech to Brazilian intellectuals in March 1990).[39] A relationship exists between local participation and national policy—municipal delegates are among those elected to the National Assembly, for example; problems identified at the local level have contributed to new policy—for example, the housing law in the 1980s. Traditional academic concern with centralization and the limits on local-level participation focus on Castro's role, the party's place in *Poder Popular* and in society, and the existence of opposition or dissent. The relationship of decentralization and representation is a provocative theoretical issue, although the official objective of decentralization and expanding participation goes beyond representation.

Administrative reorganization promised a relocation of functional responsibilities that would permit access to state decisionmaking, access that would help resolve the economic and political problems of excessive centralization. As Raúl Castro explained in 1974, "The existence of the organs of *Poder Popular* should signify, without fail, the eradication of the bureaucratic centralism existing in many parts of our state apparatus and its substitution with democratic centralism, the Marxist-Leninist groundwork for the functioning of the state."[40] The decentralization of state functions left a preponderance of policymaking and initiatives at the center and with the PCC but provided new mechanisms for control over administration at each level of the administrative hierarchy. New forms of participation were to be, in Haroldo Dilla's words, an "antidote to the bureaucratic and administrative deviations then existing."[41]

The conception of participation as an antidote to problems of bureaucracy has roots in the antibureaucratic attitudes of the 1960s and continues into the rectification period. Antibureaucratic attitudes surfaced immediately following the revolution in 1959, reflecting the legacy of colonial and neocolonial political corruption organized through the state bureaucracy. By March 1959, thousands of bureaucrats had been removed or had abandoned positions in the central government.[42] Within the centralization of direct democracy, problems of state administration and politics reshaped inherited antibureaucratic attitudes.

The technical and political dimensions of socialist administration proved troublesome in the 1960s. The exodus of technically trained Cubans drained the island of potential administrators.[43] The practices of "guerrilla administration" by revolutionary but unskilled managers were criticized, as were the attempts to counteract them with a centralized planning system imported from Czechoslovakia. Party-building efforts begun in 1961 led to Castro's criticism in 1962 of sectarianism and bureaucratism, of favoritism and privileges.[44] Concern over the political dimension of administrative problems overshadowed attention to an underdeveloped technical capacity during the 1960s.

In 1965, the Offensive Against Bureaucracy was organized to combat *burocratismo*. Surplus officials, insulation, and bureaucratic work methods were criticized, and party Commissions for the Struggle Against Bureaucracy were created. A second stage began in late 1966, and a series of editorials in 1967 presented a critique of *burocratismo* as a problem of socialism.[45] Because the state bureaucracy has a special relationship to the means of production that "might convert bureaucratic posts into comfortable, stagnant or privileged positions," there was the danger of the development of a "special stratum of citizens." More explicitly stated in Part 4 of the editorial series, "We must confront this bureaucracy directly with militant working class spirit. Past experience in struggle against this evil indicates that bureaucracy tends to operate as a new class. Certain bonds are formed among bureaucrats themselves, close ties and relationships characteristic of every social class."[46] The formal responses to bureaucratism were "ideological struggle" and the mobilization of the people under the party's leadership.

Bureaucracy was and is viewed as a profoundly political problem, not simply a technical one or one of Cuba's old order. The technical capacity of administration did become a priority in the state-building period; the new emphasis on efficiency required a more capable administrative system. The design of *Poder Popular* was informed by perceptions of the multiple problems of bureaucracy, however, as Cuba remained—and remains—aware of the problems of *burocratismo* and privileged, isolated bureaucrats. "We are all in agreement," explained Carlos Rafael Rodríguez in a 1980 interview, "that bureaucracy is one of the permanent risks of socialism. In places where all the problems of society are in the hands of those who represent society, and as a result very little occurs outside the sphere of decisions made at the local or national level, the forms of leadership and decision-making become determinant."[47] *Burocratismo* was seen as intimately related to decision-making arrangements. "In the final analysis," said Rodríguez, "the essence of bureaucratism is substituting for the role of the masses in the decision-making process."[48]

Administrative reforms accompanying the state-building process included efforts to reduce personnel and to make improvements in technical training as well as decentralization. The reduction in the number of personnel was important in conducting the experiment in Matanzas and in developing subsequent policy on administration. Yet between 1973 and 1984, the number of state bureaucrats more than doubled.[49] The technical preparation of administrators and workers was prioritized.

Schools and programs for technical and professional education multiplied after 1971, a National School of Economic Management emerged in the mid-1970s, and the 1975 Congress produced a Resolution on Cadres as the first systematic party guidelines. It was only in 1984, however, that the legal foundations of the System for Work with State Cadres emerged.

*Poder Popular* provides mechanisms for control over administration at each of the three levels of the system. These mechanisms are explained by a principle of dual subordination that allows for two dimensions of control: vertical or administrative control of administration, and horizontal control to be achieved through assemblies and representatives at each level. Control of administration at the local level is formally offered in the structure and procedures of municipal assemblies and their executive committees as well as by the role and activity of delegates.

Much as central state bodies plan, inspect, and evaluate performance of their subordinate units, municipal assemblies plan, inspect, and evaluate the performance of the administrative departments established to manage activities within local jurisdictions. The municipal assembly's executive committee appoints and removes municipal administrators. Between July and September 1978, 79 of the 1,599 department heads in Cuban municipalities were "substituted," 30.4 percent due to poor work. A June 1979 report showed that within two years, 683 changes had occurred among 1,662 municipal department heads.[50]

In addition to the supervision exercised by the municipal assembly— which is actually the sole site of authority over local administration— two additional features of *Poder Popular* express Cuba's commitment to popular control through decentralization. Elected delegates, who do not have "individual leadership authority" and must not "personally carry out administrative tasks," are expected to participate directly in the resolution of problems identified by their constituents.[51] Delegate activity might include personal discussion of problems with relevant administrators, the mobilization of mass organizations and residents to tackle a specific problem, or the solicitation of help from the assembly and executive committee. Municipalities have different methods for supporting delegate activities, although constitutional and statutory guidelines ensure basic uniformities. In one municipality in Ciudad de La Habana province in the mid-1980s, for example, there were periodic meetings of administrators, delegates, and the executive committee member charged with attending to a specific group of delegates and areas of administration.[52] Administrators may sometimes attend an accountability session, although an early proposal in the National Assembly that they be obliged to attend was rejected because it was seen to interfere with the direct relationship of the community and the delegate. Ultimately, the "elimination of a deficiency is an administrative responsibility."[53]

Second, the permanent and ad hoc commissions of *Poder Popular* are "one of the most critical mechanisms . . . for the control of the state apparatus," according to Marta Harnecker.[54] Composed of delegates and local specialists, the commissions' purpose is to aid in the supervision and evaluation of local administrative activity; they conduct special or long-term studies and give advice on the routines and deficiencies of administrative performance. In 1979, 1,853 standing and ad hoc commissions were functioning in Cuba. In the electoral term between 1981 and 1984, 1,686 commissions at the municipal level accomplished 9,999 studies or inspections.[55]

Decentralization has occurred in Cuba, accompanied by high rates of voting and postelection activity that are evidence of the successful expansion of participatory opportunities aimed at both representation and popular control of administration. On that basis, participation is more democratic and democratization has occurred. Yet centralization persists, delimiting the formal scope of representation and local decisions. Reforms begun in the mid-1980s reflect Cubans' criticisms of the performance of their institutions. Turning to rectification to offer some final questions about democratization, we will see how international and domestic conditions as well as Cuban decisions contribute to the dynamics of centralization and participation.

## Questioning Old Conclusions

Although the Cuban Revolution radically altered social, economic, and political relationships among the Cuban people, centralization indicates that political inequality has yet to disappear—the state has not withered away. Since the 1960s, Cuban standards have recognized the threat posed to democracy by socialist centralization; the participatory and antibureaucratic approach of the rectification process reflects both continuity and evolution in Cuba's perception and practice of socialist democracy. A final look at rectification suggests why old models and conclusions about what democracy is and is not must give way to questions about power, participation, and people.

Criticisms and modifications of *Poder Popular* often go unnoticed, as the economic dilemmas of rectification and differences with other socialist reforms are more dramatic. Although rectification first began with economic measures, its political dimension is summarized in the Call for the IV Congress of the PCC, which proposes a fresh look at the functioning of socialist democracy *and* the perfecting of *Poder Popular*, including more authority for municipal delegates, stronger popular control of state activity, and better responses to *planteamientos*. Yet critical evaluation of the system predates rectification. A 1985 study of institutionalization, for example, identified such problems as overly formal accountability sessions, inadequate participation by delegates in assembly debates, and deficiencies in the composition and functioning of work commissions.[56]

Modifications and improvements have included the reduction of accountability sessions from four to two per year in the early 1980s, the adoption of a unified system of information, and, more recently, experimentation with a new administrative level within several municipalities with large populations. Study of *Poder Popular* continues, organized through the system itself: A national office attends to the functioning of the system, conducting studies and helping to ensure proper relations between central and local bodies; one example of local efforts is the study by the Las Tunas provincial assembly of the processing of *planteamientos*.[57]

The strengthening of the hierarchical capacity of administration continues into the rectification period, as does the critique of bureaucracy and *burocratismo*. By 1989 there were several new Centers for the Study of Management Techniques and information bulletins for state cadres; reduction in personnel had been pursued with some notable successes. Competence was doubly emphasized as small- and large-scale corruption was sought out, exposed, and punished. In 1987 Castro criticized those who have a blasé attitude and who ignore the fact that in socialism "we must build things and care for people."[58] Rectification seeks to eliminate technocratic and economistic attitudes as well as *burocratismo*.

Cuba's theory of socialist democracy has not changed, although the party now calls for research and scholarly studies of it, active participation in it, and experimentation with and improvement of the theory. Because rectification occurs within existing institutions rather than by replacing them with liberal democratic procedures, the result of reform is not easily judged. The UJC has opened its work center evaluation meetings to nonmembers; generational differences are openly recognized; by September 1989, 16,515 housing units had been constructed by microbrigades; serious debate about improving the press has occurred; and teaching methods now stress dialogue and discussion rather than lectures and rote learning. The problem of measurement can be partially resolved by expanding our understanding of the dynamics of centralization in Cuba to include the active participation *and* commitment of ordinary people. A 1982 study for the U.S. government identified the "development of a relatively well-disciplined and motivated population with a strong sense of national identity" as one of Cuba's accomplishments.[59] In 1986, Azicri argued that "the majority of the Cuban population sees Socialism as the natural, for many even the ideal, culmination of over 100 years of struggle for the country's independence," suggesting that rectification was greeted favorably.[60] Yet the international context has changed, and economic difficulties have not disappeared. The popular participation and support that have been a source and a signal of legitimacy are critical indicators of the past *and* the future of democratization in Cuba.

The attitudes of the Cuban people toward centralization, the state, and their participation help measure the legitimacy of centralization and the potential of current reforms. As argued above, however, democratization is not a simple function of centralization and formal institutions; it is a process determined by active participation that is also antibureaucratic. We must return to contemporary theoretical concerns about democracy in socialism and three unanswered questions derived from our approach to see whether democratization so defined is necessary, sufficient, and realizable.

Increasing the power of the Cuban people in relation to the state and its organization of power has been considered here to be a process of democratization. What, however, is the measure of power in a centralized system that underpins standards of its "democratic" nature? Control has been offered as a general measure, preliminary evidence of participation has been presented, and the importance of the legitimacy granted the state has been asserted. Yet a more specific standard *and* a measure of power must be used to evaluate changes in Cuba and to substantiate the empowerment of the Cuban people. This is even more important if we wish to debate whether political pluralism *alone* is a means for democratization, whether mass organizations are potential political mediations, and whether power must or should be considered in "zero-sum" terms.

Second is the question of necessary and unnecessary restraints on democratization. Abstract goals and principles must be entertained, but existing conditions of power are the basis for all possibilities of democratization. These conditions are not simply domestic; nor are they a matter of choice. We must allow that they can and do affect participation. Thus, as John Hoffman suggests, we should probably "ask how people *should* participate in light of how they *do* participate."[61] This means more study of real people, real participation, and the range of real constraints on the choices available to both the state and the people. The study of what exists, not what is missing, requires that the always normative discussion of democracy inspect the abstract interests that are assumed in the "shoulds" of participation.

Finally, in rejecting models of whole democracies as a way *to study* democratization and noting the absence of a perfect democracy of any type, it is necessary to ask where democratization begins. Perhaps it must be built rather than legislated or decreed from within or without. Who is the agent—the subject—of democratization? Although it is commonly agreed that socialist centralization circumscribes initiatory and representational opportunities at the national level, we are still looking for autonomous participation and opposition. What counts for agency, and where is it found? Is it that "participation which fails to issue in end-products, monuments or great deeds—all those terminal finalities that are associated with heroism in the Western world—seems incoherent to us?"[62]

In all of these questions about democratization, centralization is the theoretical problematic, and decentralization—I contend—is the practical problem of democratic reform. An approach that focuses on the state and the power of participation *can* shed light on the meaning and dynamics of reform in socialist democracy—in Cuba and in any other socialist society. It asks us, however, to continue the reexamination of a traditional debate with arguments about the "democraticness" of different types of reform, with attention to the organization and dynamics of power, and with shared concern for the active participation of ordinary people as the critical element of the theoretical and practical project of both socialist *and* liberal democracy.

## Notes

1. For example, Fidel Castro's reference to a "return to political democracy" in "History Will Absolve Me," in Rolando E. Bonachea and Nelson P. Valdés, eds. *Revolutionary Struggle, 1947–1958. Volume I of the Selected Works of Fidel Castro* (Cambridge, Mass.: The MIT Press, 1972), p. 187, and Ché Guevara's comments on elections in "Interview by Telemundo Television," in Rolando E. Bonachea and Nelson P. Valdés, eds., *Ché: Selected Works of Ernesto Guevara* (Cambridge, Mass.: The MIT Press, 1969), p. 327.

2. Ernesto Ché Guevara, "The Alliance for Progress," in Bonachea and Valdés, eds., *Ché*, p. 382.

3. Fidel Castro, "This is Democracy, May 1, 1960," in *Fidel Castro Speeches. Vol. 3: Our Power Is That of the Working People. Building Socialism in Cuba* (New York: Pathfinder Press, 1983), p. 32.

4. Ernesto Ché Guevara, "Socialism and Man in Cuba," in Bonachea and Valdés, eds., *Ché*, pp. 161–162.

5. Fidel Castro, "Report on the Cuban Economy [Speech Delivered on July 26, 1970]," in Rolando E. Bonachea and Nelson P. Valdés, eds., *Cuba in Revolution* (Garden City, N.Y.: Anchor Books, Doubleday & Company, Inc., 1972), p. 355.

6. *Constitución de la República de Cuba. Tesis y resolución* (Havana: Departamento de Orientación Revolucionaria, Comité Central, Partido Comunista de Cuba, 1976), p. 84. Similar discussion occurred with the 1975 Family Code.

7. Raúl Castro, "Discurso Pronunciado por el Comandante de División Raúl Castro Ruz, en la clausura del seminario a los delegados del Poder Popular que se celebró en Matanzas el 22 de agosto de 1974," in Fidel Castro and Raúl

Castro, *Selección de discursos acerca del partido* (Havana: Editorial de Ciencias Sociales, 1975), p. 203.

8. *El Poder Popular, algunas cuestiones de la economía socialista* (Havana: Departamento de Orientación Revolucionaria, Comité Central, Partido Comunista de Cuba, 1974), p. 67.

9. *Constitución*, pp. 59–60. Among other explanations of *Poder Popular*, see Domingo García Cárdenas, *State Organization in Cuba* (Havana: José Martí Publishing House, 1986), an English version of the 1980 edition.

10. Jorge Alonso, *Cuba: El poder del pueblo* (Mexico City: Editorial Nuestro Tiempo, 1980), p. 109.

11. Frank Mankiewicz and Kirby Jones, *With Fidel: A Portrait of Castro and Cuba*, (New York: Ballantine Books, 1975), p. 79.

12. Olga Fernández Ríos and Gaspar J. García Galló, "The State and Democracy in Cuba," *Contemporary Marxism*, no. 1 (Spring 1980), p. 82.

13. The phrase "community of men" appears in Castro's explanation to Mankiewicz and Jones, *With Fidel*, p. 81. See also Fernández Ríos and García Galló, "The State and Democracy," p. 88.

14. Francisco Ordóñez Martínez, *La legalidad socialista, firme baluarte de los intereses del pueblo* (Havana: Ediciones Jurídicas, Editorial de Ciencias Sociales, 1982), p. 109.

15. Fernández Ríos and García Galló, "The State and Democracy," p. 83.

16. Ibid., pp. 81–82.

17. Raúl Castro, "Discurso," p. 59.

18. García Cárdenas, *State Organization*, pp. 32–34, reflecting Raúl Castro's explanation in "Discurso." Antonio Díaz, "The Participation of the Cuban People in Social-Political Life," in Edward D'Angelo, ed., *Cuban and North American Marxism* (Amsterdam: B. R. Gruner, 1984), writes that the nucleus of the dictatorship of the proletariat is the party.

19. García Cárdenas, *State Organization*, pp. 22–32; *Constitución*, pp. 42–43.

20. Fidel Castro, *Main Report: Third Congress of the Communist Party of Cuba* (Havana: Editora Política, 1986), p. 38.

21. On rectification generally, see Fernando Martínez Heredia, *Desafíos del socialismo cubano* (Havana: Centro de Estudios sobre America, 1988) and the short review by José Luis Rodríguez García, "Une imperiosa necesidad de cambios," *Cuba Internacional* (June 1990), pp. 55–60.

22. Martínez Heredia, *Desafíos del socialismo cubano*, pp. 22–24. See also Castro, *Main Report*.

23. *El futuro de nuestra patria será un eterno Baraguá; Llamamiento al IV Congreso del PCC, 15 de marzo 1990* (Havana: Editora Política, 1990), p. 3; Castro's January 28 speech at the closing of the 16th CTC Congress, *Granma*, February 11, 1990, pp. 2–4.

24. Max Azicri, *Cuba: Politics, Economics and Society* (London: Pinter Publishers, 1988), p. 247.

25. These figures are for first-round voting. William M. LeoGrande, "Participation in Cuban Municipal Government: From Local Power to People's Power," in Donald E. Schulz and Jan S. Adams, eds., *Political Participation in Communist*

*Systems* (New York: Pergamon Press, 1981), p. 283; *Granma,* May 7, 1984, p. 1, October 21, 1986, p. 1, May 8, 1989; and Juan B. del Aguila, *Cuba, Dilemmas of a Revolution* (Boulder: Westview Press, 1986), p. 150.

26. *Granma Weekly Review,* August 30, 1981, p. 3; *Granma,* May 24, 1984, p. 2, and April 15, 1989, p. 1.

27. LeoGrande, "Participation in Cuban Municipal Government," p. 284; *Granma,* May 24, 1984, p. 2, and May 8, 1989.

28. Marta Harnecker, "Los protagonistas de un nuevo poder (2): elección y revocación de delegados," *Bohemia,* vol. 70 (June 9, 1978), p. 39; and *Información estadística sobre el funcionamiento de los órganos locales del Poder Popular: resumen del primer mandato, octubre 1976–marzo 1979* (Havana: Departamento de Atención a los Organos Locales, Asamblea Nacional, June 1979), pp. 1–3. Eight deputies to the National Assembly were recalled during the first ten years.

29. LeoGrande, "Participation in Cuban Municipal Government," p. 289; Azicri, *Cuba,* p. 105; and *Granma,* May 24, 1984, p. 2.

30. *Mujeres y sociedad en cifras, 1975–1988; V Congreso de la Federación de Mujeres Cubanas* (Havana: Editorial de La Mujer, 1990), p. 91.

31. García Cárdenas, *State Organization,* p. 113.

32. William M. LeoGrande, "Mass Political Participation in Socialist Cuba," in John A. Booth and Mitchell A. Seligson, eds., *Political Participation in Latin America: Vol. I: Citizen and State* (New York: Holmes & Meier, 1978), p. 127.

33. *Granma,* August 23, 1983, p. 1, and *La nación cubana,* vol. 3, no. 12, (1987), p. 12.

34. *Granma Weekly Review,* July 9, 1978, p. 2.

35. *La nación cubana,* vol. 1, no. 3 (April–June 1985), p. 43, and *Granma,* March 12, 1988, p. 3.

36. *La nación cubana,* vol. 1, no. 3 (April–June 1985), p. 43, and *Granma,* March 12, 1988, p. 3.

37. Jorge I. Domínguez, *Cuba, Order and Revolution* (Cambridge, Mass.: Harvard University Press, 1978), pp. 285–286.

38. *La nación cubana,* vol. 1, no. 3 (April–June 1985), pp. 43–44, and *Trabajadores,* November 26, 1984, p. 1.

39. *La nación cubana,* vol. 2, no. 8 (1986), p. 37, and Castro's speech of March 18, 1990, published in *Granma Weekly Review,* April 15, 1990, pp. 2–5.

40. Raúl Castro, "Discurso," p. 210.

41. Haroldo Dilla, "Democracia y poder revolucionario en Cuba," *Cuadernos de Nuestra América,* no. 7 (January–June 1987), p. 68.

42. Hugh Thomas, *Cuba: The Pursuit of Freedom* (New York: Harper & Row, 1971), p. 1068, comments on the early months when the uncovering of corruption and administrative sinecures (*botellas*) was coupled with the voluntary exodus of many officials. Domínguez, *Cuba,* p. 234, provides a figure of 50,000, citing Alfred J. Padula, Jr., "The Fall of the Bourgeoisie: Cuba, 1959–1961," Ph.D. dissertation, University of New Mexico, 1974, p. 529.

43. Richard Jolly, "Education," in Dudley Seers, ed., *Cuba, The Economic and Social Revolution* (Chapel Hill: University of North Carolina Press, 1964), p. 177, provides a figure of some 50,000 of the 86,000 technically and professionally trained who have left.

44. Thomas, *Cuba*, pp. 1373–1381, and Fidel Castro, "Against Bureaucracy and Sectarianism," in *Fidel Castro Speeches. Vol. 3*.

45. See "Employees of State Organizations to Work in Agriculture One Week Every Month," *Granma Weekly Review*, March 26, 1967, p. 3. And, more generally, William M. LeoGrande, "Party Development in Revolutionary Cuba," *Journal of Interamerican and World Affairs*, vol. 21 (November 1979), pp. 457–480, and Nelson P. Valdés, "Cuba: socialismo democrático o burocratismo colectivista?" *Aportes*, vol. 23 (January 1972), pp. 36–38.

46. "The Struggle Against Bureaucracy: A Decisive Task (II)," *Granma Weekly Review*, March 5, 1967, p. 3, and "The Struggle Against Bureaucracy: A Decisive Task (IV)," *Granma Weekly Review*, March 12, 1967, p. 3.

47. Carlos Rafael Rodríguez, "An Interview with Carlos Rafael Rodríguez, December 1980," in *Fidel Castro Speeches. Vol. 3*, p. 320.

48. Ibid.

49. Joaquín Benavides Rodríguez indicates that 8 percent of the active labor force was management in the early 1980s. "La ley de la distribución con arreglo al trabajo y la reforma de salarios en Cuba," *Cuba Socialista*, vol. 2 (March 1982), pp. 70–74 (Benavides states that 54 percent of the labor force at the end of 1981 were workers, 18 percent were technicians, and 20 percent were administrative and service workers. The remainder is the figure for management personnel); Martínez Heredia, *Desafíos del socialismo cubano*, p. 23.

50. *Información estadística sobre el funcionamiento de los órganos locales del Poder Popular* (Havana: Departamento de Atención a los Organos Locales, Asamblea Nacional, December 1978), p. 5; *Información estadística . . . octubre 1976–marzo 1979*, pp. 5–6. There were 37 changes among 232 provincial department heads as well.

51. García Cárdenas, *State Organization*, pp. 114, 115.

52. Caridad Negrín Lantarón, "Por los municipios: Diez de octubre y la solución de los planteamientos," *Información al Delegado* (June 1985), pp. 28–29.

53. "El pueblo debe exigir la presencia del administrador cuando se le brinde mal servicio," *Información al Delegado*, no. 12 (October 1979), pp. 5–7.

54. Marta Harnecker, *Cuba: Dictatorship or Democracy?* (Westport: Lawrence Hill, 1979), p. 193 and pp. 184–193, where she provides examples of the activities of work review boards in the early days.

55. *La Nación Cubana*, vol. 1, no. 3 (April–June 1985), p. 43.

56. Angel Fernández-Rubio Legrá, *El proceso de institucionalización de la revolución cubana* (Havana: Editorial de Ciencias Sociales, 1985), pp. 58–59. García Cárdenas, *State Organization*, also provides critical summaries of the institutions he discusses.

57. García Cárdenas, *State Organization*, pp. 66–67, and *El Poder Informa: Organo informativo del Poder Popular*, Las Tunas, vol. 6, no. 3 (September 1987), p. 7.

58. *Granma Weekly Review*, July 5, 1987, p. 5.

59. Lawrence H. Theriot, *Cuba Faces the Economic Realities of the 1980s: A Study Prepared for the Use of the Joint Economic Committee, Congress of the United States* (Washington, D.C.: U.S. Government Printing Office, 1982), p. 5.

60. Max Azicri, "Cuba After Twenty-Six Years: An Appraisal," *Contemporary Marxism*, vol. 14 (Fall 1986), p. 87.

61. John Hoffman, "The Coercion/Consent Analysis of the State Under Socialism," in Neil Harding, ed., *The State in Socialist Society* (Albany: State University of New York Press, 1984).

62. Henry S. Kariel, "Beginning at the End of Democratic Theory," in Graeme Duncan, ed., *Democratic Theory and Practice* (Cambridge: Cambridge University Press, 1983), p. 253.

# 4

# Bureaucracy Versus Democracy in Contemporary Cuba: An Assessment of Thirty Years of Organizational Development

*Richard L. Harris*

This chapter provides a critical analysis, from a Marxist perspective, of the organizational development of contemporary Cuban society. After more than three decades of political, economic, and social development under a self-proclaimed socialist regime, it is appropriate to assess the organizational structures of Cuban society in order to determine the extent to which these structures approximate the basic vision of socialism held by Marxists since the first writings on this subject were produced by Marx and Engels more than a century and a half ago. Due to limitations of space, the focus of this chapter will be confined to an assessment of some of the basic organizational structures of the contemporary Cuban state and economy. These structures will be analyzed in terms of the extent to which they approximate the democratic forms of workers' self-management envisaged by both the founders and many of the contemporary adherents of Marxism.

In general, my analysis reveals that there has been an embryonic development of socialist forms of organization in Cuba, in spite of inhibiting factors. Moreover, there is evidence of increasing worker participation in the planning and management of production. However, the introduction of democratic socialist forms of organization, particularly worker self-management and democratic planning, has been blocked by the regime's continuing reliance on capitalist forms of organization and management as well as bureaucratic methods and procedures.

In order to place the Cuban case in a comparative context, references will be made throughout this chapter to the experience of the Soviet Union and certain other socialist or former socialist states. This will provide both a historical and a comparative perspective that will help to bring out the similarities and differences between revolutionary Cuba's development and that of other self-proclaimed socialist regimes.

## Cuba's Bad Organizational Habits

The development of socialist forms of organization in Cuba has been shaped by what can be described as the "bad organizational habits" that were introduced in the early years of the revolutionary regime. During these first years, a dramatic process of organizational change took place as the private sector was rapidly brought under state ownership. A kind of egalitarian and free-wheeling variant of state socialism emerged that was characterized by considerable disorganization and little central planning.[1]

Between 1959 and 1963, the government and the newly nationized (statized) enterprises were characterized by an ad-hoc style of management and improvised organizational structures. The free-wheeling administrative style of this period, called *por la libre* by the Cubans, was introduced by the former guerrilla army officers who assumed the leadership positions in most of the government ministries and new state enterprises. Few permanent organizational structures or procedures were established during this early period of the regime. New organizations emerged and disappeared. In many cases, individuals with no previous managerial or technical experience assumed important positions, and there was not even a tightly organized vanguard party to exercise centralized control over the expanding state apparatus.[2] The commanding figure of Fidel Castro dominated this *por la libre* period of organizational transformation, which was typified by Castro's audacious and free-wheeling style of leadership.

Although the new revolutionary society that emerged during the 1960s was characterized by intense popular participation, this participation was largely confined to the implementation of the policies made by Castro and the new political leadership. Political commandism and bureaucratic centralism developed in this context as did a host of organizational problems, some of which have continued until this day.[3]

The regime's failure to reach the goal of harvesting 10 million tons of sugar in 1970, despite the mobilization of much of the country's population to achieve this objective, led Castro and the revolutionary leadership to critically reassess the organizational structures of both the country's political system and its economy. Based on this reassessment, they decided that a fundamental rectification of the revolutionary regime was in order. The main characteristics of this process of rectification have recently been analyzed by Frank Fitzgerald, who summarizes them briefly in the following terms.

> As part of this process, between 1970 and 1973 the trade unions, which had virtually "withered away" in the late 1960s, were reconstituted along with other mass organizations. By the time of the first Party Congress in 1975, although the party remained interlocked with, and thereby ultimately in control of, the rest of the administrative apparatus, the organization and role of the party had been formally differentiated from the rest of the system. Soon thereafter, Organos de Poder Popular were created: elected assemblies empowered to administer the state at the municipal, provincial and national levels. In the same period, the revolutionary leadership began introducing a new *Sistema de Dirección y Planificación de la Economía* [System for Direction and Planning of the Economy], designed in part to rationalize central economic planning and to create relatively autonomous enterprises, with responsibility for realizing a profit within the limits of centrally controlled prices and credit.[4]

As this quote reveals, the early 1970s marked an important turning point in the revolutionary process. Beginning in this period, the largely improvised structures and "direct democracy" of the early years were replaced by the establishment of new political institutions, the strengthening and clarification of the role of the party, a renewed emphasis on the mass organizations created during the early 1960s, and the rationalization of the administrative and planning apparatus.

The organizational principles of democratic centralism, developed in the Soviet Union by Lenin and the early Bolsheviks, were adopted during this period of Cuba's revolutionary leadership as the basic guidelines for structuring participation in decisionmaking at all organizational levels of the state and economy. According to these principles, input into the decisionmaking process is to be solicited from the lower levels of all social organizations. This input is then supposed to provide an important basis for the policy decisions made by the leadership at the higher levels of the party, state, and economic system. Once a decision has been reached in this manner, dissent or opposition to the decision is supposed to cease, and the decision is to be faithfully carried out by everyone involved.

In practice, the introduction of these organizational principles has involved much more than the establishment of a series of procedural guidelines for making and implementing decisions. In fact, it has created a centralized, top-down decisionmaking process within the main organizational structures of Cuban society.[5] This system of democratic centralism has continued to be regarded as the correct structure for decisionmaking in all organizational structures as well as in the political system.

In the best of circumstances, this method of decisionmaking provides for a form of consultative democracy in which the people at the base of the society's political, administrative, and economic organizations are consulted on a limited range of issues both before and after decisions are made. They are consulted on how best to carry out these decisions at their particular level. In the worst of circumstances, it leads to what has been called bureaucratic centralism, which is a system of decisionmaking in which all meaningful decisions are made at the top of the party and state bureaucracy, with little or no input from the people below.

## Problems Stemming from Reliance on
## Bourgeois Forms of Organization

The tendency to rely on bourgeois forms of organization in the economic sphere has been present in all socialist regimes, including the Cuban case, since the Russian revolution. Lenin and many of the Bolsheviks made the mistake of thinking that capitalist forms of industrial organization and management could be used by the new revolutionary regime to create the conditions for socialism. Thus, in *The Immediate Tasks of the Soviet Government*, Lenin argued for the adoption of the latest forms of capitalist industrial organization, particularly Fredrick Taylor's methods of so-called scientific management.[6] Lenin went even further than the Taylorists by arguing that *"unquestioning subordination to a single will is absolutely necessary for the success of processes organized on the pattern of large-scale machine industry"* (emphasis added).[7]

Moreover, Lenin saw "absolutely *no* contradiction in principle between Soviet democracy and the exercise of dictatorial powers by individuals" in Soviet organizations (emphasis added).[8] Lenin strongly opposed the demands of the Workers' Opposition for worker self-management of the production process under the control of the unions, and when Bukharin introduced a resolution for industrial democracy (democratic management of industrial enterprises) in the Central Committee of the party, Lenin reacted furiously because he felt this could undermine the party's dictatorship and the management of the state enterprises by individuals.[9] Following the Kronstadt rebellion in 1921, the Workers' Opposition was banned, the trade unions were reduced to the task of ensuring labor discipline, and any further suggestion of worker self-management in the Soviet Union was precluded.

By the end of the 1920s, the *edinonachalie*, or one-man management system, became the dominant characteristic of Soviet forms of organization. Under this system, the directors of state enterprises were given absolute control over their enterprises, and all pretense of worker participation in the management of production was eliminated.[10] This form of strict hierarchical organization was consistent with the dictatorial nature of the Soviet regime under Stalin and with the "economism" that characterized the regime's approach to transforming Soviet society. In this approach, the transformation of the social relations of production (forms of ownership, management, the division of labor, and the like) was subordinated to the transformation of the forces of production (narrowly conceived as technology, technical know-how, the productive infrastructure, and similar elements). Thus, the rapid development of the country's material forces of production took precedence over the development of new forms of organization and ownership.

Charles Bettelheim, in referring to the economism of the Soviet regime, has argued that this is "the form which bourgeois ideology takes within Marxism."[11] He further claims that the Soviet experience makes it clear that unless the social relations of capitalist production are replaced by socialist relations of production, the exploitive nature of capitalism will survive and a new bourgeoisie will emerge.[12] In analyzing why the Soviet Union has failed to undergo a genuine socialist transformation, Bettelheim argues that it is due in part to the fact that the Soviet system is based on what are in essence capitalist relations of production.

In other words, only an across-the-board implantation of genuinely democratic forms of organization in the production process can prevent the survival of capitalist social relations and the revival of class exploitation. This appears to be increasingly recognized by Marxists who have critically assessed the Soviet, Chinese, and Eastern European experiences. For example, Branko Horvat argues:

> A socialist organizational model must be structured so as to eliminate hierarchy, which inevitably generates class stratification. This is achieved by closing the organizational structure in a very specific way: no countervailing power, which generates competing bureaucracies; no party bolt, which gives rise to one single omnipotent bureaucracy; but the combining of management and work by the same people—that is, self-management.[13]

According to Horvat, self-management is the basic organizational form on which socialism is based.

The fundamental institution of socialism is self-management. . . . By participating in management (and in local government), by fighting for a continuous extension of participation until it reaches self-management, workers can learn in their daily lives how to control their destiny, how to overcome the fragmentation and decomposition of labor, how to achieve meaningful social equality, and how to destroy antiquated hierarchies. They do this without the tutorship of omniscient leaders. They prepare themselves for self-determination. . . . Self-management clearly cannot be established overnight. But neither was the capitalist market. And just as the development of the market, however gradual or irregular, could not be anti-capitalist, the growth of participation from its primitive forms of joint consultation toward full-fledged self-management cannot be anti-socialist, in spite of the attempts to misuse it for the preservation of the status quo.[14]

If Horvat is right and the fundamental organizing principle of socialism is democratic self-management, then the introduction of self-management can be viewed as an indispensable step in the transition from capitalism to socialism. It follows that without this form of organization, socialist relations of production cannot be developed and a socialist democracy cannot be realized.

As Horvat indicates, self-management cannot be established overnight. It requires the increased participation of workers in organizational decisionmaking. Horvat contends that the development of worker participation generally can be said to pass through three stages: (1) joint consultation, (2) codetermination, and (3) self-management.[15] The development and institutionalization of self-management involve an organizational revolution. This revolution requires the abolition within the units of production of the hierarchical structures of decisionmaking and management inherited from capitalism as well as the elimination of the division of labor that divides the work force into different strata of intellectual and manual workers.

However, by itself self-management cannot guarantee a successful transition to democratic socialism. Self-management at the enterprise level needs to be linked effectively with democratically constituted national and regional planning bodies to ensure that the decisions made by the workers in each enterprise and unit of organization are conditioned by socially recognized needs and goals.[16] Without these structures of planning and coordination, self-management can degenerate into a type of workers' capitalism that obstructs social planning and the further socialization of the relations of production. This is what has happened in Yugoslavia. On this point, Bettelheim has warned that "decisionmaking power must not be *atomized,* if the very foundations for building socialism and planning are not to be destroyed."[17]

If one applies to Cuba the three-stage conception of the development of worker participation offered by Horvat (joint consultation, codetermination, and self-management), then it appears that worker participation in Cuba has reached stages one and two. In Cuba, organizational arrangements exist at the enterprise level that have brought workers and management together to discuss the formulation and implementation of production plans as well as working conditions and related matters.[18] In addition, there are laws and regulations that require worker representation on the management boards or directive bodies of most enterprises—the formal basis for what is known in Western Europe as codetermination, or *co-gestión* in Latin America. In its most developed form, codetermination involves joint management.[19] However, this degree of worker participation does not yet exist in Cuba.

The workers do not control either production decisions or production planning in Cuba, but since the 1970s there has been a notable increase in worker participation in the discussion of production issues as well as in the elaboration of work center plans. On matters concerning the terms of their employment, the workers within each enterprise tend to exert considerable influence on the enterprise management. This is due in part to the introduction of new forms of collective organization at the base of both the manufacturing enterprises and the state farms. Following the experience of other countries such as the Soviet Union and China, the rank and file workers have been organized into production brigades called Permanent Brigades of Production in the agricultural sector and Integral Brigades of Production in the manufacturing sector.[20]

These basic units of production are on the verge of becoming the primary organizational structure within Cuba's state enterprises and farms. They have the authority to organize their own labor and are to be given the resources necessary to complete their productive tasks. Beyond these basic features, one study of worker incentives in Cuba by the Cuban economist, Alexis Codina Jiménez, indicates that these new forms of organization have the following characteristics.

1. The workers are brought together to carry out a group job, the result of which constitutes a final product or a certain part of it (article, work, project, volume of loading and unloading, agricultural activity, or similar result).
2. A brigade works on the basis of an annual plan that all the members are involved in drawing up. This plan must concur with the principal economic and production indicators and is broken down into trimesters and at times, months or days, according to the characteristics of the brigade's activity.

3. Each brigade is assigned the technical, material, wage, and human resources that are indispensable to the fulfillment of its productive tasks.
4. The brigade's collective task is distributed among its members according to the division and cooperation of labor it has established.
5. A significant portion of the brigade's wage is tied to the final results of its work, by which is understood the fulfillment of the planned indicators that define its activity. Wages are distributed among the members according to their participation in the collective task.
6. The brigade possesses a certain degree of operative autonomy in the execution of its task; the direction and overseeing of its achievement is provided by the brigade chief, elected by the brigade members.[21]

These brigades have been organized to increase both the volume and quality of production as well as to reduce costs. They are also supposed to increase the skills of the workers involved and develop Communist attitudes toward work.

Direction and control of the production brigades by the enterprise are accomplished largely through the planning process instead of through direct supervision. Each brigade must fulfill its part of the enterprise, farm, or production unit plan that corresponds to it. Moreover, payment for work is related to the output produced by each brigade as well as the complexity of its tasks, the conditions under which it works, and the established work norms. The preferred system of payment is one that is based on the output of the brigade in terms of a specified product or service that meets a certain standard of quality.

The brigade system provides a basis for socialist emulation because it makes it possible to stimulate competition between collective work units in the same enterprise or industry. Standards for emulation are usually based on labor productivity, quality of production, efficient use of resources, work discipline, safety records, innovations, and the like. Individual emulation within the brigades is also stimulated on the basis of demonstration of initiative and contribution to the collective's output.

Prizes are awarded to brigades and individuals from the stimulation fund created by each enterprise. The use of material awards for emulation within a collective framework provides a mutually reinforcing combination of materials and moral incentives that stimulates increased performance and productivity as well as Communist principles of work and social consciousness—*conciencia*.

The formation of production brigades throughout the various branches of industry and sectors of the economy was given importance in the

1986–1990 Five-Year Plan. It was conceived of as an important means of improving the organization of production and labor productivity. However, it is significant that it was not explicitly presented as a means of increasing worker participation in the control and planning of production. This is unfortunate because the brigades could function as the essential building blocks of worker self-management and the democratization of decisionmaking and planning at the enterprise level. In other words, these brigades could function as the kind of semiautonomous work units that Horvat and others argue must form the base of a self-managed enterprise.[22] Combined within a federative structure of such groups and a bottom-up hierarchy of representative councils, they could control and plan the production process at the enterprise level and elect delegates to the multilevel democratic planning and coordination structures set up at the enterprise, economic sector, and national levels.

## Selection of Cadres

Apart from opportunities in the decisionmaking process, one of the most important factors that determine the distribution of power in any hierarchical organization is the manner in which the individuals in the upper levels of the hierarchy are selected. If they are selected by the lower levels then an essential condition of democratic organization is fulfilled. However, if they are not selected by the lower levels, and instead are appointed by one person or a few persons at the top of the organizational hierarchy, then the organization is essentially undemocratic in nature. Therefore, the manner in which the directive personnel of organizations—generally referred to as cadres in the existing socialist societies—are selected is a critical element of the organizational system that determines whether it is democratic or authoritarian.

Mihailo Markovic's critique of the *nomenklatura* system in the Soviet Union is relevant in this regard. As the following quote reveals, if the selection of cadres is dominated by a single leader, the latter can and often does assume dictatorial powers.

> The experience of all twentieth century revolutions shows that those leaders who were responsible for the selection of cadres were able to dominate the scene, to defeat their rivals and assume dictatorial powers. The cadres policy cannot remain so important in a system of self-government where personnel cannot be simply nominated, promoted or fired but must be democratically elected. . . . There is a social need to have a survey of available talent and different kinds of competence for different functions, to record the achievements and failures of individuals in their elected public functions, to propose how the most important functions within a

body of self-government should be distributed. Responsibility for cadres policy is a decisive power, and therefore it should not be in the hands of those who already have other powers—it should be separated.[23]

The selection of cadres in the Soviet Union, China, Vietnam, Cuba, and most existing socialist societies has been dominated by the party leadership, and this has guaranteed their centralized control over not only these administrative elements but the rank and file members below them as well.

In Cuba, the selection of the directive cadres in the state administration and state enterprises is under the control of the top leadership. Only the lowest-level cadres are appointed on the nomination and approval of the rank and file. This is one of the most serious obstacles to the democratization of the basic organizational structures of Cuban society. It should be noted, however, that in recent years, emphasis has been placed by the top leadership on the recruitment of more women, blacks, and young people into cadre positions in the Communist party. Moreover, there is talk of introducing the election of the lower levels of the party's leadership. In the main report of the Third Congress of the party in 1986, Castro criticized the recruitment of party cadres. The report also emphasized that the leadership of the party should reflect the ethnic and racial composition of the population. This was an important admission of the continuing importance of racial discrimination in Cuba and the party's responsibility for rectifying "historical injustices" such as racism and sexism through increasing the recruitment of blacks and women into leadership positions, both within the party and in the state and mass organizations.

Thus, certain important changes appear to be taking place in the recruitment and selection of key personnel for leadership positions in the party, state administration, state enterprises, and mass organizations. The main intent of these changes, however, is to confront the managerial deficiencies and increasing problems of lack of creativity and commitment among the cadres as well as the rank and file in the various organizational structures of the economy[24] rather than to extend the democratization of the organizational structures of Cuban society.

## Organizational Deficiencies and Managerial Problems in Cuba Today

The underlying causes behind Cuba's present organizational deficiencies and managerial problems include: (1) a cultural tradition of hierarchical and authoritarian relations that reinforces paternalistic interactions and inhibits creative decisionmaking or problem solving, except for those at the top of the hierarchy; (2) an educational system based on passive learning and the acquisition of knowledge rather than the development of creative thinking and independent inquiry; (3) the force of Castro's personality, which, although motivational and inspirational, reinforces the passivity and paternalism already rooted in the culture; and (4) the absence of cost-consciousness among cadres and workers as a result of the virtual abandonment of cost accounting after the revolutionary triumph and the subsequent separation of considerations over production from concerns about costs.

Some of the more specific managerial problems stem from the low social recognition given to managerial activity; the fact that managers often receive inadequate training in management philosophy and practices and workers receive none (especially noteworthy is the absence of any knowledge of democratic styles of management); the fact that many managers are paid less than technical personnel such as engineers; the fact that most managers spend too much time in meetings with external authorities who control and limit their power; and the fact that managers do not have the time or the encouragement to think creatively. In addition to these factors that contribute to poor management, one must add the complexity of labor legislation, job categories that are too rigid and narrow, the almost total absence of career development plans and opportunities for many workers, the absence of incentives for night and swing shifts in order to encourage people to work them, the fact that many jobs are filled on the basis of seniority rather than merit, and a personnel decisionmaking process that is often too long and bureaucratic. As a result of these conditions and a high rate of personnel turnover among the work force, management in Cuba is extremely mediocre.

At the enterprise level in Cuba, a series of vexing organizational problems undermines the effectiveness and smooth operation of the enterprises and other units of production. Due to some of the deficiencies in the managerial cadres and in the work force mentioned above, there is often inadequate inventory control, poor production scheduling, inadequate health and safety procedures, and poor planning. In fact, the main purpose of the enterprises is not clear due to the fact that they are confronted with conflicting demands—providing buses to transport local school children, building community infrastructures, providing workers for microbrigades, and producing profits. Resolution of these conflicting demands often means negotiating with national, provincial, and local government authorities. This takes an enormous amount of time, energy, and resources. In addition, the enterprises do not have direct contact with their domestic and foreign customers, and as a result they find it difficult to serve them adequately. They are also faced with too many regulations, procedures, and directions that they must follow.

The System for Direction and Planning of the Economy is too centralized and does not give the enterprises enough participation in the strategic decisions that affect their productivity and the quality of their production. In fact, often the enterprises are not consulted about the many changes that are made in the plans that affect their operations. Finally, there are often serious logistical problems due to both domestic and international factors. As a result, indispensable supplies frequently fail to arrive on time or in sufficient quantity, thereby delaying the production process and undermining the morale of the work force.

These problems are generally related to or caused by the effects of bureaucratic centralism in the political and major economic structures of the country. As Fitzgerald has noted, this phenomenon "arises in part from the proximate impact of systemic factors, but it also arises from socio-historical factors," particularly the period during the 1960s of "hypercentralized decision-making, in which the workers had little voice and in which the watchword was to mobilize for production rather than to debate problems or alternatives."[25]

Cuba's increasing economic difficulties have led to the present campaign of rectification, which seeks to root out the bureaucratism, various deficiencies, and corruption that have developed within the basic organizational structures of Cuban society. However, as the preceding analysis has suggested, this process of rectification does not give priority to extending the democratization begun in the 1970s to the planning and management of the production process, which is needed in order to get at the roots of the organizational and ideological causes of many of the country's present problems.

## Moral Versus Material Incentives

In order to understand the current effort at rectification that is taking place in Cuba as well as the basic organizational culture in Cuba, it is necessary to examine the debate over moral and material incentives that has been a continuing theme in the country since the early days of the revolutionary regime. The present renewal effort and the errors that are now being criticized by Cuba's leaders go back to the first years of the revolutionary regime when Ché Guevara was Cuba's leading theoretician and protagonist of the use of radical measures to bring about the socialist transformation of Cuban society. Ché Guevara as well as other radical members of the revolutionary leadership such as Raúl Castro, Osvaldo Dorticós, and Antonio Núñez Jiménez, argued that Cuba's small size and relatively well-developed communications system made it possible to introduce central planning and do away with the pricing mechanism of the market. Ché Guevara adopted a radical Marxist perspective and opposed attempts to build socialism that used capitalist methods.

> The pipe dream that socialism can be achieved with the help of the dull instruments left to us by capitalism (the commodity as the economic cell, profitability, individual material interest as a lever, etc.) can lead into a blind alley. And you wind up there after having traveled a long distance with many crossroads, and it is hard to figure out just where you took the wrong turn. Meanwhile, the economic foundation that had been laid has done its work of undermining the development of consciousness. To build communism it is necessary, simultaneous with the new material foundations, to build the new man.[26]

Ché Guevara argued that moral incentives should be given primacy over material incentives and that the finances of the state enterprises should be part of the state budget. He was opposed to the Soviet *khozraschet* system in which the state enterprises operate much like capitalist enterprises and function as independent accounting units responsible for making profits and covering their costs.[27] He felt Cuba should rapidly establish a centrally planned economy and make a clean break with capitalist ideas and methods.

Ché Guevara forcefully advocated the perspective that the transition from capitalism to communism requires linking transformations in the economic structure of society with transformations in the social consciousness of the population. More specifically, he argued that in the period of socialist transition, the use of capitalist methods corrupts the process and that it is necessary to create a new Communist consciousness in order to bring about the socialist transformation of society. In other words, Ché Guevara was acutely aware that the transformation of the motivations and consciousness of men and women is as important as the transformation of the structures of production and distribution. Therefore, he believed that "communism is a phenomenon of consciousness and not solely a phenomenon of production."[28]

Ché Guevara played a major role in the great debate over alternative models of socialism that took place in Cuba during the early 1960s. Among the various models considered by the Cubans was the Yugoslav model of decentralized market socialism, involving a regulated market, commodity relations, profit-making enterprises, decentralized investments, and material incentives.[29] Ché Guevara appears to have shared Paul Sweezy's views on this system[30]—namely, that this type of economic system produces individuals with goals and motivations no different from those of capitalism.[31]

In 1965 Ché Guevara left Cuba under a cloud of secrecy, and shortly afterward the debate over alternative models was settled in favor of a centralized model of socialism in which the primacy of nonmonetary and moral incentives was a distinctive feature. This was the egalitarian variant of administrative (centralized) socialism Ché Guevara had advocated, and he left behind many ideas as to how it could be implemented in Cuba—including the use of voluntary work brigades, fraternal competition between workers and work groups called "socialist emulation," and a budgetary finance system for the efficient management of the country's state enterprises and the production process in general.

The Cuban model that came into being by the end of the 1960s was based on a narrow range of wage levels and the satisfaction of basic necessities through the provision of free services (such as health care and education) and the rationing of basic goods at subsidized low prices. It also emphasized the need for collective forms of consumption as opposed to private consumption, the distribution of certain goods such as refrigerators and televisions on the basis of the decisions of worker assemblies, and the establishment of an elaborate system of nonmonetary awards for persons and groups displaying exemplary attitudes and performance (socialist emulation). Ché Guevara's ideas were responsible in particular for the mobilization of the population to freely give up some of their leisure time to participate in voluntary work projects and public education campaigns aimed at developing communist morals (*conciencia comunista*) in place of the values of egoistic individualism.[32]

Ché Guevara's views have often been characterized as romantic and idealistic, and his approach has been criticized as giving rise to "voluntarism."[33] Critics ask how long people can be expected to substitute moral fervor for improved material consumption, and they question whether the use of moral incentives is anything more than a means of extracting unpaid labor from workers who feel psychologically coerced to give up their leisure time.[34] Moreover, it is argued that the Marxist-Christian ideal of men not living by bread alone overlooks the fact that in reality there is often a trade-off between material well-being and moral behavior, especially under conditions of scarcity.

However, Ché Guevara and his supporters knew full well that moral incentives had to be combined with material incentives and that it was not enough to rely on the development of a Communist work ethic among the working population. They in fact advocated the establishment of a wage system in which wages would be tied to qualifications and the fulfillment of prescribed work norms. Ché Guevara believed, however, that the wage system during the transition to socialism should not overemphasize material incentives, and he stressed that it should be used in combination with moral incentives to build a Communist work ethic. For him, the development of a new consciousness about the social significance of work was critically important because he saw this new consciousness as a material force in the construction of socialism.

The influence of Ché Guevara's ideas on moral incentives is still strong in Cuba, even though it has been more than a quarter of a century since he left the country. However, during the late 1970s and early 1980s, voluntary work and the prior emphasis on moral incentives were displaced by an increased emphasis on individual material incentives and administrative methods. Now, as part of the rectification campaign launched in 1986, Cuba's leaders have revived voluntary work brigades and begun to attack the problems they believe were created by the retreat from the ideals and methods introduced in the 1960s.[35] The rectification campaign seeks to use both material and moral incentives in such a way as to elicit high productivity, commitment to quality, labor discipline, the pursuit of collective goals as opposed to selfish individual interests, efficiency, conservation of resources, honest and professional management, and respect for the consumer-public. It remains to be seen whether this campaign will be able to overcome these problems through a revival of the kind of moral and material incentives that were advocated by Ché Guevara and introduced during the late 1960s.

## Market Reforms and Decentralization

Since the introduction of perestroika in the Soviet Union and the collapse of the state socialist regimes in Eastern Europe, there has been a great deal of discussion about the need for market reforms and decentralization in Cuba. The tendency in this discussion has been to assume that market reforms and decentralization are the solutions to the kind of economic and organizational problems that beset contemporary Cuba. However, this assumption is highly questionable.

The evidence has tended to indicate that when a centralized planning body imposes detailed production targets on individual enterprises, the enterprises are commonly presented with tasks that they either cannot fulfill or can easily fulfill without using their full capacity. Thus, centralized planning takes away from the main units of production the flexibility they need in order to function effectively. However, a socialist solution to this problem does not lie in decentralization or a return to the enterprise autonomy of capitalist firms. Greater enterprise autonomy does not resolve the problem; it merely creates new problems. What is needed is for the national planning process and the production relations *within* each enterprise to be brought under the *democratic control* of the producer.[36]

Yugoslavia's experience with so-called market socialism, decentralization, and worker-managed enterprises reveals the important issues underlying the centralization versus decentralization debate. The key structures in the Yugoslav system are the worker-managed enterprises, which operate as independent profit-maximizing economic units that are "owned" by their workers. They operate in a market context much like private enterprises elsewhere. This means that those units with the most advantages (favorable access to finance capital, resources, markets, and an appropriate supply of labor) tend to increase their incomes at the expense of those with the fewest advantages.[37]

In other words, a form of exploitation takes place in which the workers and managers in the more favored enterprises increase their incomes at the expense of those in the less favored enterprises. This also has contributed to the lopsided development and unequal distribution of national income among the different regions of the country. Moreover, because the workers and managers of each enterprise seek to maximize their individual incomes through maximizing the net income (profit) of their enterprise and then distributing this income to themselves in the form of wages, these worker-managed enterprises have chosen largely to use the earnings of their enterprises for short-term wage increases rather than investing a major portion of these earnings into their enterprises or other productive economic activities. In fact, when they do undertake investments in their enterprises, they tend to finance these investments through loans secured from the state banks at low interest rates rather than from setting aside savings from their earnings for investments. This has had negative effects on the country's economy by giving rise to a low rate of savings, high inflation, and insufficient as well as inefficient investments.

Furthermore, the profit-oriented, market-determined nature of the Yugoslav system has reproduced bourgeois capitalist ideas and relations, while undermining the development of socialism. I quote the conclusions of one of the more insightful studies on this issue:

The Yugoslav-Soviet dispute and the subsequent Cominform blockade, real threats of external and internal subversion, the serious drought of 1950 and 1952 and the mismanagement of the economy by the League of Communists—all combined to bring about chaotic economic conditions during 1950–52. The communist party intellectuals became "disillusioned" and impatient with the existing order of things within a surprisingly short period of time. Abetted and encouraged, no doubt, by the covert bourgeois elements within the party, these intellectuals advocated curtailing the scope of central planning and replacing it by the market mechanism in allocating resources and distributing incomes. The restoration of the market mechanism was accompanied by the establishment of profit-seeking labor-managed enterprises. Such quick rehabilitation of the ubiquitous profit motive to propel the economy forward not only retained and revived the old bourgeois values but also corroded the socialist ideals before they had a chance to spread roots in the society. The integration of the Yugoslav economy with the world market dominated by the capitalist countries came as a natural result of the process.[38]

As this study indicates, the autonomous enterprises and the reliance on market relations went hand in hand with the restoration of bourgeois values and the integration of the Yugoslav economy into the capitalist world market. As a result, the society "has gradually stratified, naturally embracing in its fold the beneficiaries of the new system," which represents what is essentially a new bourgeois ruling stratum veiled by the ideological facade of "workers' self-management."[39] In many ways, the transformations taking place in Eastern Europe today appear to be a déjà vu of what has taken place to some degree in Yugoslavia.

Greater decentralization, market relations, and enterprise autonomy in the Cuban context would most likely lead to the same kinds of results as in Yugoslavia. They would aggravate Cuba's economic difficulties, undermine the accomplishments of the revolution, and most likely lead to a restoration of capitalism. Although the present regime clearly suffers from the hypercentralization of economic decisionmaking and a centralized planning system that functions on the basis of bureaucratic centralism, the solution is not to turn away from socialism but to extend the democratization of the basic organizational structures of the society and establish a federative, bottom-up planning process in place of the existing bureaucratic top-down planning system. This would empower the Cuban working class, unleash the full productive and creative potential of the population, free the economy from many of its bureaucratic shackles, and rapidly rid the country of many of the ills created by its "bad organizational habits."

## Conclusion

In this chapter, the elements have been introduced for concluding that the continued development of Cuba's forces of production under socialist conditions requires the institutionalization of worker self-management and democratic participation in the planning and direction of production—neither of which can be developed overnight. These important democratic socialist relations of production require extensive preparation and a lengthy learning process in which workers, managers, the general citizenry, state officials, and the political leadership develop the necessary organizational consciousness and skills—including those associated with collaborative forms of problem solving, consensus decisionmaking, and democratic planning.

As with the Soviet and Eastern European experiences, the Cuban case reveals that the elimination of private property does not by itself bring about socialism because capitalist ideology, practices, and organizational forms remain and must be totally eliminated in order to prevent the reproduction of bourgeois ideas and behavior. Bureaucratic decisionmaking and hypercentralized forms of organization are clearly not the means for achieving socialism. In the Cuban case, these factors have been offset somewhat by embryonic forms of worker participation and partial democratization at the local government level. However, the revolutionary regime and the socialist development of the country are increasingly threatened by the numerous problems and ills caused by the bureaucratic centralism that reigns in the major structures of the state and the economy. Only an across-the-board implantation of democratic forms of organization and planning can eliminate the restoration of capitalist relations of production and prevent increasing bureaucratization. In short, the Cuban experience since 1959 indicates that effective worker self-management at the point of production, democratic planning in the interests of society, and a popular democratic state constitute the organizational prerequisites for a successful transition from capitalism to socialism.

## Notes

1. Robert M. Bernardo, *The Theory of Moral Incentives in Cuba* (University: University of Alabama Press, 1981), p. 22.

2. Edward Boorstein, *The Economic Transformation of Cuba* (New York: Monthly Review Press, 1968).

3. See William LeoGrande, "Mass Political Participation in Socialist Cuba," in Philip Brenner, et al., eds., *The Cuba Reader: The Making of a Revolutionary Society* (New York: Grove Press, 1989), pp. 186–199, and Frank Fitzgerald, "The Reform of the Cuban Economy, 1976–86," *Journal of Latin American Studies*, vol. 21 (1989), pp. 283–310.

4. Fitzgerald, "The Reform of the Cuban Economy," p. 285.

5. Ibid., pp. 286–287.

6. V. I. Lenin, *Selected Works* (New York: International Publishers, 1976), p. 417.

7. Ibid., p. 425.

8. Ibid., p. 424.

9. Branko Horvat, *The Political Economy of Socialism* (New York: M. E. Sharpe, 1982), p. 140.

10. Ibid., p. 142.

11. Charles Bettelheim, *Class Struggles in the U.S.S.R.: First Period, 1917–1923* (New York: Monthly Review Press, 1976), p. 35.

12. Ibid., p. 17.

13. Horvat, *The Political Economy of Socialism*, p. 189.

14. Ibid., pp. 426–427.

15. Ibid., pp. 166–167.

16. Charles Bettelheim, *The Transition to Socialist Economy* (Sussex: Harvest Press, 1979), pp. 117–118.

17. Ibid., p. 118.

18. See Marta Harnecker, *Cuba: Dictatorship or Democracy?* (Westport: Lawrence Hill, 1979), pp. 1–27; and Michael Lowy, "Mass Organization, Party and State: Democracy in the Transition to Socialism," in Richard Fagen, Carmen Deere, and José Luis Coraggio, eds., *Transition and Development: Problems of Third World Socialism* (New York: Monthly Review Press, 1986), pp. 268–270.

19. Horvat, *The Political Economy of Socialism*, pp. 172–173.

20. Alexis Codina Jiménez, "Worker Incentives in Cuba," *World Development*, vol. 15, no. 1 (1987), p. 135.

21. Ibid., pp. 135–136.

22. Horvat, *The Political Economy of Socialism*, pp. 239–242.

23. Quoted in Paul Bellis, *Marxism and the U.S.S.R.* (Atlantic Highlands, N.J.: Humanities Press, 1979), p. 43.

24. See Darío Machado, "Para un estudio del fenómeno del burocratismo en Cuba," *Cuba Socialista*, vol. 9, no. 6 (November–December 1989), p. 61.

25. Fitzgerald, "The Reform of the Cuban Economy," p. 301.

26. Quoted in Carlos Tablada, *Ché Guevara: Economics and Politics in the Transition to Socialism* (New York: Pathfinder Press, 1989), p. 136.

27. Bernardo, *The Theory of Moral Incentives in Cuba*, p. 28.

28. Tablada, *Ché Guevara*, pp. 215–216.

29. Bernardo, *The Theory of Moral Incentives in Cuba*, pp. 16–17.

30. Ibid., p. 9.

31. See Leo Huberman and Paul Sweezy, "The Peaceful Transition from Socialism to Capitalism?" *Monthly Review*, vol. 14 (March 1964), pp. 569–590.

32. Terry Karl, "Workers' Incentives in Cuba," *Latin American Perspectives*, vol. 7 (1975), p. 39.

33. Tablada, *Ché Guevara*, p. 174.

34. Bernardo, *The Theory of Moral Incentives in Cuba*, p. 27.

35. Thomas Angotti, "The Cuban Revolution: A New Turn," *Nature, Society and Thought*, vol. 1, no. 4 (1988), pp. 527–549, and Tablada, *Ché Guevara*, pp. 26–27.

36. See Wlodzimierz Brus, *Socialist Ownership and Political Systems* (London: Routledge & Kegan Paul, 1975), pp. 148–171, and Gordon White, et al., *Revolutionary Socialist Development in the Third World* (Lexington: University of Kentucky, 1983).

37. Mohammad Ali Taslim, "The Evolution of Market Socialism in Yugoslavia: A Critical View," *The Insurgent Sociologist,* vol. 12, nos. 1–2 (Winter–Spring 1984), pp. 48–49.

38. Ibid.

39. Ibid., pp. 52–53.

# PART 2

# Whither the Cuban Economy?

# Introduction to Part 2

## Andrew Zimbalist

Cuba has long been accustomed to being the only centrally planned socialist country in the Western Hemisphere. As Cuba enters the 1990s, it is confronting the prospect of being the only centrally planned socialist country in the world. To be sure, Cuba still has company in China and North Korea, but Cuba's trading partners in COMECON—with whom Cuba has conducted around 85 percent of its trade in the last few years—are all eschewing central planning. The rapid disintegration of the Soviet economy and the severe economic dislocations throughout Eastern Europe along with the introduction of a new trading regime are creating major supply disruptions and ubiquitous shortages for the Cuban economy. The U.S. blockade continues and, if anything, has been tightened under President Bush. Cuba's isolation has created the country's worst crisis since 1959 and has put the question of the revolution's mutability and survivability on the tip of the analyst's tongue. The authors of Part 2 seek to cast some light on this situation.

### Trade and the Cuban Economy

As is true for all small economies, international trade is very important for Cuba. Socialist Cuba's reliance on trade, however, has often been overstated. First, it is important to note that before the revolution, the Cuban economy had an above-average (and rising[1]) dependence on trade for a country of its size and per capita income. Second, the comparison of the pre- and post-1959 periods has often been made without making the necessary accounting adjustments to render the figures commensurable. Carmelo Mesa-Lago, for instance, has compared the pre- and post-revolutionary periods' import shares without adjusting for the fact that Gross Domestic Product (GDP)—from the Western national income accounting system—is much larger than Gross Material Product[2]—from the COMECON system.[3] As can be seen in Table 6.1, when the unadjusted import share is used, it appears that Cuba's import dependence has grown markedly during the revolutionary years. The adjusted share, however, suggests similar levels of trade dependence in the 1950s and 1980s. In fact, the adjusted share in the 1980s is slightly below that in the 1950s even though it does not adjust for the upward bias resulting from import values being in current prices whereas GDP estimates are basically in constant prices. In both the adjusted and unadjusted series, one notes a sharp initial drop in import shares as Cuba realigned its trading partners during the 1960s, followed by a distinct upward trend.

Although higher import shares are associated with trade dependence, higher shares per se do not denote economic weakness. To be sure, conventional trade theory would argue that higher import shares are consistent with greater international specialization and thus represent a positive development. To some extent, this is the case for Cuba, but it must also be noted that Cuba's exports did not keep up with its growing imports, and this led to growing foreign indebtedness, as Archibald R. M. Ritter illustrates—hardly a salutary development. The primary point here, however, is that Cuba's high import share enhanced Cuba's vulnerability to the present perturbations in its trading relationships. In a similar sense, it can be argued that Cuba's vulnerability to the post-1960 U.S. economic blockade was great, and hence the costs of this blockade were extremely high.[4]

## Trading Partners

Despite its overwhelming quantitative importance, trade with CO-MECON was never a qualitative replacement for trade lost with the United States since 1960. Cuba's 1959 machine park was made in the United States, and Cuba needed then (as it does now) Western technology and parts to keep its economy running. Despite limitations—many imposed by the politics of the U.S. blockade—Western Europe, Canada, and Japan have stepped in with vital products at crucial junctures to provide a lifeline for the Cuban economy.[5]

After a recession during 1986–1987, the Cuban economy resumed growth (albeit very modest) during 1988–1989. The newest impediment to Cuban economic performance emerged primarily from supply disruptions resulting from transitional economic policies and sociopolitical instability within COMECON rather than from doctrinal disputes with Gorbachev or Eastern Europe.[6] Delays in the shipment of oil, wood, wheat, paper, and many other goods exacerbated an already severely bottlenecked Cuban economy.[7] Recent estimates suggest as much as a 35 to 40 percent shortfall in Soviet oil deliveries to Cuba during 1990.[8] In the light of these trade developments, Cuba can take little comfort in its formal 1990 trade protocol with the Soviet Union, which called for an 8.7 percent increase in trade turnover between the two countries.

Further, it is clear that the U.S. invasion of Panama in late December 1989 has curbed Cuba's use of front companies in Panama's Colón Free Zone to trade in U.S. goods. I estimate that Cuba imported an average of roughly $6 million yearly through these companies during 1986–1988.[9] Although it is difficult to predict at this point how much of a crackdown on this activity the U.S. will impose, the Cubans will probably be able to turn to other free trade zones in the Caribbean to reestablish some of this trade. More difficult to replace would be the trade between Cuba and subsidiaries of U.S. companies based in third countries. This trade has been allowed since 1975 and amounted to an annual average of approximately $250 million between 1982 and 1987.[10] In 1989, however, Senator Connie Mack of Florida introduced an amendment to an appropriations bill to prohibit such trade. The Mack measure failed to carry, but the senator reintroduced it in 1990 (as Gareth Jenkins points out in Chapter 7). The measure's dubious standing in international law and political pressure from a variety of countries make its future uncertain.

### Aid and Debt

Along with COMECON trade came preferential prices and development aid. Soviet aid to Cuba has been extraordinarily important in promoting the Cuban economy. The aid has taken the form inter alia of payments for Cuban sugar at prices considerably above those of the world market since the mid-1970s, charges for Soviet petroleum considerably below world prices until 1986, project aid, and balance-of-payments loans. Although the centrality of Soviet aid cannot be denied, its magnitude has been vastly overstated by Western sources. The Central Intelligence Agency (CIA) has given the Western media faulty estimates that rely on artificially inflated exchange rates, untenable assumptions about opportunity costs, and suppression of the fact that Cuba must buy often overpriced, shoddy Soviet goods with most of the Soviet sugar payments. For instance, a 1990 article in *Pravitelstvenniv Vestnik*, the official weekly publication of the Soviet Council of Ministers, stated that the prices for Soviet machinery and equipment exports to Cuba have been double world market prices and that in 1988 alone, Cuba overpaid 600 million rubles for these goods.[11]

Among other goods, Soviet export prices charged to Cuba also exceeded world market prices for wheat, tires, cut lumber, tin plates, butter, and powdered milk.[12] Poor quality and deficient goods have been pervasive. According to González Vergara, many Soviet investment projects in Cuba have turned out to be white elephants. In the first nine years of construction of the Soviet-designed nuclear power plant in Cienfuegos, which is still far from completion, costs were already 800 million rubles above projection. A new nickel plant built in Cuba with Soviet technology is at least twice as inefficient as plants built in Cuba in the 1950s, and, citing energy shortages, the Cubans recently decided to shut it down.

Similar problems exist in Cuban trade with Eastern Europe, another traditional source of economic aid for Cuba. In his speech to the closing session of the Federation of Cuban Women on March 7, 1990, Castro detailed several instances of low-quality or unusable goods from Eastern Europe.

We were the only ones in the world who bought Bulgarian forklifts. They're so worthless and have so many problems that no one but us bought them. . . . There are hundreds, even thousands of these forklifts standing idle in our warehouses. . . . We're now studying part by part to see which ones work and which ones don't, so we can buy what we need elsewhere or else make it ourselves and install it to get the forklifts running.

The Hungarian buses get six kilometers to the gallon. They fill the city with exhaust fumes, poisoning everybody. . . . They come with a gearbox manufactured in Czechoslovakia [with] two speeds. Our own bus, the one we're now manufacturing and that is to replace all that junk in the future, gets 11 kilometers to the gallon.[13]

More reasonable estimates would show Soviet aid to Cuba to be at the upper end of foreign aid to Latin American countries, taken as a share of national income. If one also included the aid implicit in the Soviets' repeatedly delaying the repayment date for Cuban debt (around 15 billion rubles), then Soviet aid to Cuba would surpass Western aid to other Latin American economies, with the exception of Puerto Rico, on a per capita or GDP share basis. However, before inferences are made about the Cuban economy's ability to sustain itself without outside aid,[14] it is well to remember both the tremendous cost of the U.S. blockade and the proportionately extravagant foreign aid program to other developing countries maintained by the Cubans.[15]

To be sure, overall Soviet price subsidies have diminished in recent years. Since 1976 Cuba's price for Soviet oil has been set equal to the average of the five previous years' prices on the world market. Until

1986, this meant that Cuba was paying below the world price; however, since 1986 the Cubans have been paying an average of 27.02 pesos per barrel for Soviet oil, which is considerably above the world price (measured at official exchange rates). The article in *Pravitelstvenniv Vestnik* mentioned above estimates that the annual cost of Cuba's over-payment for Soviet oil since 1985 has been 1.3 billion rubles. In fact, Archibald R.M. Ritter makes the case in his chapter that terms of trade with the Soviet Union have been turning against the Cubans since 1980.[16]

Cuba's increasing difficulties with COMECON have been compounded by shrinking Western markets and growing hard currency debt. Unlike the rest of Latin America, however, the Cuban economy grew strongly between 1980 and 1985. This was not because Cuba avoided building up a sizable debt during the 1970s but was because rather than borrowing money and then squandering it on capital flight or luxury imports, Cuba used the loan capital to invest in productive assets. By 1985–1986, however, a combination of external factors interrupted Cuba's growth and saddled the island with an increasingly acute foreign exchange crisis. Cuban hard currency imports in nominal terms were one-third below the 1985 level in 1987 and 1988; in real terms the drop was closer to fifty percent. Medium- and long-term debt service payments have been irregular since 1986, and no new rescheduling agreement with Cuba's creditors has been reached since 1987. By mid-1990, the hard currency debt was nearly $6.5 billion. Combined with Cuba's debt to COMECON, this placed Cuba among Latin America's most heavily indebted nations in per capita terms.

Excepting short-term suppliers' credits, new hard currency loans have not been forthcoming since 1985. Instead, as Gareth Jenkins indicates in Chapter 7, Cuba has attempted to attract direct foreign investment, but given the U.S. blockade, foreign countries have been reluctant to invest in Cuba outside of the tourist sector.

The foregoing discussion provides some context for the interpretations that follow. Economists continue to debate the extent of internal mis-management in Cuba and the appropriateness of Cuba's development strategy. Sergio G. Roca, for example, discusses Cuba's economic problems with a focus on planning blunders and micromanagement, and Archibald R.M. Ritter details the weak performance of Cuba's foreign sector as well as the weaknesses in its domestic economy.

Gareth Jenkins analyzes the important structural changes as well as the present predicament of Cuba's economy. Jenkins makes it clear that Cuban investments in capital goods, biotechnology, agriculture, minerals, and tourism have propelled the economy forward in the past and offer some positive prospects for the future. He also offers an extended and up-to-date account of Cuba's efforts to expand its tourist sector. Although the sector has grown commendably in recent years, Jenkins sees some problem areas that will need attention if Cuba's goals for the end of the 1990s are to be approached. He elucidates the tensions engendered by the growth of a parallel dollar economy to service the foreign guests. The appearance of material luxury in the tourist sector and the infiltration of tourist dollars into the nontourist sectors of the economy run against the grain of the purity of socialist consciousness elevated by the ideology of the rectification campaign.

Jenkins reminds us of the contradictory nature of Cuba's success. His point is well taken and can be easily extended: Cuba produces sophisticated biotechnological products but lags miserably in packaging and marketing these products for foreign markets; it produces buses, a rarity for a developing country, but provides woefully inadequate public transportation services to its population; it produces large and growing quantities of construction materials, but its housing stock is deteriorating with alarming alacrity; it produces generally adequate amounts of foodstuffs, but one-third of its food output never makes it to the market. These are the problems of a central government trying to do too much. The economic plan would do well to concentrate on key sectors and strategic products, leaving the rest of production and most services to be handled by the market. Distributional and equity concerns can be addressed by other government policies.

Together the chapters in Part 2 give a current and balanced view of the problems and prospects for the Cuban economy in the 1990s. It is premature to predict what course the economy will follow, but strong and growing forces within Cuba are calling for economic reform. The 1991 Party Congress will likely debate proposals for structural reform in a more critical and open fashion than socialist Cuba has heretofore witnessed.[17] This debate will take place in a context of stringent austerity and growing economic hardship.

The majority of the Cuban population under thirty did not experience the pervasive prerevolutionary poverty or know the ebullience of the revolutionary struggle. The population is ready for bold steps of reform. Yet Castro's intransigence is sustained and partly justified by unabated hostility from the United States. This is one reason there is a clear consensus among Cuban scholars about the importance of a change in U.S. policy: Lifting the counterproductive and hypocritical embargo and normalizing diplomatic relations would be the most effective means of promoting liberalization in Cuba's economic and political system. Only then can the true measure of Cuba be taken.

## Notes

1. The import share averaged 31.7 percent between 1952 and 1956 and then rose to 34.0 percent in 1957 and 36.6 percent in 1958.

2. Gross Material Product is *ingreso nacional disponible* plus depreciation. It does not include nonmaterial services and hence is at least 25 percent below GDP.

3. Carmelo Mesa-Lago, *The Economy of Socialist Cuba* (Albuquerque: University of New Mexico Press, 1981), p. 79.

4. In 1982 the Cuban National Bank estimated that through 1980, the blockade had cost Cuba some $10 billion. More recently, the Cubans published updated estimates that suggest an ongoing cost of nearly $500 million per year during the 1980s. See Banco Nacional, *Informe Económico, 1982* (Havana: Banco Nacional de Cuba, 1983), and Latin American Regional Reports, *Caribbean Report*, May 12, 1988.

5. See Alistair Hennessey and George Lambie, eds., *Cuba and Western Europe: Breaking the Blockade* (London: Macmillan, 1990).

6. Soviet oil deliveries to Cuba actually rose from 7.37 million metric tons in 1986 to 7.85 million in 1987 and 8.50 million in 1988. Total Cuban imports from the Soviet Union in value terms remained basically flat at around 5.4 billion pesos between 1986 and 1988. *Resumen Estadístico del Comercio Exterior* (Havana: Ministry of External Commerce, 1989), pp. 12, 199.

7. A related problem for Cuba has been that it has been in arrears in its contracted sugar deliveries to the CMEA. This necessitated borrowing from European sugar brokers in 1988–1989 and paying them back in 1989–1990, which prevented Cuba from taking full advantage of the higher market prices for sugar in 1989–1990. Cuba, then, has not reaped the expected benefit from its large 1989 *zafra* of over eight million tons.

8. According to Ramón González Vergara, the former vice-secretary of the State Committee on Economic Collaboration (CECE) who defected in July 1990, the Soviets in principle have terminated oil shipments to Cuba in excess of their internal consumption needs. Howard French, "Cuban Defector Tells of Soviet Cuts," *New York Times*, September 13, 1990, p. A3. Cuban reexports of surplus Soviet oil provided roughly 40 percent of the country's hard currency earnings during the early 1980s.

9. Based on data presented in Ministerio del Comercio Exterior, *Resumen Estadístico del Comercio Exterior*.

10. Estimate from study by School for Advanced International Studies, *Opportunities for U.S.-Cuban Trade* (Washington, D.C.: SAIS, June 1988), p. 14. Morris Morley estimates this trade at $89.4 million in 1979, $303.2 million in 1980, and $73.8 million in 1981. See Morley, *Imperial State and Revolution: The United States and Cuba, 1952–1986* (Cambridge: Cambridge University Press, 1987), p. 339.

11. Cited in *Bohemia*, July 6, 1990, p. 62. For a full discussion of the problems with the CIA's estimates of Soviet aid to Cuba, see Andrew Zimbalist and Claes

Brundenius, *Revolutionary Cuba: The Challenge of Growth with Equity* (Baltimore: Johns Hopkins University Press, 1989), Chapter 9. See also the discussion by Ritter in Chapter 6.

12. Zimbalist and Brundenius, p. 153.

13. *Granma Weekly Review*, March 18, 1990, p. 1.

14. Ibid.

15. Details on Cuba's foreign aid programs can be obtained from Zimbalist and Brundenius, ch. 9, and Julie Feinsilver, *Cuba as a World Medical Power* (Cambridge, Mass.: Harvard University Press, 1990).

16. For different estimates of the extent of this deterioration, see José Luis Rodríguez, "Thirty Years of Economic Relations," *Cuba Business*, vol. 3, no. 6 (December 1989), p. 6.

17. The data on market opening and economic reform are far more prevalent and extensive than suggested by Ritter. The actual implementation of reform ideas is another matter.

# 5

# Cuba's Socialist Economy at Thirty: Assessments and Prospects

*Sergio G. Roca*

The Cuban revolution at thirty is long consolidated and unquestionably strong. It is firmly entrenched and well defended. It confronts a formidable adversary yet faces no credible external threat. Its supporters can point proudly to significant achievements in the provision of social services and the generation of economic equity. Yet there have been disappointing, even deplorable, results in political liberalization, cultural diversity, and human rights. In these areas the revolution remains, without defensible arguments, intransigent and recalcitrant.

More to the topic at hand, the Cuban revolution thirty years later exhibits fundamental shortcomings in economic organization, production structure, economic performance, and international economic relations. Why? Primarily because the revolution is fettered and constrained by a leadership of similar vintage. After three decades the revolution is *again* confronted by what sociologist Edward Shils calls the struggle between "charismatic authority" and "the routine social order."[1] The question, however, is not whether the revolution will survive the passing of the founding fathers (and mothers) because it clearly will—although not in unchanged form. Rather, the issue concerns the viability of the revolution under the continued stewardship of the Moncada generation, a question dealt with in 1988 by Rhoda Rabkin.[2]

## Economic Strategy and Accomplishments

Basically, over the past three decades Cuba has followed an export-promotion and import-substitution development strategy. In general this strategy has been appropriate and wise, fitting Cuba's objective conditions (resource endowment and comparative advantage) and subjective quandaries (international political forces). The strategy has suffered, however, from uneven implementation, inefficient operational plans, and wasteful utilization of resources. All of these factors (together with the burden of U.S. trade sanctions in the early years) have resulted in detraction from rather than contribution to the development effort.

In terms of economic growth, there is an uneven record based on an unsure footing, and questions have arisen about the quantity and nature of that growth. This is a controversial topic; final results are not yet in, and they may always be in dispute.[3] A brief summary of growth performance suggests the following outline: The early years (the early 1960s) may be discounted due to political consolidation and economic confusion, but the Moral Economy of 1966–1970 meant negligible or negative growth in Gross Social Product (GSP). In the early 1970s performance was strong, but the GSP suffered after the involvements in Angola and Ethiopia. The 1980s replicated the pattern of the previous decade. GSP growth started strong but deteriorated quickly and sharply after 1985, due largely to the rectification process. From 1986 to 1989, total real GSP was virtually stagnant but declined 3 percent per capita.

Cuba's economic structure exhibits continued excessive sugar specialization (sugar exports represent more than 75 percent of total exports), very limited export diversification (despite strong growth in the 1980s, nontraditional exports accounted for 2 percent of total exports), and a vulnerable open economy (total trade equals 40 to 50 percent of GSP). More critically, the foreign sector has been deficit-producing rather than surplus-generating. Since 1959, there have been only two years of (miniscule) merchandise trade surpluses. The cumulative total trade deficit stood at about 19 billion pesos through 1988. Cuba has been unable to self-finance its development and has become increasingly dependent on Soviet economic aid (subsidies and grants) plus loans and military assistance. Since the mid-1970s, the island has heavily increased its reliance on Western sources of financial and real capital. In 1989, Cuba's hard currency debt stood at $6.5 billion, representing a heavy burden on its international relations.

Economic efficiency, the cornerstone of sustainable long-term economic growth, is not yet firmly established in socialist Cuba. Since the early 1960s, with a respite in the mid-1970s, the revolution has suffered from low labor productivity. There have been innumerable campaigns to reduce absenteeism, increase work hours, improve work effort, control bloated payrolls, and increase quality. Castro recently estimated the underemployment rate in Havana at 12 to 25 percent of the work force. In addition, there has been a long history of poor capital efficiency: from Chilean economist Alban Lataste's remark about "gross junk accumulation" in the 1960s, to investment and production setbacks in nickel, cement, and textile plants in the 1970s, and finally to long (over ten-year) gestation periods for several investment projects in the 1980s.

In the realm of social achievements, Cuba has made significant, remarkable, and commendable improvements in the amount, quality, and coverage of education, health, and social security services. The exception is housing, which requires massive resources just to keep up with maintenance needs and demographic pressures. In the future, Cuba will need to emphasize quality over quantity in both education and health. It also may be approaching the point of diminishing returns for continued investments in social services. How much lower should the infant mortality rate be driven, at what cost, and at what opportunity cost? A strong case can be made for diverting resources to occupational safety and environmental cleanup concerns.

## Current Dilemmas

The Cuban economy is facing two key dilemmas: one domestic and one international, although they are not unrelated. What is the domestic economic model, and what is its international economic role? The much-vaunted rectification process is *not* a model, and in fact it represents the absence of a model, the denial of a system. Hard evidence points increasingly to the resurgence of a personalist style of economic decisionmaking involving both excessive centralization and detailed micromanagement: In essence, Fidel Castro has taken the economy in hand. The September 25, 1989, issue of *Granma* contained a three-page spread on the "new operative work style" of the Executive Committee of the Council of Ministers under Castro's leadership, which has been in place since September 1988. A careful reading of this account (plus Castro's two speeches to construction sector workers published in the October 2 and 3, 1989, issues of *Granma*) clearly reveals the nature of economic planning in Cuba today.

Traditional central planning processes and institutions are not operational at this time. JUCEPLAN was superseded by the Central Group from late 1984 until September 1988 and since then by the Executive Committee of the Council of Ministers. There were few public references to the progress of the 1986–1990 five-year plan (FYP) and none about preparations for the 1991–1995 period. In fact, Cuban officials have admitted privately that the current FYP has been "virtually abandoned" and that annual plans have become "emergency plans." Moreover, special plans (reminiscent of the 1960s operational style) unveiled by Castro in mid-1987, one year prior to the formal restructuring of the Council of Ministers, are now guiding major sectors of the economy and the appropriations of massive capital and human resources (mostly reallocated from other planned uses and largely reassigned personally by Castro). These special plans include water resources, selected agricultural products (sugarcane, pork, eggs, rice, milk, tubers, and vegetables), the construction sector (highways, housing, and tourist facilities), and the transportation sector (bus production and urban services).

In addition, output targets and timetables of these special plans appear to have been overambitious and strained. The construction rate of child care centers in Havana was accelerated to forty times the planned rate and generated a 25 percent overfulfillment of the needed level of service. Confronted with a 30 percent spoilage rate of agricultural products in Havana, Castro decided to build four wholesale markets "in a few months . . . instead of waiting until 1995." Construction contingents and brigades are said to put in 12- to 14-hour workdays plus weekend time during 1989 and 1990.

Finally, Castro and the Executive Committee of the Council of Ministers are involved in a process that could be described as micromanagement of the economy. This Executive Committee has dealt at length with items such as the industrial yield of tomatoes, imports of frozen chicken, distribution of diet powdered milk, production of sesame seeds for the parallel market, and developing the detailed medical history of one Cuban soldier who was accidentally wounded in Angola. Whereas this committee has met close to biweekly (32 times from September 1988 to September 1989), Castro has had weekly meetings with *one* construction brigade chief (114 meetings over a two-year period). It is highly likely that Castro is again directly involved (as he was in the 1960s) in technical decisions and is dealing with issues such as paving highways with cement rather than asphalt, constructing causeways, and developing sheep-raising schemes in specially reconstituted soils. Particularly alarming was the decision to implement the field drainage system in sugarcane plantations, extending the program to 50 percent of planted acreage on the basis of only one experiment at the Urbano Norris complex.

If the policies of the rectification process are maintained, Cuba will continue to suffer from the allocation, coordination, and motivation problems associated with the mobilization of radical economic models, in sharp contrast to the pragmatic reform paths chosen by most other socialist countries. We may have insufficient information on current developments. Economists and government officials in Cuba might discuss alternatives and criticize policies, but such efforts apparently have no demonstrable effect or impact on public policy. And internal debate remains largely beyond the reach of scholars. In sum, the key issues for Cuba are to find, define, and retain an economic model, a coherent system of organizing economic tasks that is efficient, applicable, and acceptable.

In view of the ambivalent views and conflicting policies reflected in the Cuban press and Cuban journals (and in recent writings of Susan Eckstein, Andrew Zimbalist, and Marifeli Pérez-Stable), it is germane to ask: If economic mechanisms are immortal *and* socialist values are inefficient and undeveloped, what happens then? What is the Cuban economic model? Why should we suppose that such a model would do a better job than existing-working socialist alternatives at either economics or morality?

Moreover, it is difficult to argue that the internally induced and systemically driven economic and political changes in the socialist world are exceptional to Cuba and that the revolution will be immune to them. When the Soviet Union, China, Eastern Europe, Vietnam, and Angola have been forced to question and to reexamine core socialist values, structures, and policies, why should anyone think that Cuba is an exception—a *sui generis* case? Another fundamental question has to do with Cuba's international economic role in a new world economic order in which market objectives and criteria appear to be in ascendancy and solidarity may be scarce. The USSR and Eastern Europe give every indication of moving toward greater integration into the world economy and appear amenable to play by the rules of that economy. The EEC is about to coalesce into a formidable, perhaps impenetrable economic giant. The United States and Canada have signed a trade pact, and Mexico is showing interest in joining. Where and how will Cuba fit into these developments?

Several issues are poised at critical junctures, and some have already affected the performance of the Cuban economy. How will Soviet enterprises seeking profit under perestroika deal with Cuban units seeking purity under *rectificación*? Cuban officials are understandably concerned about this issue. José Luis Rodríguez of Cuba's Center for the Study of the World Economy stated in 1989 that "certain transitional mechanisms must be implemented which would prevent [Soviet and East European] state enterprises, operating in a decentralized way, from being disinterested in dealing with Cuba."[4] Rodríguez confirmed the existence of a formal "hold harmless" provision for Soviet enterprises dealing with the island, but admitted that it is being applied casually and irregularly.

What will be the Cuban terms of trade with Eastern Europe? How reliable will the socialist supply pipeline continue to be? In September

25, 1989, *Granma* reported "complexities" in commercial relations "with some socialist countries which have resulted in shortages of certain products." Throughout 1990 and 1991, this trend has continued unabated. Rodríguez recently acknowledged that several industrial sectors were operating at 40 to 60 percent of capacity due to import restrictions (shortages of raw materials and spare parts). He added, "We have no control over the Western or Eastern flow of external supplies to the Cuban economy. This is very problematic for us."[5] According to Jaime Crombet, secretary of the Communist party, a national forum on spare parts was held in December 1990, in part to remedy "the lack of supplies of many spare parts of socialist equipment."[6] In the summer of 1990, Czech and Rumanian delegations went to Havana to discuss revisions of the 1990 trade agreements and to design new ways of conducting bilateral commercial relations.[7]

How long will Soviet largesse continue, at what level, and under what conditions? Since 1985, Soviet merchandise deliveries to Cuba have remained flat at about 5.4 billion pesos annually. The 1986 reduction in Soviet imports was only the fourth in the entire revolutionary period and was the first decline since 1972. Articles in *Pravda,* journal reports by Vladimir Chirkov, and parliamentary speeches by Nikolai Shmelev are just a few of many indications of Soviet discontent with the extent and efficacy of economic assistance to Cuba. Gorbachev declared his tolerance of diversity and his encouragement of experimentation in the socialist world but *not* his intention or ability to subsidize it.

In a recent study, Archibald R.M. Ritter concluded that the total level of Soviet economic assistance to Cuba has been reduced by half or more since 1985.[8] Starting in June 1990, a Soviet-Cuban working group (an offshoot of the Intergovernmental Commission formed in 1970) met to develop guidelines for the new bilateral economic agreement that was signed in early 1991. The difficult nature of these negotiations was revealed in the public statements of the principle delegates. Whereas the Cuban foreign trade minister understood the group's "strategic objective" to be "the preservation and consolidation of the conditions and achievements of our mutual collaboration developed until now, widening and strengthening them under the new conditions," the Soviet minister of external economic relations responded in a neutral manner, saying that "any problems will be resolved, as usual, in the interest of bilateral collaboration."[9]

In the near future, Cuban economic self-sufficiency will be called to the fore and will be put to the test. Pressure for change will be generated by both the worsening conditions of socialist economic relations and the increasing burden of servicing the hard currency debt. Additional pressure will come from the continued detrimental impact of rectification on economic performance. The combined crunch of external and internal forces will provide the critical impetus for the eventual dawning of an opening and *reconstrucción* in socialist Cuba. The question is not if but when, how, and by whom the second revolution—as defined by Gorbachev in the USSR and by reform elements in Eastern Europe—will occur in Cuba.

## Conclusion

In *The Constitution of Society*, Edward Shils, the distinguished sociologist, has explored with great insight the implications for the social order of what Max Weber called "extraordinary charisma." His analysis is applicable and pertinent to the Cuban case. (An unlikely source of corroboration is Gabriel García Márquez's character sketch of Castro in "El oficio de la palabra" in the October 1988 issue of *Cuba Internacional*.) Shils argues that "charismatic authority denies the value of action motivated by desire for proximate ends sufficient unto themselves, by the wish to gratify personal affections, or by the hope of pecuniary advantage"[10]—hence the promotion of internationalist solidarity, voluntary labor, and moral incentives.

Shils maintains that "charismatically generated order is . . . generated by the creativity which seeks something new, . . . by inspiration from transcendent powers"[11]—thus, the process of "rectification of errors and negative tendencies," the renewed pursuit of "the new man," and the assertion that "now indeed we're going to construct socialism." But Shils maintains, quite reasonably, that "the actions of men and women in all ongoing societies are impelled by a variety of considerations, [including] personal affections, anticipations of advantage and fears of loss, destructiveness, responsiveness to obligations, respect for concrete authority" and other, *as well as* "an intermittent flickering of charismatic responsiveness."[12] Moreover, "concentrated and intense charismatic authority transfigures [the flickering] into incandescence. . . . That is why charismatic authority, really intensely imputed and experienced charisma, is disruptive of any routine social order."[13]

It is time for Cuba to get on with the business of developing a "routine social order." It will likely be a socialist order, preferably with sufficient market elements to ensure economic efficiency and with concrete political guarantees to assure democratic rule, but it must be a routine social order. The era of charismatic disruption, whose necessity and legitimacy may be granted, must give way to the routine tasks and mundane methods required to construct the Cuban future.

## Notes

1. Edward Shils, *The Constitution of Society* (Chicago: University of Chicago Press, 1982).

2. See Rhoda Rabkin, "Cuba: The Aging of a Revolution," in Sergio G. Roca, ed., *Socialist Cuba: Past Interpretations and Future Challenges* (Boulder: Westview Press, 1988), chapter 3.

3. A major controversy developed between Claes Brundenius and Andrew Zimbalist on the one hand and Carmelo Mesa-Lago and Jorge Pérez-López on the other in the journal *Comparative Economic Studies*. See Brundenius and Zimbalist, "Recent Studies on Cuban Economic Growth: A Review," *Comparative Economic Studies*, vol. 27, no. 1 (Spring 1985), pp. 21–45; Mesa-Lago and Pérez-López, "Imbroglios on the Cuban Economy: A Reply to Brundenius and Zimbalist," *Comparative Economic Studies*, vol. 27, no. 1 (Spring 1985), pp. 47–83; Brundenius and Zimbalist, "Cuban Economic Growth One More Time: A Response to 'Imbroglios,'" *Comparative Economic Studies*, vol. 27, no. 3 (Fall 1985), pp. 115–131; Mesa-Lago and Pérez-López, "The Endless Cuban Economic Saga: A Terminal Rebuttal," *Comparative Economic Studies*, vol. 27, no. 4 (Winter 1985), pp. 67–82; and Brundenius and Zimbalist, "Cuban Growth: A Final Word," *Comparative Economic Studies*, vol. 27, no. 4 (Winter 1985), pp. 83–84. Brundenius and Zimbalist have published a condensed and updated version of their arguments as "Cubanology and Economic Performance," in Andrew Zimbalist, ed., *Cuban Political Economy: Controversies in Cubanology* (Boulder: Westview Press, 1988).

4. José Luis Rodríguez, "Las relaciones económicas entre Cuba y los países socialistas: situación actual y perspectivas," Conference on Thirty Years of the Cuban Revolution, Halifax, Nova Scotia, Canada, November 1989, p. 9.

5. José L. Rodríguez, Panel on Economic Aspects of the Rectification Process, Halifax Conference on Thirty Years of the Cuban Revolution, November 1989. (Reply to question in the discussion period.)

6. *Granma*, January 13, 1990, p. 1.

7. *Granma*, June 4, 1990, p. 2 and June 7, 1990, p. 2.

8. Archibald R.M. Ritter, "The Cuban Economy to the Year 2000: External Challenges and Policy Imperatives," *Journal of Interamerican Studies and World Affairs*, vol. 32, no. 3 (Fall 1990), pp. 117–149.

9. *Granma*, June 6, 1990, p. 1.

10. Shils, *The Constitution of Society*, p. 111.

11. Ibid.

12. Ibid.

13. Ibid.

# 6

# Cuba in the 1990s: Economic Reorientation and International Reintegration

*Archibald R.M. Ritter*

At the beginning of the 1990s, Cuba faces severe economic difficulties, great uncertainty, and powerful geopolitical forces for domestic economic and political change. Ultimately, Cuba will likely respond to the new situation with a major although gradual reorientation of the domestic economy—its structure, functioning, and general development strategy— and with a new attempt at integration into the international geopolitical and economic systems. Fundamental changes are unavoidable for Cuba in the long term because of the imminent demise of its special relationship with the Soviet Union, the unsustainability of its current economic institutions and development strategy, and the imperative to achieve financial self-reliance, or to pay its own way, in the international system.

The first and primary objective of this chapter is to review some of the central forces currently impelling change in the Cuban economy and Cuba's integration into the international system, emphasizing both external and internal factors. A second objective is to explore a number of possible policy options and types of economic change that undoubtedly will be increasingly prominent as Cuba seeks to reinsert itself in the international system and to modify its economy so that goals of sustained and authentic economic growth and diversification can be achieved.

## The New International Economic Environment

The international economic environment within which Cuba must exist has changed with a velocity that was unimaginable, at least until late 1989. The phasedown of the Cold War, the conversion of the economic and political systems of the countries of Eastern Europe toward Western European orthodoxy, and the ongoing economic and political changes in the Soviet Union have reshaped the international geopolitical system. Furthermore, much of the world is launched on an accelerated transformation toward global economic integration. This process is driven by the changes in Eastern Europe, by "Europe 1992" (that is, the creation of a full common market and the achievement of a closer political as well as economic union among the member countries of the European Community) and by the general shift by most developing countries toward externally oriented development strategies.

## The End of the Special Relationship with the Soviet Union

The central feature of Cuba's special relationship with the USSR has been the high level of implicit and semihidden USSR subsidization of Cuba. This subsidization has permitted Cuba to live beyond its means, to enjoy rapid economic growth according to aggregate economic measures of Gross Social Product and *ingreso nacional creado* (at least until 1985), and to run an activist and interventionist foreign policy of a type normally associated with major powers. There is little doubt that the volume of Soviet assistance will decline in the 1990s and will probably be phased out completely.

Estimating the magnitude of Soviet assistance is difficult and imprecise in both conceptual and practical terms. The lack of economic realism in the exchange rates of both the Cuban peso and the Soviet ruble together with a lack of precise knowledge of the relative cost and quality of Soviet exports to Cuba compound the difficulties in estimating implicit subsidization. A quick review of this subsidization is presented below prior to a discussion of why and how this subsidization is being phased out.[1] The concept of subsidization used here is the value of the various components of the special relationship in comparison with the value of these components if Cuba participated in the world economy in a manner and degree similar to its economic exchange with the Soviet Union.

A major component of Soviet assistance has been the merchandise trade deficit Cuba has been permitted to run almost continuously since 1960. These deficits have been lower than they would have been if Cuba's sugar and nickel exports and petroleum imports had been valued at world market prices rather than at the special prices of the bilateral relationship with the USSR. This deficit was high in the 1980s, especially in 1986–1987 when it averaged nearly 1.5 billion Cuban pesos (see Table 6.1, row 5).

This bilateral trade deficit is the principal source of Cuba's debt to the Soviet Union. Although the Cuban-Soviet financial relationship has been shrouded in secrecy for over thirty years, the magnitude of Cuba's debt was placed at 15 billion rubles by former Soviet Prime Minister Ryzkov.[2] It is not presently clear whether this debt will ever be repaid. If in the future Cuba must generate a trade surplus and repay the USSR, then the annual trade deficits could not be considered assistance. But if the debt were forgiven or if Cuba refused to repay the debt, then presumably it would represent aid rather than a loan. When asked if the Soviet Union was likely to forgive the debt, a high-ranking Cuban official recently stated, off the record, "I don't know if they are going to forgive it; in any case we are not going to pay it."[3] On the other hand, González Vergara, a prominent Cuban official, said prior to his defection in July 1990 that the USSR expected Cuba to begin repayment of the debt in 1995 in dollars at a rate of exchange to be determined in 1990. Thus, the situation is not clear. Interest payments on Cuba's debt to the Soviet Union have also been continuously postponed and rolled into the 15 billion ruble debt or perhaps been forgiven.

A second component of Soviet assistance is embedded in the pricing of Cuban sugar exports to and petroleum imports from the USSR. The USSR has paid a peso price for Cuban sugar that for most years and at official exchange rates has been a multiple of the world free-market price. Similarly, petroleum import prices have been below world market prices, at least until 1986. Cuban analysts and officials reject the idea that such pricing arrangements contain hidden subsidies for Cuba, arguing that Cuba engages in a type of exchange that is fair and equitable within the international socialist division of labor rather than at the exploitative and unfair prices of the international capitalist economy.[4] However, such pricing has created direct opportunity costs for the Soviet Union, which could have sold petroleum for convertible currencies and at higher prices before 1986 and which could have purchased sugar more cheaply, albeit in hard currency.

An estimate of the value of the sugar subsidy to Cuba is presented in line 1 of Table 6.1. It is calculated as the difference between the world free-market price and the Soviet price multiplied by the total volume of Cuba's net sugar exports to the USSR (deducting reexports of sugar purchased from other producers by Cuba for resale to the USSR).[5] The value of the petroleum subsidy is estimated as the world price less the Soviet price multiplied by net petroleum exports from the USSR to Cuba (allowing for Cuban reexport of Soviet petroleum for hard currency earnings). Estimates of Soviet subsidization through petroleum pricing are shown in Table 6.1, row 2.

A further component of Soviet assistance has been the reexportation of sugar and petroleum. In the 1980s, Cuba was permitted to buy sugar on the international market at the free-market price for resale to the

TABLE 6.1  Estimation of Soviet Economic Assistance to Cuba, 1980-1987 (in millions of Cuban pesos, unless noted otherwise)

| | 1980 | 1981 | 1982 | 1983 | 1984 | 1985 | 1986 | 1987 |
|---|---|---|---|---|---|---|---|---|
| 1. Sugar subsidy | 831.5 | 974.2 | 2,164.0 | 2,368.8 | 2,046.4 | 2,329.5 | 2,017.1 | 2,574.7 |
| 2. Petroleum subsidy | 2,078.7 | 1,993.8 | 1,664.6 | 1,009.4 | 489.7 | -182.0 | -711.7 | -664.7 |
| 3. Sugar reexports | 0 | 0 | 44.3 | 146.3 | 745.9 | 1,281.4 | 615.1 | 664.3 |
| 4. Petroleum reexports | 0 | 70.2 | 105.7 | 105.6 | 19.7 | -38.6 | -325.8 | -190.5 |
| 5. Bilateral trade deficit | 650.2 | 876.5 | 454.8 | 363.5 | 830.2 | 937.3 | 1,401.8 | 1,577.2 |
| 6. Total | 3,560.4 | 3,914.7 | 4,433.4 | 3,993.6 | 4,131.9 | 4,327.6 | 2,996.5 | 3,961.0 |
| 7. Subsidy per capita (Cuban pesos) | 367.3 | 401.4 | 450.2 | 401.5 | 411.4 | 426.3 | 292.5 | 382.5 |
| 8. Subsidy per capita at official exchange rates (U.S. dollars) | 512.3 | 499.3 | 524.1 | 462.1 | 457.1 | 463.4 | 352.4 | 382.5 |
| 9. Subsidy as percent of *ingreso nacional creado* | 36.1 | 34.0 | 36.4 | 30.9 | 30.2 | 31.0 | 23.3 | 32.2 |
| 10. Adjustment for over-pricing of imports from USSR | -580.6 | -646.8 | -754.9 | -849.1 | -965.5 | -1,074.6 | -1,062.8 | -773.5 |
| 11. Revised total subsidy | 2,979.8 | 3,267.9 | 3,678.5 | 3,144.5 | 3,166.4 | 3,253.0 | 1,933.7 | 3,187.5 |
| 12. Subsidy per capita (Cuban pesos) | 307.4 | 335.1 | 373.5 | 316.2 | 315.3 | 320.4 | 188.7 | 307.8 |
| 13. Subsidy per capita at official exchange rates (U.S. dollars) | 428.7 | 416.7 | 434.8 | 363.8 | 350.3 | 348.3 | 227.4 | 307.8 |
| 14. Subsidy as percent of *ingreso nacional creado* | 30.2 | 28.4 | 30.2 | 24.3 | 23.1 | 23.3 | 15.0 | 26.0 |

TABLE 6.1 (continued)

*Assumptions:* (1) Official exchange rate of Cuban peso and 1990 U.S. dollar used; (2) debt (interest and amortization forgiveness excluded.

*Calculations:*

1. Sugar subsidy: [Soviet price less world free-market price] times [total Cuban sugar exports less reexports to the USSR]; estimated for 1986 and 1987.
2. Petroleum subsidy: world price less Soviet price times total Soviet crude petroleum exports to Cuba less reexports.
3. Sugar reexports. See Archibald R.M. Ritter, "The Cuban Economy in the 1990s: External Challenges and Policy Imperatives," *Journal of Interamerican Studies and World Affairs,* vol. 32, no. 3 (Fall 1990), pp. 117-149.
4. Petroleum reexports. See Archibald R.M. Ritter, "The Cuban Economy in the 1990s."
5. Bilateral merchandise trade deficit with the USSR (*Anuario,* 1988, pp. 419-423).
6. Per capita subsidy: total subsidy divided by population (*Anuario,* 1988, p. 57).
7. Per capita subsidy in U.S. dollars: subsidy in Cuban pesos converted to U.S. dollars at Cuba's official exchange rate.
8. Per capita subsidy in U.S. dollars: subsidy in Cuban pesos converted to U.S. dollars at Cuba's official exchange rate.
9. Subsidy as percent of *ingreso nacional creado* (*Anuario,* 1988, p. 99).
10. Adjustment for overpricing of imports from USSR: 20 percent of the value of Cuban imports from the USSR, assuming that Soviet exports are overpriced and quality is inferior to alternate suppliers.

11.-14. Calculated similarly to rows 6 to 9.

*Sources:* Comité Estatal de Estadísticas, *Anuario Estadístico de Cuba, 1988* (Havana: CEE, 1989); Economic Commission for Latin America and the Caribbean, *Statistical Yearbook, 1988* (New York: U.N., 1989); Banco Nacional de Cuba, *Economic Report,* successive issues, 1982-1989.

USSR in fulfillment of long-term sugar export commitments. This allowed Cuba to receive a profit, the magnitude of which depended on the price differential and the exchange rate at which the U.S. dollar free-market price was converted to Cuban pesos. Similarly, the USSR permitted Cuba to reexport petroleum on the basis of an agreement that provided that if petroleum consumption and importation levels declined vis-à-vis previously planned levels due to energy conservation, the petroleum that was "saved" could be reexported at world prices and in convertible currency. This transaction has been a paper transaction only, with the petroleum traveling physically from the USSR to Eastern and perhaps Western Europe. Detailed calculations of reexport profits to Cuba are summarized in Table 6.1, rows 3 and 4.

Soviet assistance to Cuba has been exceedingly generous, amounting to 1.9 to 3.7 billion Cuban pesos—that is, $225 to $430 per capita, or 15 to 30 percent of *ingreso nacional creado*—from 1980 to 1987. This subsidization has shielded Cuba from the vagaries and instabilities of the international economy, especially from the volatility of sugar and petroleum prices. Such assistance increased the levels of aggregate economic activity Cuba experienced in the 1980–1985 period and created an appearance of economic prosperity and growth that was in part illusory. A reduction of assistance occurred in 1986; this reduced foreign exchange availability, reduced imports in relative terms, and led to a strangulation of economic growth—which was sharply negative during that year.

The real value of Soviet economic assistance to Cuba is likely to decline in the 1990s, with or without the continuing implementation of perestroika in the USSR. The petroleum import price subsidy to Cuba, which basically disappeared after 1985, will likely be insignificant or will disappear altogether. Petroleum reexport profits to Cuba will also remain low or will disappear. The sugar export price subsidy to Cuba will decline because the Cuban export price is determined in part by an index of prices of Cuban imports—including petroleum—from the USSR. Sugar resale profits to Cuba will be lower in the 1990s than they were in the 1980s due to lower Soviet ruble purchase prices and world free-market hard currency prices, which will probably continue to be higher than the depressed prices of the mid-1980s.

Intensification of the implementation of perestroika in the Soviet Union could lower the real value of Soviet assistance in a variety of ways. First, greater reliance on the market in exchange rate determination, which would mean a devaluation in the ruble and presumably the peso as well, would lower the U.S. dollar equivalent of the ruble and the peso price of sugar. This would reduce the margin between the Soviet price and the free-market price, thereby reducing the hidden sugar subsidy and eliminating the profits from reselling sugar bought at the free-market price from other sugar producers for reexport to the Soviet Union. Moreover, at the January 1990 COMECON meeting in Sofia, the Soviet delegation under then–Prime Minister Ryzkov proposed that trade among members be conducted in convertible currencies and at market prices.[6]

Second, the Soviet move toward a realistic exchange rate will undoubtedly be accompanied by a move toward realistic (market-determined) pricing for major traded goods such as petroleum, sugar, nickel, and other commodities. This would diminish and perhaps eliminate hidden subsidization and reexport profit opportunities unless Soviet-Cuban pricing arrangements remained exceptional. However, although Cuba would lose some or all of its subsidization as a result of ruble convertibility and market-based pricing of its main trade items with the USSR, it may gain in that its foreign exchange earnings with the Soviet Union could become fully convertible and be usable anywhere in the world.

A third manifestation of perestroika is the greater power allocated to Soviet firms in an April 1989 law to market their products abroad independently. This could result in some enterprises choosing to supply only those foreign purchasers who can pay a hard currency price or a premium price. This phenomenon has already occurred with the Icarus bus enterprise in Hungary, which has effectively stopped further shipments to Cuba because of increased prices.

Fourth, the general orientations of Soviet policy under Gorbachev—namely, greater concern with reestablishing dynamism within the sluggish Soviet economy, reduced emphasis on fostering socialist and Communist regimes in the rest of the world, and greater recourse to decentralization and the market mechanism in economic organization—all lead to the conclusion that heavy subsidization of the Cuban economy is unlikely to last. Furthermore, as the domestic economy weakened in 1990, the Soviet Union became more interested in obtaining low-cost credits and perhaps outright assistance from the West to facilitate a transition toward greater marketization of the economy. It is unlikely that the United States or other developed economies would assist the USSR if this merely meant a flow-through of assistance to Cuba. In consequence, by mid-1990 the USSR was under pressure to reduce its subsidization of Cuba—pressure that has continued through 1991.

## Global Economic Integration

The international community is launched on a project with great potential historical significance. There is a powerful momentum toward a closer economic union of all the major countries of the world. This momentum has been generated by a number of factors operating concurrently. The process will likely continue, at least as far as the establishment of nearly free trade on a global basis and in the more distant future toward the establishment of a global common market. Policymakers and analysts in Cuba are reasonably aware of the advantages of expanded exports and of the national economic gains to be reaped from having a comparative advantage in a global trading environment. However, for Cuba to obtain appropriate benefits from the movement toward a closely integrated international trading system, a variety of policy initiatives will be required. It is imperative that Cuba enter this new global project with determination and persistence if it is to fulfill its long-term economic developmental potential.

A number of forces are at work in propelling the global economy toward a more intense level of economic integration. These have important implications for Cuba. The first factor is the movement of the countries of Eastern Europe toward a market orientation and greater integration into the global economy. There are unprecedented and rapid institutional changes away from central planning, with its relatively limited interconnections to the world economy, toward a greater reliance on decentralized market mechanisms internally and intensified economic interactions with the rest of the world. These changes will have significant effects on Cuba. The direct effect will be a reduction of Cuba's exports and imports within the socialist bloc.

Eastern Europe's trade relations will be driven increasingly by economic or commercial motives within the broad international system rather than by political motivations within the socialist bloc. This has already begun to happen, as in the above-mentioned case of the Hungarian Icarus trade in buses with Cuba. Moreover, the movement of the countries of Eastern Europe into the convertible currency market will mean that Cuba will be under pressure to follow suit. To the extent that Cuba's exports to Eastern Europe are based on a genuine comparative advantage, this represents an advantage to Cuba because it can earn hard currency for existing exports and can use such foreign exchange earnings anywhere in the world, breaking out of the enforced bilateralism of trade in inconvertible currencies. It is also important to note that the institutional changes in the economies and politics of the countries of Eastern Europe can only weaken the confidence with which Cubans adhere to their current institutions, which were copied in large part—although with some modifications—from those countries.

It would be highly damaging to Cuba in the long run to remain outside of the process of intensifying global economic integration. To postpone or abstain from this process or to enter it only half-heartedly would mean that Cuba would gradually fall further behind other countries—and perhaps most of the rest of the world—in terms of the evolution of its economic structure and institutions. A more complete insertion of Cuba into the global integration process, the policy implications of which are discussed below, would permit real improvements in productivity, specialization, and expansion in a diversified range of export commodities; increases in real foreign exchange earnings; and ultimately improvements in living standards.

## Reassessing Institutional Structures in the Cuban Economy

### Development Record

Cuba's achievements since 1958 in the areas of education, health, the reduction of open unemployment, and the equity of income distribution are well known. It is important to note, however, that other countries in Latin America, following different development paths, have also been reasonably successful in achieving social development objectives and in meeting basic human needs. In the recently published United Nations Development Programs (UNDP) human development index, which includes components for life expectancy, adult literacy, access to material resources, and real GDP per capita, Cuba ranks sixth among Latin American countries for the period 1985–1987.[7]

Although Cubans clearly would not want to sacrifice the improvements in social development, it is unlikely that they would want to rest on their laurels and not make further improvements in material levels of living. Casual observation suggests that there is a general hunger for material improvement. This demand can only intensify in the future as the demonstration effect of the Cuban elite and foreign tourists continues to intensify, as knowledge of other countries improves, and as (or if) further material improvements occur in Eastern Europe and the Soviet Union following their processes of economic change.

Cuba's growth record since 1958 has been mixed. Following unsatisfactory growth in the 1960s, the 1970–1985 period was one of steady improvement. In this period, the annual rate of growth of *ingreso nacional creado* (INC) was 5.7 percent, or 4.8 percent in per capita terms. From 1985 to 1988, however, real economic growth as measured by INC was negative at −1.6 percent per annum, or −2.6 percent per capita per annum.[8] We might note that the INC measure of economic activity differs from GNP or GDP in that it excludes services such as education, health, administration, and finance. Because these sectors have expanded rapidly, the estimates of the growth of INC are lower than estimates of GDP growth. The INC measure also excludes informal sector activities, such as the sale of handicrafts and some services such as plumbing or general carpentry, which are significant in Cuba. On the other hand, estimates of INC are exaggerated because the implicit Soviet subsidization through higher sugar and nickel export prices inflates the value added in those export activities, whereas subsidization through lower pre-1986 petroleum prices reduced import costs and thereby inflated domestic value added. Petroleum and sugar reexports have increased INC in a similar way. In the absence of such subsidization, INC and GSP would be much lower than the actual estimates, but the impacts on the estimates of growth rates over time are ambiguous.

Cuba's strong growth performance from 1970 to 1985 was based on a number of external as well as internal factors. Its favorable and stable import and export prices with the USSR, together with debt financing of a proportion of Cuba's imports from nonsocialist countries and the USSR, were of major benefit. Internally, Cuba's investment efforts in human development and infrastructure as well as machinery and equipment were important sources of growth. The general stability of economic policy, increasing pragmatism in the running of the economy, and continuing emphasis on improving productivity were important contributions. A specific factor worthy of note was the major improvement in labor productivity made possible by the continued mechanization of the sugar harvest, which released a large proportion of the agricultural labor force for employment elsewhere.

The negative growth experience from 1985 to 1988 resulted from two main external factors. First, the previously manageable convertible currency debt crisis became serious: Cuba was unable to service such debt and declared a moratorium in 1985 that was still in effect in 1990. The country was therefore cut off from further lending by virtually all of the public and private financial institutions in the nonsocialist countries. Second, the real value of the assistance from the Soviet Union declined sharply in 1986. These factors resulted in reduced imports of essential inputs, component parts, and capital equipment with consequent negative effects on levels of output.

Cuba's prospects for economic growth in the 1990s are not bright. The likely termination of the special relationship with the Soviet Union will clearly have negative consequences. The need to come to an agreement with the Paris Club of Creditors and to begin to reduce the hard currency debt will also reduce the availability of foreign exchange for imports of all sorts. In facing this eventuality, Cuba is not well prepared to expand and diversify its exports. Indeed, one of the least successful aspects of Cuba's development performance is in the area of export diversification. Cuba continues to be dependent on its traditional exports—notably on

TABLE 6.2   Importance of Exports: Cuba in Latin American Perspective, 1960-1988[a]

|  | 1960 | 1970 | 1980 | 1988 |
|---|---|---|---|---|
| **Cuba** | | | | |
| Sugar products | 80.6[b] | 76.9 | 83.7 | 74.6 |
| Minerals | 3.8 | 16.7 | 4.9 | 8.2 |
| Tobacco | 6.7 | 3.2 | 0.9 | 1.8 |
| Fishery products | 0.8 | 1.8 | 2.3 | 2.7 |
| Other agricultural | 1.9 | 0.1 | 2.0 | 4.5 |
| Other | 6.1 | 1.4 | 6.3 | 8.2 |
| Total exports[c] | 733.5[b] | 1,049.5 | 3,966.7 | 5,518.3 |
| **Brazil** | | | | |
| Coffee | | 34.6 | 12.4 | 7.5[d] |
| Total exports[e] | | 2,714.4 | 20,079.5 | 26,228.1 |
| **Colombia** | | | | |
| Coffee | | 65.8 | 59.9 | 32.6 |
| Total exports[e] | | 735.7 | 3,940.9 | 5,026.2 |
| **Chile** | | | | |
| Copper | 69.8 | 75.5 | 46.1 | 47.1 |
| Total exports[e] | 490.0 | 1,111.7 | 4,670.7 | 7,048.3 |
| **Mexico** | | | | |
| Oil | 1.8[f] | 2.6 | 62.3 | 38.4[d] |
| Total exports[e] | 944.0[f] | 1,174.5 | 15,515.3 | 20,531.2 |

*Sources:* U.N. Economic Commission for Latin America, *Anuario Estadístico de América Latina y el Caribe, 1989* (Santiago, Chile: United Nations, 1990), pp. 116-133; Comité Estatal de Estadísticas, *Anuario Estadístico de Cuba, 1988* (Havana: CEE, 1990), p. 426.

[a]  Figures for all products are the percentage the product represents of the country's total exports for the stated year.
[b]  1958 figures.
[c]  Millions of Cuban pesos.
[d]  1987 figures.
[e]  Millions of U.S. dollars.
[f]  1962 figures.

sugar, as indicated in Table 6.2. The high level of dependence on sugar depicted in Table 6.2 is exaggerated, however, due to the fact that the subsidized Soviet sugar price inflates the value of sugar exports and, thus, of sugar's weight in total exports. This is also true of nickel exports. Cuba has been able to develop and expand citrus exports and has begun to export a variety of other products such as a few consumer goods, cement, and some sugar-sector machinery and equipment. Unemployment did not seem to increase during the 1985–1988 recession and rectification process but remained at about 6 percent throughout the period.[9]

Cuba faces a number of interlocking economic problems rooted ultimately in the nature of its economic system. These problems have damaged and stunted Cuba's economic performance. Their impacts will intensify in the future, reducing the country's ability to provide for the material well-being of the Cuban people. The problems also contribute to further economic backsliding vis-à-vis the rest of the world. I will outline some of the more severe of these problems, but I cannot attempt to undertake a comprehensive analysis of Cuba's overall system of economic management and its development strategy.[10]

## The Private Sector

Perhaps the most serious weakness of the Cuban economy is the near-absence of a private small enterprise sector. In the revolutionary offensive of March 1968, many middle-sized private businesses—approximately 56,000 in all—were nationalized or abolished. This included 9,600 small manufacturing firms; the rest were services of various sorts. (In the province of Pinar del Río, 51 percent of the 1,834 private enterprises affected by the offensive were simply shut down.)[11] By 1970, the only business enterprises still in operation were informal sector microenterprises in such areas as transportation, barber and beauty shops, and customized clothing-making. The total number of officially recognized enterprises outside of agriculture—assuming that each self-employed individual represented a microenterprise—was 28,600 in 1988 (see Table 6.3). Since 1970, the volume of employment in the private nonfarm sector has declined steadily, from 2.7 percent of the total in 1970 to 1.1 percent of the total in 1988. The situation in the private agricultural sector was similar: Major inducements have been offered and some pressures applied to convince farmers to move from the private to the public sector, and private farmers have been encouraged to join cooperatives.

There is a significant unregistered informal, or microenterprise, sector in Cuba. Unfortunately, according to Francisco Almagro, vice-minister of the Comité Estatal de Estadísticas in a 1990 interview with the author, no estimates of the magnitude, growth, or economic significance of this sector have yet been made by the Comité Estatal de Estadísticas or by independent analysts. In 1990, this sector included a number of types of microenterprise self-employment such as garment-making; auto mechanics; shoemaking and repair; house construction, renovation, and repair; tradesmen's services (carpenters, electricians, plumbers, masons,

TABLE 6.3   Employment Structure by State and Private Sectors, 1970-1980

|  | 1970 | | 1984 | | 1988 | |
| --- | --- | --- | --- | --- | --- | --- |
|  | Number (000s) | % | Number (000s) | % | Number (000s) | % |
| Total employment | 2,408.9 | 100.0 | 3,364.3 | 100.0 | 3,740.6 | 100.0 |
| State sector | 2,078.8 | 86.3 | 3,122.0 | 92.8 | 3,531.3 | 94.4 |
| Nonstate agriculture | 264.9 | 11.0 | 190.3 | 5.6 | 167.9 | 4.5 |
| private farmers | (264.9) | (11.0) | (118.0) | (3.5) | (101.9) | (2.7) |
| cooperative farmers | 0 | 0 | (72.3) | (2.1) | (66.0) | (1.8) |
| Private sector (nonagricultural) | 65.2 | 2.7 | 52.0 | 1.6 | 41.4 | 1.1 |
| Self-employed | (30.0) | (1.2) | (39.5) | (1.2) | (28.6) | (0.8) |
| Employees | (35.2) | (1.5) | (12.5) | (0.4) | (12.8) | (0.3) |

*Source:* Comité Estatal de Estadísticas, *Anuario Estadístico de Cuba, 1985*, p. 187, and *Anuario Estadístico de Cuba, 1988*, p. 192 (Havana: CEE, 1986 and 1990).

metal workers); domestic services (housecleaning, child care); electric and electronic repair services (television, radio, stereo, refrigerator, stove); transport services; secretarial services; and gardening.

Despite the vibrance of parts of the microenterprise sector and the pervasiveness of the black market, the abolition of most small and medium-sized private businesses has hurt Cuba badly. By abolishing and either shutting down or incorporating such enterprises into the state sector—with the owner-operators dispossessed—a large amount of human capital was effectively eliminated. This human capital included varying combinations of entrepreneurship, managerial skill, technical knowledge, and marketing expertise. The effects of this loss over time have been serious: Twenty-five to thirty years' worth of pragmatic learning by small business entrepreneurs has been lost. The innovation, learning by doing, and response to changing circumstances that entrepreneurs normally develop in order to remain in business have been absent. The bureaucratized and centralized planning system in the public sector has not replaced the decentralized initiative and self-activation of hundreds of thousands of small business owner-operators.

There are a number of other harmful economic consequences of this situation. First, the range and quality of material goods and services available to citizens are far below what would be possible with a different structure. Second, the economy has been sluggish and slow to respond to new opportunities created by technical changes and changing consumer demand in comparison with other countries at roughly similar levels of development. Third, the ability of the economy to diversify and expand exports in a range of new, nontraditional areas has been impeded because the continuous trial and error and learning by doing inherent in small business have not occurred. Fourth, the division of labor within the economy and the creation of numerous new specialist enterprises as firms "spin off" particular functions to such enterprises have also been blocked, with consequent productivity losses that are magnified increasingly over time.

## Markets, Prices, and Centralization

Cuba's economic system and institutions were in large part borrowed, with modifications, from the countries of Eastern Europe and from the Soviet Union. By mid-1990 those countries had begun the process of restructuring and replacing the old systems of centralized planning with more decentralized systems that rely more heavily on markets and the price mechanism to orchestrate and rationalize the economic activities of myriads of producers with the choices of consumers. Cuba would be unwise to ignore for much longer the objective merits of a decentralized mixed-market system in favor of the current demarketized and highly centralized system that has demonstrated its shortcomings and unsustainability in Eastern Europe.

The absence of normally functioning markets creates great difficulties for the Cuban people in their day-to-day existence. Many examples might be cited, but only one or two can be outlined because of space limitations. In Cuba, there is no legal, smoothly functioning market for housing. As people move through the life cycle—growing up, marrying, raising families, and retiring—their housing needs change. But without an active rental or ownership market for housing, it is extremely difficult for people to change houses—unless they are officially allocated or reallocated. The entire system has become inflexible to the point of paralysis. This problem is compounded by a general housing shortage with sub-subdivision of housing units and numerous family units and all generations sharing small accommodations. The result of this shortage and inflexibility is that minimal housing and privacy needs for married couples and families are often unmet. This is often cited as one reason for Cuba's alarmingly high divorce rate and the predominance of single-parent families.

A second general and continuing weakness in Cuba's economic system is the extreme degree of centralized control in decisionmaking about resource allocation. Hypercentralization was a serious problem in the 1960s. The most publicized and particularly damaging examples were (1) the 10 million ton sugar harvest objective of 1964–1970, and (2) the

Havana Greenbelt program. In these cases, the hierarchical structure of the command of economic management permitted decisions reached at the level of President Castro to reorient the energies of much of the population into massive programs that turned out to be ill-conceived, economically foolish, and exceedingly costly to the Cuban people. These programs were subsequently reversed.[12] In the 1970s and early 1980s, it appeared that Cuba and President Castro had learned from the experiences of the 1960s and had become more pragmatic and deliberative in economic matters. However, some examples of the extreme centralization of decisionmaking that occurred in the 1980s suggest that this phenomenon is inherent in the structure and functioning of the economy and the political system.

One of the more well-known recent projects that illustrates the excessive degree of centralization in Cuban political-economic decisionmaking is the Biotechnological Institute, a huge, ultramodern research facility on the outskirts of Havana. Other recent examples of the hypercentralization of decisionmaking include the decisions to invest massively in infrastructure such as the continuing extension and expansion of the trans-Cuba highway, the continuing large investment in costly high-technology medicine, and the decision to close the farmers' markets.

It appears that the roots of hypercentralization are systemic in nature. Essentially, President Castro wields so much power and influence through the party, the Council of Ministers, and the National Assembly that his decisions can be quickly adopted and implemented without serious criticism or evaluation anywhere within the political system or the system of economic management. This degree of centralized decisionmaking creates a certain macroflexibility in Cuba's economy and society: Decisions can be reached and implemented rapidly so that natural, human, and capital resources can be mobilized and deployed quickly. The weakness of hypercentralization is that when mistakes occur, they tend to be massive and exceedingly costly.

An additional consequence of the demarketization of the Cuban economy is what appears to be a nearly irreversible and almost unstoppable tendency toward bureaucratization in the system. This phenomenon has been particularly severe in Cuba because bureaucracies are supposed to perform all of the control, coordination, allocation, and activation functions conducted with high automaticity and spontaneity by the price mechanism in a market system. Bureaucratism manifests itself in a variety of ways: expansion of the number of personnel throughout the economic management system, conversion of managers from entrepreneurs to order-takers (in a 1990 interview with the author, Carlos Rafael Rodríguez lamented that what Cuba needed was *empresarios socialistas*), extreme subdivision of functional tasks among bureaucrats with a resulting lack of flexibility and an absence of general managerial savoir faire, promotion on the basis of political criteria more than on aptitude,[13] a loss of sight of the real purpose of an enterprise (to serve Cuban citizens), and preoccupation with procedures and immediate private rewards. Much of the current rectification process has been aimed at making the current system work more effectively, but the results so far are discouraging.

Finally, the absence of an economically rational structure of prices represents a serious problem. Without prices that accurately reflect economic scarcities, enterprises cannot ascertain with accuracy whether they are using inputs effectively and efficiently in producing outputs that have the greatest relative value to the Cuban people. The absence of a meaningful and unified exchange rate—that is, a relative price for all foreign vis-à-vis domestic goods and services—means that no enterprise can know if it is using foreign and domestic inputs in optimal combination. Indeed, the allocation of foreign exchange and of all inputs and outputs becomes a task of the planning bureaucracy. At this time there appears to be no workable alternative to the price mechanism for allocating resources efficiently in a complex economic system. No country, and certainly not a middle-income country, can afford to waste or in effect to destroy its scarce natural, capital, and human resources decade after decade by abstaining from using the price mechanism and relying on a bureaucratic central planning system that is being discredited and discarded by its original adherents.

## Redesigning the Economic System for Reintegration into the Global Economy

As argued earlier, recent changes in the international economic environment—namely the prospective end of the special relationship with the USSR and the ongoing process of global economic integration—require that Cuba reconsider and revise its position in the international system so that it can participate in and gain from that system as it actually exists and functions. It was then argued that the current domestic economic system, although strong in some senses, was essentially flawed and unsustainable in the long term.

A central imperative for Cuba is to become self-financing in the international system. Declining Soviet subsidization and the need to reduce the convertible currency debt and perhaps the debt with the USSR as well mean that Cuba must increase its hard currency foreign exchange earnings by expanding exports of goods and services. Failure to increase export earnings in the future would lead to economic contraction or slowdowns in growth as a result of insufficient imported inputs. (At this time, Cuba has few luxury imports that could be cut back quickly and painlessly.) The opportunities for developing industries to produce commodities in substitution for those previously imported is now limited due to the extreme level of import substitution pursued in Cuba in the past. The need for export promotion, the diversification of markets, and the diversification of the range of export commodities is well understood in Cuba and has been emphasized for some time. Indeed, there was some success in 1988 and 1989 in entering Latin American markets and in expanding nontraditional exports, although this process is still in a relatively early stage.

Cuba's export potential is quite good. In time, with the right policy and institutional frameworks and with tenacious market development, Cuba could produce as broad a range of exports as Florida or Chile. For example, a broad range of tropical and subtropical fruits and vegetables could be developed and expanded for foreign and in some cases domestic markets. The international markets for exotic tropical fruit juices and concentrates (passion fruit, mango, papaya) could become as large as the market for citrus products. Cuba could also export a wide range of middle-quality consumer goods including baseball equipment, and it could expand exports of a number of types of machinery and equipment such as sugar-cultivation and milling equipment.

A second imperative for Cuba is to maintain and raise levels of material well-being. As noted earlier, Cuba's achievements in this area are impressive. Basic human needs fulfillment has improved markedly, especially with respect to health, education, and the establishment of a minimum floor or safety net with respect to real income levels. Further significant and sustained improvement in real income or real material well-being (aside from education and health) will require major institutional innovations and important policy changes. Fortunately, the above-mentioned external and domestic imperatives can be achieved with the same set of institutional and policy changes.

The types of institutional and policy changes that are appropriate now and that will undoubtedly be introduced in time include the following:

1. A major expansion of the private sector in a mixed-market system with a large state sector and pluralistic ownership forms
2. Further decentralization of decisionmaking in the state sector
3. Expansion of the role of the market mechanism and the price system in orchestrating economic activities
4. More reliance on market forces in the macroeconomy, including the establishment of a single realistic and unified exchange rate and a realistic rate of interest

5. Further opening up of the economy including a phaseout of current absolute bureaucratic protectionism, unification of internal and world prices for tradeables, and an easing of policies regarding foreign investment and joint ventures
6. Public-sector innovations necessary in a mixed-market economy such as income taxation, some regulatory activities, and establishment of a sugar earnings stabilization fund

Each of these institutional and policy areas merits more analysis than can be included here, but a few observations will be made. The Eastern European experience shows that there are important political dimensions and concomitants to these types of changes. It appears that centralized political control through a monopoly political party dominated by one person and operating through monopoly control of the media, the civil organs of society, and the political system is ultimately incompatible with the decontrol and liberalization of the economy. It is significant that in all of Eastern Europe, the move toward political pluralism has accompanied the movement towards economic liberalization and marketization. These political dimensions of economic changes make the suggested policy and institutional reforms discussed here doubly controversial in Cuba at this time. Indeed, the very term *market* is currently disdained in Cuba. Virtually none of the economic changes mentioned above were in mid-1990 within the range of acceptable political discourse (with the exception perhaps of the exchange rate regime). In sum, the probability of Cuba instituting the types of market-oriented changes discussed here is exceedingly low. On the other hand, as the reform process in Eastern Europe proceeds, when the difficulties of its transition recede, and when the external and domestic imperatives discussed above are fully perceived, adherence to Cuba's traditional economic system will be inviable. After President Castro's departure from the political scene, we can expect rapid, deep-cutting changes. It is not inconceivable that Castro may learn from the Eastern European experience, reappraise the international and domestic economic realities, modify his understanding of economics, and introduce some moves toward marketization, decentralization, and economic liberalization. However, this is improbable; there are reasons for Castro to fear any type of economic decontrol because of its political ramifications and concomitants.

Of central importance in the process of economic change is the pluralization of ownership firms—that is, the legalization of small, private businesses in a range of manufacturing and service activities and the legalization of cooperative ownership (outside of agriculture), all co-existing with state ownership. Expansion of the private sector would liberate the entrepreneurial energies that are currently diverted and deformed in black market activities, locked and stunted in the informal sector, or suppressed through the current prohibition of small or medium-sized formal business activity. This expansion would increase the range and quality of goods and services available to the populace, increase the productivity of resource use, increase productive employment, increase competitive pressures on large, state-sector enterprises, and generally permit real incomes to increase. On the negative side, the emergence of a flourishing private business sector would create high entrepreneurial incomes, especially during transitional periods before large numbers of similar businesses emerged or until the state sector responded (so that competition would lower the initial high enterprise profits). This impact on income distribution would require the establishment of an income tax. But initial incomes are in fact the signal and incentive for enterprise proliferation and expansion in specific activities.

An increased role for the market mechanism and price system is also necessary and would have to accompany the liberalization of ownership firms. Rather than attempting to fix all input and output prices in the system, the state should allow prices to perform a larger share of the task of resource allocation. The price system is indispensable as the means of orchestrating the activities of the private sector and a decentralized state sector. However, because of the large stock of cash for which consumers have no current use (a result of the suppressed past inflation or the imbalance between the value of wages and salaries paid and the value of goods and services available for purchase), uncontrolled prices would initially rise, contributing to overt inflation and high private-sector incomes. This is clearly a problem, but it can best be handled by eliminating the large cash overhang and reducing the income-to-expenditure imbalance (something Cuba has been trying to achieve for some years).

A range of policies that would open the economy to the international system is also necessary. Adoption of a unified realistic exchange rate—which means a significant devaluation—will improve the relative competitiveness of Cuban exports and make imports more expensive. Accompanying this should be a gradual phaseout of extreme protectionism. These policies would bring Cuban and foreign prices into agreement and would provide an incentive structure for a rationalization or restructuring of Cuban economic activity or, more specifically, of those sectors producing tradable goods and services. They are perhaps the most crucial policies in achieving a genuine economic opening to the world economy and in permitting or stimulating domestically oriented enterprises to become internationally competitive and to expand and diversify exports.

An additional valuable policy would be some liberalization of regulations governing foreign investment and joint ventures. Some transfer of entrepreneurship, managerial expertise, technology, and capital through foreign investment in defined areas could accelerate the process of economic diversification for domestic and foreign markets. Of particular usefulness in this respect would be the Cuban community abroad, some members of which have been successful in a variety of areas of enterprise and would have an interest in ventures in Cuba.

An important component of any long-term reorientation of the Cuban economy toward greater trade- and external-orientation ultimately will involve the reestablishment of trade relations with the United States, which is undoubtedly part of Cuba's natural geographical market sphere. This would benefit Cuba as an exporter, but it is not without economic as well as sociological risks. However, Cuba would be in a stronger position to benefit from normalization with the United States if it is well advanced in establishing a successful export-oriented economic structure and trading system. Normalization of relations with the United States depends on that country as well. So far, the United States has been singularly uncooperative in establishing normalization.

The central challenge for Cuba in the future is to gradually modify its economic orientation toward marketization and openness to the international system while maintaining the achievements of the revolution with respect to social equity and the provision of basic human needs in education, health, and nutrition. These goals are generally considered by Cubans to be incompatible and the experiences of many countries— especially in Latin America—appear to confirm this. However, Cuba's investment in people as well as infrastructure can help serve as a foundation for the move to an open market economy. In my view, Cuba can achieve efficiency and economic growth in the world economy with equity and also pay its way in the international system. This will not be easy, but there is no clear reasonable alternative.

## Notes

1. For a more complete discussion of Soviet subsidization, see Archibald R.M. Ritter, "The Cuban Economy in the 1990s: External Challenges and Policy Imperatives," *Journal of Interamerican Studies and World Affairs*, vol. 32, no. 3 (Fall 1990), pp. 117–149. For a discussion presenting an opposing point of view, see Chapter 9 of Andrew Zimbalist and Claes Brundenius, *The Cuban Economy: Measurement and Analysis of Socialist Performance* (Baltimore: Johns Hopkins University Press, 1989).

2. *Izvestia*, March 3, 1990.

3. Author's interview with respondent, Havana, July 1990.

4. Such concepts were developed in interviews with Vice-President Carlos Rafael Rodríguez and José Luis Rodríguez, vice-director of the Centro de Investigaciones sobre la Economía Mundial, in 1990. President Castro, cited in the March 9, 1990, issue of the *Journal of Commerce*, summarized the concepts concisely: "No one gives us things. We buy them and we pay for them. If our sugar receives a higher price than the world dumping price, it is still a fair price, because it put an end to the phenomenon of unequal terms of trade" (p. 1).

5. What would happen to Cuba's sugar exports to the USSR if the special relationship with that country were terminated is open to conjecture at this time. The most probable outcome is that as the USSR moves toward ruble convertibility, market determination of the prices of tradable commodities, and greater openness to international trade, it would continue to import similar or perhaps increased volumes of sugar from the world free-market suppliers generally. This means that although Cuba might lose special access to the Soviet sugar market, Soviet purchases from other sources would make space for Cuban sales to other purchasers in the world market. If both Cuba and the USSR shifted their sugar exports and imports to the world free market, the average world market price would not change much, if at all—although it would become a good deal less unstable. It is therefore reasonable to use the sugar price in the world free market in comparison with the special price of previous decades in order to estimate the value of the subsidy rather than to use other prices such as the higher U.S. or European Community protected prices.

6. Carmelo Mesa-Lago, F. Gil, and I. Brenes, "Relaciones económicas de Cuba con la URSS y la CAME: Pasado, presente, y futuro," unpublished manuscript, 1990.

7. This UNDP report, published in 1990, was cited in the May 26, 1990, issue of *The Economist*, pp. 80–81.

8. Comité Estatal de Estadísticas, *Anuario Estadístico de Cuba, 1988* (Havana: CEE, 1989), p. 103.

9. José Luis Rodríguez, "Aspectos económicos del proceso de rectificación," *Cuba Socialista*, no. 44 (1990), p. 98.

10. For a more comprehensive examination, see Archibald R.M. Ritter, *The Economic Development of Revolutionary Cuba: Strategy and Performance* (New York: Praeger, 1974); Andrew Zimbalist, ed., *Cuba's Socialist Economy Toward the 1990s* (Boulder, Colo.: Lynne Rienner Publishers, 1987); and Carmelo Mesa-Lago, "The Cuban Economy in the 1980s: The Return of Ideology," in Sergio Roca, ed., *Socialist Cuba: Past Interpretations and Future Challenges* (Boulder, Colo.: Westview Press, 1988).

11. *Granma Weekly Review*, April 7, 1968, p. 3.

12. For analyses, see Chapters 4 and 5 of Ritter, *Economic Development of Revolutionary Cuba*, and Carmelo Mesa-Lago, *The Economy of Socialist Cuba: A Two-Decade Appraisal* (Albuquerque: University of New Mexico Press, 1981).

13. Soledad Cruz, "Eliminar las causas de los azares," *Juventud Rebelde*, July 8, 1990, p. 2.

# 7

# Beyond Basic Needs: Cuba's Search for Stable Development in the 1990s

*Gareth Jenkins*

Even before the collapse of the East European regimes in the last months of 1989, the main lines of Cuba's development appeared more uncertain than at any time since the consolidation of Fidel Castro's regime in the late 1960s and early 1970s. Many of the initial aims of the revolution had been achieved, in particular the creation of a welfare state unique in the Third World that has resulted in a healthy, educated population with adequate nutritional standards. But the very success of Cuba's basic-needs approach was making increasingly urgent the need for an answer to the basic question about the next stage in the Cuban revolutionary process.

The restructuring of trade relations within the Eastern European–Soviet Council for Mutual Economic Assistance (COMECON), in particular the move toward trading in convertible currency and the phasing out of Soviet subsidies to Eastern Europe and the Third World, has dramatically increased uncertainty about Cuba's economic future. A substantial part of Cuba's trade with the former COMECON countries will likely continue, albeit on the basis of hard currency pricing and through bilateral clearing accounts. But at the very least, the prospect of losing Soviet subsidies of \$2–3 billion a year within a few years is speeding up the search for new economic mechanisms and sources of hard currency—whatever the official rhetoric about the "rectification of errors."

## Some Economic Achievements

The intensification of economic and political pressures by the United States has partially reversed the dominant trend of the 1980s. During that decade the U.S. embargo continued to hinder Cuba's development, but more through restricting access to trade and investment relations with the United States directly than through hampering Cuban trade with other Western countries. The main exception was the success of the Reagan administration in bullying West European, Japanese, and Canadian steel makers into excluding Cuban nickel from their exports to the United States. However, in the middle of the decade the embargo began to break down spectacularly as Cuba reestablished relations with most of Latin America, thus ending more than twenty years of regional isolation during which only Mexico and Canada had refused to withhold diplomatic recognition.

Cuba's relations with the developed capitalist economies in the 1980s thus began to approach the pattern of relations existing between other Latin American countries and the West. Cuba even contracted a Latin American debt problem: Its hard currency debt per capita amounted to approximately $600 by the end of 1989, which should be multiplied several times for a true comparison because Cuba's hard currency trade with non-COMECON countries is only 10–20 percent of its total trade.

European business took advantage of the strong performance of the Cuban economy in the early 1980s to increase trade, at a time when the rest of Latin America was in deep recession. Cuba in turn suffered the vicissitudes of the international financial and commodity markets, particularly the dramatic increase in interest rates in the early Reagan years. Nevertheless, Cuba remained an essentially marginal market, with total hard currency imports of around $1 billion a year. In this respect, it was not comparable with many of the markets of Eastern Europe, perceived by European business as offering a strategic escape from declining profitability and potential recession.

Most Western analysts have argued that Cuban statistics exaggerate real economic growth, that what growth there has been is the result of generous Soviet aid, and that Cuba would have done better to tie its fortunes to U.S. capital like that other Spanish-speaking Caribbean nation—Puerto Rico. This view has been strongly challenged by some Cuban economists—especially José Luis Rodríguez[1]—and by the Western economists Andrew Zimbalist and Claes Brundenius.[2] They have argued for the basic credibility of Cuban official statistics and the rationality and at least partial success of Cuba's development strategy. They have shown that given the restricted access to Western products and financial markets imposed by the U.S. embargo, sugar provided the only realistic source of surplus for capital accumulation.

They have also demonstrated the extent to which Cuba has developed a credible engineering sector out of the need to produce its own agricultural machinery and equipment and a range of industrial by-products of sugar such as paper, building materials, and animal feeds. The value of by-products has reached approximately 10 percent of the value of raw sugar production and, according to Zimbalist's calculations, the constant price share of raw sugar exports in total exports (excluding petroleum reexports) fell from 84.5 percent in 1965 to 64.3 percent twenty years later. Cuba has in fact pursued a moderately successful import-substitution program and has developed a range of hard currency export products. These include primary products such as citrus, coffee, seafoods, marble, and metals and also industrial products such as cement, iron and steel products, clothing, medicines, and non-electrical machinery. Within the last few years, it has also begun to produce sophisticated products such as video recorders, color televisions, software applications, and—most impressively—biotech products.

The success of the biotechnology program, which only began in 1981, throws into relief both the strengths and the weaknesses of Cuba's industrialization program. A group of Cuban researchers was trained in Finland on production techniques for interferon, and Cuban interferon was used in the treatment of dengue fever in June 1981. The following year, the Centro de Investigaciones Biológicas was established and soon won the personal backing of Fidel Castro. As a result, construction of a much larger research center, the Centro de Ingeniería Genética y Biotecnología (CIGB), was begun and was completed in the summer of 1986.

The CIGB is equipped with the best European and Japanese equipment, as U.S. Senate Foreign Relations Committee Chair Claiborne Pell remarked on a visit in November 1988: "I was struck by the fact that the medical research equipment used in the impressive high technology Institute of Genetic Engineering, where significant cancer research is being undertaken and genetic materials are being developed, was of Japanese, Swedish and German manufacture. Better quality and less expensive equipment, especially in terms of shipping costs, is available in the United States."[3]

Cuban researchers are well trained and highly dedicated, and they already have some impressive achievements to their credit. Cuba also has plans to market some of the products the CIGB is producing, particularly health care products for Latin America and other developing regions. This is a sensible strategy because there is a wide range of products that are not profitable for Western countries to market in the Third World but with which Cuba could reasonably expect to succeed.

The consistent support of a stable national state has made this program possible where many other developing countries have failed. Representatives of major international biotech companies such as Pharmacia from Sweden and Amersham from Great Britain acknowledge Cuba's success in this field.

## Some Economic Weaknesses

It is already apparent, however, that Cuba lacks many of the marketing networks and promotional skills necessary to take advantage of its research capability. This weakness can take very simple but devastating forms. For instance, a number of Cuba's biotech products have tested well in Brazil, Sweden, and other countries, but Cuba has failed to take the most basic steps to publicize the results, without which foreign experts will not take the products seriously. Moreover, even when Cuba has won major export contracts, delivery and quality problems have emerged. This was the case with Cuba's most important biotech export contract to date, which was worth $80 million. It was signed in late 1989 with the Brazilian conglomerate Petrobras and was for 8 million doses of the meningitis B vaccine that Cuba is the only country in the world to have succeeded in producing.[4]

A *Financial Times* survey, published in 1989, highlighted this tension between Cuba's achievements and aspirations and the shortages and inefficiencies that hold it back from realizing its potential.

Cuba is no longer what one might call a Third World country. For the advances made in health care, education and the nutrition of its people could certainly rank it among the top five in the league of developing countries. It has built a reasonably solid industrial base in energy, construction and steel. The experience gained in stainless steel manufacture for the sugar and fermentation industries, the development and diversification of oil refining capacity and its well-developed bio-medical sector give Cuba strong possibilities for expansion into the manufacture of sophisticated chemicals and pharmaceuticals. . . . It is one thing to produce interferons, it is another to sell them to the rest of the world. Can Cuba supply its customers reliably when the workers that produce these quality products have to spend much of their time waiting for a bus, or standing in a queue for tomatoes?[5]

This is the most obvious contradiction of Cuba's economic development. It is as though many of the mechanisms are in place for the functioning of a modern economy but certain crucial cogs and lubricants have been forgotten. Problems arise in one sector, and resources are allocated to resolve them, but they only reappear somewhere else.

The reasons seem to lie first in inflexibilities and lack of adequate signals to permit the efficient continuous allocation of labor and second in the country's inadequate integration into the world division of labor. These are problems Cuba shares with many other developing countries, although in Cuba's case they take a specific form as a result of its adoption of COMECON-style planning mechanisms in the mid-1970s. For instance, the attempt to control millions of individual prices through a central bureaucracy becomes increasingly hard as industrialization advances and leads to inefficient allocation of labor, equipment, and materials.

Cuba also faces other external constraints that exacerbate its internal problems of economic organization. Although it has benefited greatly from privileged access to COMECON markets for its products, it has received little comparable preference in its relations with Western economies, with the exception of Spain, which throughout the period has negotiated state-level bilateral trade agreements for all products except nickel. Even this special relationship is now coming to an end as Spain becomes fully integrated into the European Economic Community.

After the partial thaw of the Carter years, the U.S. embargo continued to constrain Cuba's development in the 1980s, mainly through restricting access to U.S. products and financial markets. In a study written in May 1981, the U.S. Commerce Department congratulated itself that "the US embargo has been and continues to be not only a major but a crucial impediment to Cuba's efforts at diversifying and expanding its hard currency trade, the key to improved economic growth and living standards."[6] This, however, was a considerable exaggeration.

In November 1980, at the end of the Carter administration, the U.S. government invoked legislation dating from 1963 to ban the import of special steels from the French company Creusot-Loire that contained Cuban nickel. The new Reagan administration tried to tighten the embargo still further. During 1981 and the first half of 1982, it exposed more than forty companies that it claimed were "pass throughs" set up specifically to enable Cuba to trade with U.S. companies through third countries. The Treasury Department labeled them "designated Cuban nationals" and withdrew their licenses to trade with Cuba. Morris H. Morley suggests that this largely explains the decline in Cuban purchases from "US third country subsidiaries" in 1981. These had increased from $89.4 million in 1979 to $303.2 million in 1980, but dropped back to $73.8 million in 1981.[7] However, it seems that Cuba quickly found ways to restore this trade, which increased to $253 million in 1982 and averaged $276 million over the seven-year period 1983–1989.

Cuba's dependence on trade with the Soviet Union and Eastern Europe became acute in the years between the recession of the mid-1980s and the collapse of the East European regimes at the end of 1989. According to the peso calculations of Cuba's national statistics, in 1988 70 percent of Cuba's imports came from the Soviet Union and a further 15 percent from Eastern Europe; 67 percent of its exports went to the Soviet Union and 15 percent to Eastern Europe. This reflected Cuba's acute shortage of convertible currency and its failure to make substantial inroads into export markets, rather than its national policy. Indeed, in the mid-1980s, Cuban economists held that the ideal situation was for 30 percent of trade to be conducted with capitalist countries. Nevertheless, the opportunity to off-load large consignments of goods onto the undemanding markets of the East with little need to invest in sophisticated packaging, quality control, or marketing was no doubt an important factor in biasing trade in this direction—over and above the influence of long-term sugar agreements.

During its economic boom of the early 1980s, Cuba's foreign trade was more balanced. In 1980 and 1981, Cuba's imports from Western Europe, Canada, and Japan amounted to 19.5 percent and 18.1 percent, respectively, of total imports in those two years, with the Soviet Union and the East European countries accounting for 75.5 percent and 77.3 percent, respectively. The total Western share remained above 11 percent between 1984 and 1986 as a result of large imports from Japan, but the rescheduling impasse since then caused it to fall to 8.2 percent in 1987 and 7.9 percent in 1988. To some extent, this decline was compensated for by increased hard currency imports from other Latin American countries, particularly Argentina and Mexico. These amounted to 331.9 million pesos in 1988—55.7 percent of the value of Western imports.

## Efforts to Expand Tourism

In order to break out of its dependence on sugar and develop more balanced foreign trading relations, Cuba needs to generate substantially greater export revenues. The key to the problem is being sought, almost inevitably, in tourism. After two decades of spurning it as a source of foreign exchange—and despite bad memories of what tourism, prostitution, and gambling did to Cuba in the 1950s—the government made the decision in the late 1970s to open up the country to Western tourism once again. The National Institute of Tourism (Intur), set up in 1959 to rescue the industry, was dusted off and set to renovating hotels, developing infrastructure, and attracting a new generation of tourists.

Although it had a ponderous, inexperienced, and inefficient bureaucracy, Intur was able to get the number of hard currency tourists visiting Cuba up from 78,000 in 1980—of whom 22,000 were from Canada and 35,000 from the United States—to 149,000 by 1986, despite the loss of the United States market when Reagan tightened travel restrictions. The main markets it succeeded in developing during this period were West Germany (23,000 in 1986), Spain (20,000), Mexico (13,000), Italy (11,000), and Argentina (7,000).

Nevertheless, Cuba still was not attracting the luxury tourists who visited other Caribbean islands and was fast running out of unused facilities. The government passed its first joint venture law (Decree No. 50) in 1982 specifically with an eye on attracting foreign investment in hotel construction and other tourist facilities. Although the names of companies in Canada, Mexico, West Germany, France, and other countries were mentioned from time to time, no substantial investments materialized until 1989 when a joint project with a Spanish hotel chain resulted in a new hotel in Varadero.

Spanish management consultants were brought in to improve the running of three hotels in Varadero, and another Spanish group undertook the highly successful renovation of the Victoria Hotel in central Havana, but these contracts were outside the joint venture legal framework. A Canadian tour operator did supply second-hand building equipment to renovate a Varadero hotel with payment from the revenue his tour groups brought in, but the project was never completed. The only other major interest expressed in negotiating a joint venture was by the French hotel chain Novotel, which was interested in contracting to manage four hotels, including the Habana Libre—the former Hilton. But talks broke down in 1986 when Novotel discovered that the staff-to-room ratio at the Habana Libre was 2.2, compared with 0.3 in their French hotels. Novotel seems to have pulled out in despair at the prospect of trying to manage the hotel efficiently.

Given the centrality of tourism by this time in Cuba's plans to generate hard currency, this experience pushed the government in 1987 to set up a new rival enterprise to Intur—Cubanacan S.A.—which would operate outside the existing structure for foreign trade enterprises. There was a precedent for this type of corporation in Cuba. In 1977 the Panamanian-registered corporation, Cimex S.A., was established to take advantage of the visits of Cuban emigres returning to Cuba from the United States to visit relatives as a result of a relaxation of restrictions under President Carter. Cimex S.A. subsequently became, through its subsidiary Havanatur, the largest tour operator selling holidays in Cuba, with offices throughout Western Europe and Latin America and in Canada. It has also diversified into general trading in the Caribbean hotel and tourist resort development, banking, and consultancy—possibly including activities connected with breaking the U.S. embargo.

Like Cimex, Cubanacan owns hotels and works as a tour operator. It differs in that it has a specific brief to attract foreign investment in joint ventures. A total of 1,442 tourist rooms, mostly in hotels in Havana and Varadero, were transferred to Cubanacan from Intur, and in addition it was given responsibility for developing the eastern half of the island for tourism—Santiago, Granma, Baracoa, Holguín, Santa Lucía, Trinidad, and the Isle of Youth. One of its most ambitious long-term projects, which provides an important clue to Cuba's foreign policy in the next decade, is the development of the virgin key Cayo Coco as a major tourist resort and free port. It is scheduled to be in full operation by the mid-1990s and is clearly intended to attract wealthy U.S. tourists once they are again permitted to visit Cuba.

No one could doubt Cuba's potential as a tourist destination, especially once relations with the United States improve. The tourism of the 1950s was narrowly based in Havana and the casinos. Cuba now has the opportunity to develop tourist centers throughout the island and on the 1,600 keys and small islands that surround its coast. In terms of geography, natural attractions, historical heritage, and the splendor of Havana—which is now being restored—Cuba could easily eclipse the rest of the Caribbean in the world tourist market.

Tourism could even eventually rival sugar as a hard currency earner. In 1989 total hard currency earnings from tourism (including airline and other revenues) were $260.4 million, roughly $1,000 per tourist. If we assume that Cuba's total sugar exports of some seven million tons a year will soon all be sold for (or at least valued in terms of) convertible currency and that sugar prices average around $300 per ton, then total sugar export revenues would amount to some $2 billion a year. Cuba's highly ambitious tourism development plan envisages attracting 1.5 million tourists in 1995. If this were achieved and the level of earnings per tourist increases, by then Cuba would be earning close to $2 billion a year from tourism—equivalent to its earnings from sugar.

However, the modern tourism industry is intensely competitive and is dominated by a handful of giant tour operators. In order to achieve its targets, Cuba will have to create the infrastructure, provide the international and domestic transportation, and develop the level of personal service demanded by these tour operators. It will have to compete with established resorts such as Cancún and the Bahamas and other rapidly developing destinations such as the Dominican Republic—with a population of six and a half million, very low wages, and extremely generous foreign investment incentives. This is well understood by those who run the tourism industry in Cuba. More attention is being paid to staff training at all levels—including language training—smart new hotels are going up, airports are being revamped, new buses and cars are being purchased, and recreation facilities are being developed.

So far the hotels have been full, and the indications are that earnings per tourist are increasing. But as Fidel Castro often complains in his speeches, Cubans have lost the habit of personal service and seem slow to relearn it, which is proving to be a major problem. Although the average West European or U.S. package tourists may not be very discerning in many respects, they do expect their meals and drinks to be served promptly, rooms to be made up on time, light bulbs to be replaced, and so on.

At present the proportion of tourists who return to Cuba after their first visit is low—probably around 7–8 percent—whereas a figure of one in five would be more typical for the Caribbean. At the moment this does not matter greatly because the main constraint is the shortage of hotels, with room occupancy rates high throughout the main season from September to April. But as more hotels are constructed and as word of mouth becomes more important, this will become a major area of concern. Return rates are closely related to the level of service and attention tourists receive, the standard of the facilities, ease of travel to the country, and the support infrastructure available—transportation, excursions, recreational facilities, shopping, and so on. These factors also strongly influence how much a country earns per tourist. On most of these counts, Cuba is clearly still a minor player in the international tourism industry.

Cubanacan opened its first new installation, Villa Los Cactus in Varadero, in November 1988. Its earnings in 1988 from the 20,956 tourists it received amounted to $20.4 million, or $974 per tourist. This compares with probable earnings per tourist for Cuba as a whole of around $720, which suggests that Cubanacan is already offering better or more highly priced facilities than Intur.

Most of the hotel construction deals Cubanacan has struck so far are with Spanish firms. For instance, in early 1989 a joint venture, Hoteles de Cuba, was set up with the Spanish firm Ibercusa. It is building two hotels with a total of 900 rooms in Havana, including the 21–story Cohiba next to the Riviera hotel, and is participating in the 1,000-room Guardalavaca Beach hotel program in the east of the island. The first joint venture hotel was opened in Varadero in May 1989. It was built by Cubanacan as a joint venture with the Spanish firm Sol Melia, which is investing a total of around $100 million in five installations. Another Spanish company, Cadena de Hoteles Unidos, overhauled the management of the Marina Hemingway complex in Havana in 1988, and a hotel school was opened under its guidance.

Cubanacan's plan for the eight years from 1988 to 1995 is to build 32,216 new rooms throughout the island. The largest developments being undertaken are in Cayo Coco (7,425 rooms), Santa Lucía (5,801 rooms),

Holguín (5,776 rooms), Varadero (4,860 rooms), Havana City (3,962 rooms), the Isle of Youth (2,150 rooms), and Santiago de Cuba (1,492 rooms). It is planned that 25,842 of these rooms will be built by joint ventures and that a further 4,636 rooms will have foreign financing, leaving 1,738 without foreign finance. By the end of 1989, 9,079 rooms had been either completed or begun.

## Problems of Debt-Rescheduling and Foreign Investment

Cuba has also made efforts to attract foreign investment in industrial joint ventures since 1988. Many of the plants Cuba purchased from Western Europe, Canada, and Japan in the late 1970s and early 1980s with the revenues earned when sugar prices were high are currently running at very low capacity due to lack of equipment and parts and marketing outlets. On the face of it, there appear to be some interesting opportunities for foreign investors, but so far few companies have shown any serious interest.[8] As long as the Cuban economy was expanding in the first half of the 1980s, the National Bank was able to negotiate new loans with Western Europe and Japan, even though pressure from the Carter and Reagan administrations seems to have frightened off some lenders. This finance was important in stimulating the expansion of trade relations with the capitalist countries in the first half of the 1980s.

Like many other developing countries, Cuba was hit by soaring interest rates in 1980 to 1982, which added over half a billion dollars to the country's hard currency debt. Even so, total debt fell from 3.2 billion pesos at the end of 1980 to 2.7 billion pesos at the end of 1982, staying below 3 billion pesos until the end of 1984. However, the slowdown of growth in 1985 created serious repayment problems for the first time, causing the debt to rise to 3.6 billion pesos at the end of the year and soar over the next three years to 6.5 billion pesos at the end of 1988. The increase in the debt during 1988 alone was more than three times the hard currency earning potential anticipated from the country's main tourist resort of Varadero when it is fully developed in the early 1990s. However, the government's austerity measures brought the growth in the debt under control, leading to a small reduction in total convertible currency debt over the first three quarters of 1989.[9]

Cuba has been effectively cut off from new Western finance since July 1986. In May of that year, the National Bank suspended debt service payments on all its hard currency debt except for short-term trade-related payments. Within two weeks, however, the National Bank told Western bank creditors that it would continue to meet payments on interest falling due, although not on principal. The banks nevertheless rejected terms put forward by Cuba for a rescheduling of debt falling due in 1986 over twelve years with six years' grace.

In July 1986 the Paris Club of creditor governments agreed to reschedule 95 percent of the $116 million in principal falling due in 1986 and to consider 1987 maturities at a later date. Later that month, Cuba began to fall behind on payments on its short-term commercial debt as well. This was unprecedented, as Cuba had hitherto been regarded as a model debtor. The banks responded with an offer to lend an additional $85 million, extend for another year $600 million in trade credits, and reschedule $75 million falling due in 1986 over ten years with six years' grace.

Since July 1986 there has been no further movement in negotiations with either the Paris Club of Western government creditors or the commercial banks, which generally follow the Paris Club's lead. The National Bank has consistently argued that no matter what measures are taken, the Cuban economy will not be able to restructure and achieve steady growth without new credits from the West to finance imports. The Paris Club and the banks, for their part, maintain that without major restructuring of the economy to improve efficiency, they would be throwing money away if they agreed to new credits. There does not seem to be hard evidence that the creditors' position is influenced by U.S. pressure, although that cannot be ruled out.

Statistics for the economy in 1988 and subsequent reports of a resumption in payments of money outstanding to private companies made it seem that a renegotiation of the debt could be in sight. Real national income (net material product) grew 3.6 percent in 1988, returning the economy to its level of 1986—although this was still 3.4 percent below the level of 1985, before the economy went into recession. The most notable aspects of the economic situation were the very high and growing level of state investments—equivalent to 26.6 percent of real national income—particularly in tourism and in attempts to complete major unfinished projects; the acute shortages of materials and parts for industry; the continued and indeed increased priority given to social spending; the rapid growth in consumer liquidity as a result of the economy's inability to satisfy demand for consumer goods; continued tight curbs on imports; and a very high growth in exports to the market economy countries.

However, growth slowed to 1.0 percent in 1989 and was likely to be only slightly—if at all—positive in 1990, as Soviet oil supplies were cut by half and the country braced itself for a major restructuring of its trading relationship with the Soviet Union in 1991. Prospects of a rescheduling of the debt and provision of fresh Western credits appear as remote as ever.

## Looking Ahead: Some Possible Developments

I began this chapter by suggesting that the Cuban economy and Cuban society more generally have come to the end of one stage of development and are now searching for ways to assimilate more advanced technologies and accelerate industrial growth. The baby boom generation of the 1960s, which has no direct experience of prerevolutionary Cuba, has grown up and is pressing for the modernization of the economy and the consumer benefits that it will bring—and it is doing so at a time of greatly increased austerity and uncertainty. It remains to be seen how the government, which is very aware of these social pressures, will adapt to accommodate them and what political and economic changes will result.

The end of this stage in Cuba's internal development coincides with the first rumblings of what could become major changes in its foreign relations. The most striking changes that took place during the 1980s were the great increase in Cuba's commitment to the war in Angola and the rapid improvement in relations with the rest of Latin America and, to a lesser extent, the Caribbean. At its peak Cuba had some 50,000 troops in Angola and played a decisive part in forcing South Africa and the United States to the negotiating table.

Cuba's reestablishment of relations with Latin America is of more long-term significance and represents its homecoming after years of regional isolation. It now has diplomatic relations with Mexico, Nicaragua, Panama, Trinidad-Tobago, the Bahamas, Jamaica, Saint Lucia, Guyana, Venezuela, Ecuador, Peru, Bolivia, Brazil, Argentina, and Uruguay and has trade relations with many others. In the twelve months following the resumption of relations with Brazil in June 1986, the leaders of Argentina, Bolivia, Uruguay, and Brazil and the prime minister of Peru all visited Cuba. Many more have visited since. Fidel Castro has again become a familiar figure in other Latin American countries, after a gap of fifteen years following his visit to Chile in 1973. In the autumn of 1988 and spring of 1989, he attended presidential inaugurations in Ecuador, Mexico, and Venezuela, and he has since visited Brazil for the inauguration of President Collor de Mello. In Caracas he met the leaders of Colombia and the Dominican Republic, with which Cuba still has no diplomatic relations. He also spent more than three hours with Jimmy Carter, the former U.S. president.

Argentina and Mexico are Cuba's main trading partners so far, but it is also rapidly expanding commercial ties with Venezuela, Peru, Ecuador, and Brazil. Brazil in particular, with its large domestic market, is seen as an important outlet for trade and for cooperation in areas such as electronics, biotechnology, health care, and agriculture—all areas in which Cuba has placed much emphasis on developing technology.

Western observers have been anticipating a major restructuring of Cuba's relations with the Soviet Union and its other COMECON partners ever since President Gorbachev introduced his policy of perestroika. During the first half of 1990, the Soviet Union cut supplies of oil to all of its COMECON partners—by close to one-half in the case of Cuba. From 1991 onward, COMECON will effectively cease to exist, and the Soviet Union will require hard currency for its oil. In many respects Cuba, as an exporter of commodities (sugar, citrus, nickel, and the like) that can be sold in world markets, is in a better position to cope with this transition than the weak industrial economies of Eastern Europe. Moreover, until the Gulf crisis of August 1990, Cuba had been paying above world prices for Soviet oil under the 1986–1990 plan, although not in convertible currency.

Nevertheless, the renegotiation of Soviet-Cuban trade on the basis of world prices and in convertible currency—even if it will be, as is likely, on a clearing account basis—will effectively reduce the Soviet subsidy. Soviet price subsidies have declined in recent years, and the terms of trade with the Soviet Union moved against Cuba throughout the 1980s, although project and balance-of-payments aid increased. No moratorium has been announced on Cuba's debt to the Soviet Union— estimated at 15.4 billion rubles in the Soviet press—but it is unlikely that it will ever be repaid. It is more likely that it will gradually be written off in the course of renegotiating trade and aid relations. Cuba has already introduced new exports to the Soviet Union such as medical supplies and will treat up to 10,000 children who were victims of the Chernobyl nuclear disaster. There are also discussions of Soviet-Cuban joint venture resorts for Soviet tourists.

Uncertainty within COMECON is compounded by continuing uncertainty in Cuba's relations with the United States. At the beginning of the Bush administration's term in office, the logic of U.S. regional interests and détente with the Soviet Union combined with George Bush's supposed pragmatism seemed to point toward a cautious normalization of relations with Cuba. However, the U.S. invasion of Panama, the collapse of the East European regimes, the loss of power by the Sandinistas in Nicaragua, and an increasingly aggressive U.S. stance toward Cuba seem to have put normalization beyond reach for the time being. At the Houston summit of leading capitalist countries in July 1990, George Bush even called for the granting of Western aid to the Soviet Union to be tied to a reduction of Soviet aid to Cuba. Among the exile community, for the time being, the virulently anti-Castro Cuban

American National Foundation under the leadership of Jorge Más Canosa has had the president's ear.

The situation could change again, however, if the Cuban regime is able to stabilize the economy and adapt to popular pressures without a major upheaval. After stridently claiming throughout the first half of 1989 that the Castro government was about to collapse, the Más Canosa exile faction lost some credibility, and there were signs that Washington was prepared to begin to listen to other voices within the Cuban community. After a year or two, pressures for normalization of relations could become significant once again.

Since it was first colonized by the Spanish, Cuba's economy has been closely tied to international trade as a sugar exporter. Today, as it tries to build up its industrial base and capitalize on the development potential its education, health, and other social programs have given it, Cuba is as dependent as ever on making its way in the world. The government is aiming for a soft landing: a gradual reduction in support from the Soviet Union; a reorientation of trade toward Western Europe, Latin America, Canada, and China in particular; increased food self-sufficiency; and a rapid development of tourism to replace potential lost sugar revenues. If Cuba succeeds in these goals, it could be in a position by the middle of the 1990s to reestablish trade relations with the United States, which, depending on when this is done, could give a major boost to Cuba's industrial development. If, however, a catastrophe in the Soviet Union or in the world economy should develop, the Cuban economy would be very vulnerable, and its future development would be in jeopardy.

## Notes

1. José Luis Rodríguez, *Crítica a nuestros críticos* (Havana: Editorial de Ciencias Sociales, 1988).

2. See especially Andrew Zimbalist and Claes Brundenius, *The Cuban Economy: Measurement and Analysis of Socialist Performance* (Baltimore: Johns Hopkins University Press, 1989).

3. Senator Claiborne Pell, "The United States and Cuba: Time for a New Beginning," a report of a trip to Cuba made to the Committee on Foreign Relations of the United States Senate, Washington, D.C., December 1988.

4. See the report in *Cuba Business*, vol. 4, no. 1 (February 1990), which details some of the problems the contract encountered.

5. See the *Financial Times*, February 17, 1989, p. 37.

6. Quoted in Morris H. Morley, *Imperial State and Revolution: The United States and Cuba, 1952–1986* (Cambridge: Cambridge University Press, 1987), p. 371.

7. Ibid., p. 339.

8. See Gareth Jenkins, "Western Europe and Cuba's Development: The 1980s and Beyond," in H. Michael Erisman and John M. Kirk, eds., *Cuban Foreign Policy Confronts a New International Order* (Boulder, Colo.: Lynne Rienner, 1991), pp. 183–201.

9. Banco Nacional de Cuba, *Informe Económico Trimestral*, September 1989.

# PART 3

# Everyday Life in Contemporary Cuba

# Introduction to Part 3

*Carollee Bengelsdorf and Jean Stubbs*

Texts on Cuba that present themselves as assessments of the revolution too often suggest a balance sheet: On one side of the ledger is a list of achievements, on the other a list of problems—as if they could be added and subtracted. Aside from the static, unlifelike paradigm this scenario provides, implicit in it is the assumption that the revolution is a continuum: a process that began in 1959 and has traveled along a straight line to the present. Once one accepts this assumption, then one accepts the notion that at any one point, the revolution can be stopped—frozen—and measured in its totality.

The tendency to do exactly this has been nowhere so tempting as when dealing with the kinds of issues discussed in Part 3. "Social" problems seem, for some reason, to lend themselves to this kind of treatment. Whereas it would be difficult, if not absurd, to speak of economic policies or of political structures without taking account of the decisive shifts in direction represented by the 1970s institutionalization process or the 1980s rectification campaign and the impact of such shifts on these policies and structures, this omission is precisely what does occur in the social realm. Thus, for instance, in the majority of the literature appearing on women, the 1975 Family Code is generally seen as a station along the steady Cuban march toward women's equality. Yet in reality it also signified a return to the notion of the family as a major arena of child socialization, which had dissipated in the first decade of the revolution. Perhaps even more critically, it represented an attempt to prescribe a particular concept of the family—the nuclear family—that was and is, it could be argued, *not* the dominant family type in Cuba. Seen in historical and contemporary social perspective, the nuclear family is far removed from observable family and kinship patterns, and it raises fundamental conceptual questions concerning race, gender, social provision, and sociocultural values within a national policy prescription inscribed in revolutionary ideology.

Social historians have long had to come to grips with disaggregating notions of Cuban nationhood and national Cuban institutions in a society of huge divisions. The most obvious division in the context of nineteenth-century sugar plantation society was race, and this carried over in new forms into the twentieth century. Equally evident were cleavages along regional, class, gender, cultural, and religious lines. The late-nineteenth-century abolition of slavery and formal political independence from Spain, labor uprisings in the 1930s, the 1950s insurrection, and the revolutionary euphoria of the 1960s were key moments in contemporary Cuban history when levels of unity and social cohesion were achieved that subsumed the divisions. The return to a more routine social order almost inevitably entailed the resurfacing of the cleavages, albeit in newly defined forms. This resurfacing is a major challenge for the Cuban revolution as it enters the 1990s.

As we look beyond the state to civil society, we must widen our definitions of democracy beyond the narrowly political to include the dynamics of corporatism. Through state institutionalization, elective People's Power, and mass organizations, the corporate policy of revolutionary Cuba has been heavily imbued with notions of political centralism that arguably are derived as much from Martí as from Lenin. Within this centralism, channels for representation and accountability could, and in practice at key moments did, challenge conventional ideological and political wisdom, resulting in significant shifts in policy. Analysis needs to focus on which groupings within civil society have become empowered or disempowered through the use of those channels. Parallel arguments can be drawn in looking beyond economic planning or "the market" to civil society.

Democratization can no longer stop at populist notions of the people, or at the worker-peasant alliance. It must be more differentiating and thereby more encompassing of ethnic and racial groups, of the public and private spheres. One of the lessons of the 1980 Mariel exodus was that many who left were motivated by social, familial, and individual frustrations rather than by any strongly articulated political hostility. Within Cuban society, similar frustrations are being played out. Support for revolutions arises from expectations of improvements in living standards, and ultimately the scope and quality of available goods and services influences public opinion. In the "boom" of the early 1980s, social consumption rose by 7.1 percent and individual consumption by only 2.5 percent. Since then, both have declined. Cuba, like many other socialist societies, has had good long-term vision but has been short on delivery. This proved crucial in the reaction to socialism in Eastern European countries and is something Cuba is having to contend with in the context of a tightening in the political and economic spheres both internally and externally.

The 1980s closed at a critical moment in the practice of socialism in Cuba. It was critical not only as it was being experienced by policymakers or planners but as it reverberated through every arena of life in Cuba—on streets and in homes throughout the island. Moments of crisis can be two-edged swords: One edge portends extreme difficulty, but the other holds the promise of new possibilities. The crisis of socialism both permits and makes it incumbent on us to readdress the texts of Marxism as historical documents that need to be rethought in the light of contemporary developments. Nowhere is this more pressing than in the sphere of daily life, where democracy becomes practice rather than mere form. A pertinent example is the Engelsian paradigm that has remained entirely untouched as the theoretical structure underlying socialist state policy on the question of women. Engels's service in his time was to take the family out of the realm of timeless nature to which it had been consigned and to insert it in history and tie its evolution to changes in production. Nonetheless, his vision, as with that of Marxism in general, was bound by a nineteenth-century Eurocentrism. The linear progression from barbarism to civilization has much in common with mainstream Western development thinking about modernization. The two combined in twentieth-century revolutionary experience to create serious obstacles to the depth of analysis not only on gender and patriarchy but also on race and broader value systems within the socialist experiment.

Our purpose here has not been to focus on the full range of what is generally found under the category of social. Rather, we intend to suggest the beginnings of structuring a framework that allows us to put in order the threads of discourse already going on within civil society at a multiplicity of levels and in a variety of contexts. Each of the four chapters in Part 3 points in its own way to some common threads that define the language and categories into which this discourse is molded.

The field of social work is often seen as encompassing eminently empirical, practical issues, yet Marguerite G. Rosenthal alerts us to serious conceptual considerations. She makes clear in her analysis of the implications for social policy of the high incidence of female-headed households in Cuba (approximately 40 percent of the total) and the single-mother syndrome that female-headed households need a voice in their affairs. A crucial point to be made here is that single mothers may be an emerging concern for national social policy, but they are certainly not an emerging phenomenon. This brings us full circle to a realization of how heavily circumscribed the nuclear family type has been in Cuba in historical, class, and race terms. The obviation of this fact in the revolutionary period contributed to a process wherein the non-normative family, which is by no means in the minority found itself on the margin of change.

The Cuban revolution swept to power with an overwhelming sense of moral prerogative and codes of behavior and a vision of human motivation and redemption. Taking this as a point of departure, Lois M. Smith charts the ways in which policies concerning sexual codes and the institution of the family have been both conservative and contradictory. Sexual policy, as it has evolved over time, has been overwhelmingly moralistic in its model of appropriate sexuality, which is geared more to social stability than to sexual fulfillment with a substantial gap between sexual knowledge, behavior, and values on the one hand and policy aspirations on the other. One is left with the provocative impression of patriarchal state power and a potentially more democratic family in crisis.

Whether in the realm of social or sexual policy, family or state, a glaring gap in our knowledge hinges on race, and Gayle L. McGarrity alerts us to the pressing need for Cuba to address—not subsume—the race question. The issue is not so much the potential paradox of persisting racism but the extent to which racism can be an unwritten ideology and can surface in new ways, a situation that is encouraged by the failure to deal with the race issue in all its ramifications. In Cuba's goal of a people united in revolution, no race-specific, affirmative action policy was implemented until the mid-1980s, and then at the level of the party. Although there is an ongoing reassessment of history and culture along racial lines in Cuba there have been no published studies to date whose express intent has been to assess contemporary racial composition or attitudes. Ethnic democratization of Cuba's new political, economic, and sociocultural structures must tackle the racism inherent in obscurantist and derogatory notions about Africa and Afro-Cubans. The theoretical contributions of black liberation as much as national or class liberation need to be revisited.

Nelson P. Valdés provides a thoughtful and fascinating analysis of Cuban political culture, one that straddles the social and political spheres. Most of all, however, his chapter is a valuable study of Cuban social psychology. A variety of codes are examined—the generational question, an emphasis on idealism, the issue of "permanent betrayal," and the importance of death—all of which, contends Valdés, are omnipresent concerns in the Cuban psyche. If we are to better understand the social reality of Cuba (or indeed of the revolution's political concerns), it is invaluable first to grasp the psychological premises on which it is based.

Blacks and women appear to be the major groups in Cuban society that have the fewest illusions about any switch to Western-style market democracy or Eastern-style perestroika. The resurgence of racism and sexism in both of those camps belies the paradigm. The problem in Cuba is how to make functional an option that, for all its contradictions, has provided Cubans with the groundings for an alternative agenda. Cuba's new social critics and dreamers come from some predictable but also unforeseen quarters. Among the more predictable are the youth. Over one-half of the population has been born since the 1959 revolution: Their problems are its problems. Among the more unforeseen developments is the religious revival. This revival is not like the latter-day U.S. evangelism of born-again Christians; rather, it is a questioning societal spirit that is strong in ecumenical terms and that serves as the grass-roots social force of Afro-Cuban religions. The artists and musicians, more than the writers, have produced some of the most biting social comment. All of these areas demand careful study but, we would suggest, in disaggregate fashion. There are vast differences within the generic categories. The problems and tastes of black youths are not the same as those of white youths. Seen from the viewpoint of gender, *santería* is more progressive than its Christian counterparts. When it comes to cultural trends, will postmodernism have a Cuban face? The lines are being redrawn in more ways than one.

# 8

# The Problems of
# Single Motherhood in Cuba

*Marguerite G. Rosenthal*

Current literature concerning the status of women in Cuba points to an emerging concern about the increase in teenage pregnancy and single parenthood. Stories in the press discuss the sorry plights of young women who leave their studies to marry young or, in an even worse scenario, bear a child alone. The Federation of Cuban Women (FMC) recently conducted a study to learn about the economic circumstances of single mothers, with the intention of making recommendations for laws to assist them. Spokespersons for the women's organization decry the irresponsibility of fathers who fail to support or help raise their children. They are also alarmed that segments of the young generation of women fail to properly integrate themselves into the new society in which all adults are expected to participate in productive and communal life. There is concern that a portion of the population is becoming dependent—in fact, is becoming a "culture of poverty."

These concerns echo those of demographers and policy researchers in other parts of the world who are increasingly aware that families headed by single mothers are particularly vulnerable to economic and social stress. Without specific governmental interventions, these families are likely to be poor and isolated from the mainstream of society.[1] Such families are not new to Cuba, but the country appears to be recognizing that their existence is a growing problem for which social and economic policies are needed.

This chapter focuses primarily on social and economic policies that contribute to and alleviate the economic burdens faced by single mothers.

Several issues concerning the general position of women in Cuban society as well as some particular questions that pertain to single mothers will be examined, specifically the articulated social goals that affect women in Cuban society; women's labor activity; demographic trends, concentrating on fertility and marital patterns; and current and proposed social and economic policies for single mothers. Where relevant, experiences of other countries in managing the economic and social concerns of single mothers will be discussed.

## Social Goals for Women in Cuba

Postrevolutionary ideology in Cuba has emphasized participation in the labor force as the basis of citizenship and economic rewards. This ideology has had an enormous impact on the lives of Cuban women who have been exhorted and, in many substantial ways, assisted to enter the world of paid work—to leave the *casa* for the *calle*, as one writer has put it.[2]

Although the Cuban leadership has consistently emphasized the importance of women's labor participation, it has not promoted the idea that women should be able to perform all jobs. By law, numerous jobs (three hundred in 1974, reduced to approximately one hundred in the late 1980s) are prohibited to women because they are harmful to their reproductive functions, although many jobs are reserved specifically for women.[3] Gender equality and a "separate spheres" philosophy are not seen as contradictory. Indeed, social development is seen as a matter of discouraging confrontation with men over specific women's interests in favor of harmonious development in order to benefit the overall society.

Since the rectification campaign began in 1986, women (as well as men) are also expected to demonstrate their integration into the revolution by participating in voluntary labor, generally organized around construction projects. Already pressed for time to manage work and home responsibilities, women have found participation in rectification activities arduous, if not impossible.[4]

The specific domain of women, however, remains the home. Although the Family Code enacted in 1975 provides an ideological basis for egalitarian relationships between men and women in the home, it also sanctifies the nuclear family as the basic, unassailable unit of society—and it is within the private sphere of the family that divisions of labor between men and women are most difficult to eliminate. Cuban law has supported the primacy of women's caretaking, domestic roles in specific ways: Maternity leave is provided, but not paternity or parental leave; until recently, only women could take time off from work to care for sick children or attend to sick relatives who are hospitalized.[5] Although Cuba is moving toward more sex role equality in these areas, tradition and law have combined to reinforce the notion that these duties properly belong to women. Cuba has created programs to alleviate the double burden borne by working women, as discussed below, but the women-only provisions cited above reinforce cultural patterns that emphasize women's reproductive roles. Evidence from other countries indicates that so long as women bear the primary responsibility for home and care of family, they cannot participate as equals in community and political life.[6] Although the extended family undoubtedly assists working women and single mothers in Cuba, help is provided in a sex-segregated way (grandmothers assist in child care or do the shopping, for instance), which itself reinforces the primacy of women's obligations to housework and child care.

## Women's Labor Activity

At the time of the revolution, women in Cuba participated in the work force at a relatively high percentage compared to women in other Latin American countries; nonetheless, most women were not employed, and those who were held menial jobs such as domestic work and jobs in seasonal agricultural production. Following the revolution, specific retraining policies designed to integrate women who had been working as domestics and prostitutes into the paid work force and into the rapidly expanding fields of public health and education resulted in a dramatic growth in the number of women in the labor force. These changes, which flew in the face of traditional patterns of female domesticity, caused considerable upheaval for many families. The divorce rate rose, and the burdens women had to bear as workers and as the primary keepers of the home caused many to drop out of the work force soon after joining it. A Cuban study done in 1972 showed that married women represented a very small percentage of women in the labor force: Of all women working, 82 percent were unmarried (43 percent were divorced, 30 percent were single, and 9 percent were widowed).[7]

In 1989 women made up 38 percent of the Cuban work force,[8] up from about 25 percent in 1974. In 1981, about 50 percent of women between the ages of 25 and 44 were employed, a dramatic change from the prerevolutionary period, when only around 20 percent of women in this age range worked.[9] However, these figures indicate that large numbers of women still depend on other family members for support. Women living in urban areas are much more likely to work for a wage than women in the rural areas: In 1981, 17 percent of women in a Havana district listed themselves as housewives, whereas 42 percent of women in a rural area of Guantánamo did so.[10]

This influx of women into the Cuban labor force reflects for the most part the rapid and dramatic growth of the service sector (which in capitalist countries is often called the "public sector"), where women have largely filled new positions in public health and in the expanded educational system. In this respect, the changes in the Cuban labor sector resemble those that have occurred in capitalist and mixed economies, which in the 1970s also showed dramatic increases in the numbers of women entering the work force—although in these economies the percentages of women working tend to be higher than those in Cuba. In the formerly socialist countries of Eastern Europe, the mass entry of women into the paid labor force occurred much earlier—following World War II and the assumption of power by Communist governments.

In Cuba, as elsewhere in the world, women have largely entered a sex-segregated working world. Although women have been making slow but gradual gains in the manual, technical, and managerial fields, the vast majority work in support or service jobs, such as secretaries, day care workers, public health personnel, and the like. An analysis of the composition of the Cuban labor force along gender lines is revealing. If we accept five basic categories of the work force, it is interesting that 25 percent of women are workers (compared with 65 percent of men), 30 percent are technicians (14 percent for men), 17 percent are administrators (only 2 percent for men), 22 percent are employed in the service sector (8 percent for men), and 6 percent are at the level of directors (9 percent for men).[11] A small number of women have been able to enter new areas of "intellectual work," but the great majority of women—although achieving well beyond basic literacy—have not been prepared for unusual fields of work and are therefore consigned to the occupational arenas that in nearly all countries are the sphere of women. This situation may be changing, however, because younger women are achieving levels of education well above those of previous generations, and urban women are well represented in occupations requiring skill and training.

The situation of sex segregation in the work force is magnified by the job restriction laws cited above, which prohibit women from working in positions considered dangerous to their reproductive role (these include jobs involving heavy machine vibration as well as ones in which heavy insecticides and other materials potentially dangerous to fetuses are used). These restrictions keep women out of many areas of manual and agricultural work that tend to be better paying. Sex segregation in the work force is clearly associated with lower compensation for women. Although there has been considerable wage leveling in Cuba, the lowest salaries tend to be concentrated in the range of jobs women disproportionately fill. (A minimum wage of 100 pesos was established in 1987.)

Although the social wage (subsidies for food, housing, education, and health care) substantially reduces the effects of income inequalities, the relatively low wages available to most working women place comparative burdens on them when they must support their families alone. A member of the FMC stated during a discussion in January 1989, that it takes two incomes to live comfortably in Havana today; the corollary is that it is difficult to support a family on one income, particularly one that is low. In this regard, the fact that work is compensated according to "effort" and not "need" (including the number of people one must support) works to the disadvantage of families with one earner and of all families that have many members.

Although the social values encouraging women to work are clearly articulated, there is evidence that women continue to suffer from job discrimination. This discrimination appears to be based on a combination of traditional attitudes of male superiority on the part of male managers and on structural and legal arrangements that dissuade managers from hiring women. Policies in regard to maternity leave and, until the recent change, the care of sick children and relatives are particularly cited as reasons for preferring men to women workers, especially since the mid-1970s when efficiency has been required within the various enterprises. Such discrimination is part of the reason women have a considerably higher rate of unemployment than men: 7.8 percent compared with 2.5 percent in 1980.[12]

Single mothers do have a special place in the Cuban labor market. In particular, whereas some minimum social assistance is given to unemployed single mothers, the major thrust of social policy is to seek work for women in this position. The FMC and the Committees in Defense of the Revolution (CDRs) are responsible for obtaining work for single mothers, who have priority for any job openings. Despite this policy, a 1989 study showed that only about 54 percent of single mothers assisted monetarily were incorporated into jobs in the previous year.[13] The problem has been particularly acute for young women with children, who experience job discrimination and exclusion from school. One recent "solution" has been to provide them with piecework sewing to be produced at home; compensation is based on the quality of the goods produced.[14]

## Demographic Trends in Family and Marital Status

Women become single mothers through widowhood, through divorce and separation from either formal or consensual unions, and through childbirth without an involved partner. Although it is difficult to obtain precise information about the trends of these various demographic occurrences, we do know that there has been an increase in the number and percentages of single mothers, or *madres solteras*. Increases in longevity in the Cuban population combined with declines in fertility have resulted in few widows caring for minor children, and the phenomenon of widowhood will not be specifically examined here. The focus will be on separated, divorced, deserted, and never-married mothers.

Birth rates in Cuba have declined rapidly and remarkably since 1965 when the rate was 34.3 per thousand inhabitants (although the birth rate increased during a temporary baby boom in the early 1970s). In 1984 the birth rate was less than half that of 1965 at 16.6 per thousand. Based on 1981 figures, it appears that Cuban women between the ages of 15 and 49 had an average of 1.83 children each. This decline in the birth rate is related to a number of factors, including the involvement of women in work and education; the availability of health care, including birth control and abortion; and the facility with which divorces can be obtained. (In 1981 women from rural and eastern provinces and those with less education had more children: Women from Guantánamo with little education had, on the average, 5.1 children, whereas university-educated women from Havana had .82 children each.)[15]

The divorce rate in Cuba is high, affecting about 50 percent of all marriages.[16] Couples who marry under the age of 20 are especially likely to divorce.[17] But remarriage or recoupling is also fairly common so that only a minority of the population at any one time is listed as divorced or separated. Figures for 1981 showed that 59 percent of women over the age of 14 were married or living consensually with a mate, 12 percent were divorced or separated, 7 percent were widowed, and 22 percent were single. Taken as a whole, 8.9 percent of the adult population (14 years and older) were listed as divorced or separated in 1981, compared to 3.2 percent of the population in 1970 (although the method of counting was somewhat different at that time).[18] An in-depth analysis of women in different areas of the country in 1982 found that 19 percent of those in central Havana, 11 percent in semiurban Buenavista, and 12 percent in rural Guantánamo were divorced or separated.[19]

Unfortunately, available statistical tables do not show the total number or percentage of single parents. One estimate puts the number at 200,000.[20] It seems safe to say that virtually all single parents are single mothers and that a large percentage of divorced and separated women are mothers; at least 10 percent—and more likely between 15 and 20 percent—of households with children are headed by women alone.

## Teen Parents

Of great concern to Cuban researchers and officials is the perceived growth in the number of births to young, unmarried mothers and the divorce and separation rates of young women with children.[21] The concern is particularly focused on teenaged mothers who now account for one-third of births and who, when they give birth out of wedlock, challenge the officially encouraged model of the stable two-parent nuclear family. Lois M. Smith discusses some of the major issues that attend the problem of teenage pregnancy: conflict between traditional and newer social and sexual values; failure to integrate substantial numbers of young women into the preferred roles of work and social participation; and the financial burden for the state, which must often provide monetary assistance to families unable to support themselves—an apparent majority of which have been deserted by the fathers.[22]

Although officials have been focusing on the high percentage of births to teen mothers (approximately one-third of total births in 1984), it appears that the birth rate itself actually remained rather stable in the 1980s after its dramatic decline in the 1970s. (The current rate is about what it was in 1958.) One reason the teenage birth rate appears to be high is that births to women over the age of 25 have declined dramatically. Another is that those born during the baby boom of the late 1960s and early 1970s are now having children. Women in Cuba have reduced their fertility to about the same rates as women in industrialized countries. However, unlike women in the industrialized world, Cuban women continue to have their children at a young age. The constant rate of births to teens thus translates to a greater percentage of the total births and a perception that an overwhelming number of babies are being born to young women. Women ages 20–24 have the highest birth rates— about 140 per thousand—whereas the birth rates for women aged 15–19 and 25–30 are about equal at approximately 80 per thousand. Again, there are distinct regional differences, with urban women postponing childbirth longer than rural women.

Bearing children at a young age is associated with discontinuation of education and restricted occupational mobility and participation. Perhaps for these reasons, there is a sense of a teenage fertility crisis in Cuba, and there are considerable official efforts under the auspices of the National Working Group on Sex Education, established in 1977, to develop effective techniques to dissuade youths from early sexual involvements and hasty marriages while encouraging the use of birth control measures and abortion. Young mothers are likely to become single parents in two ways: Many young women do not marry (although precise data are not available), and many who do marry experience early separation and divorce. The legal age at which girls in Cuba can marry is 14, which reflects traditional Cuban patterns, particularly those in rural areas. In 1984, about 25 percent of girls under the age of 20 were married,[23] and 32 percent of all women marrying were between the ages of 12 and 18; 68 percent were under the age of 25.[24] The age at which women feel they should marry rises with educational level and status and the extent of occupational participation.[25] These differences in attitudes no doubt influence the leadership in its concern about early marriage and childbirth. (It should be indicated that young women are also likely to divorce: Of all women divorcing in 1984, one-third were ages 12–19 and 63 percent were under 25.[26] In a detailed population study of three neighborhoods conducted in 1982, between 10 and 12 percent of women under age 30 were divorced.)[27]

### Role of the Extended Family

Precise information about Cuban household composition is not available, although one 1981 study showed that about 20 percent of households included grandchildren, in-laws, other relatives, and unrelated adults.[28] Informal discussions with Cubans revealed that percentages of multigenerational households are probably considerably higher than this figure, largely because of the housing shortage. In addition, traditional patterns of mutual aid and reliance, which typify Latin cultures and economically distressed peoples generally, create an environment in which the sharing of resources—including housing—is expected among family members. Although this situation may ease economic and caretaking responsibilities for the single mother, it can also cause economic hardship and social strain—particularly in those cases in which single mothers must return or continue to live with their parents.

Role expectations within the extended family structure may also be undergoing change. As women are encouraged to participate in the paid labor force, they may be less willing to serve as baby-sitters for their grandchildren. In this respect the pattern of early childbearing may be particularly problematic: A 60-year-old grandmother may be willing to care for her grandchildren while her daughter goes to school or works, but a 45-year-old grandmother may not. In the absence of universal child care, one of the women in households with young children will have to stay at home.

### Economic and Social Policies
### for Single Mothers

Postrevolutionary Cuba has been diligent and inventive about creating social policies aimed at furthering more equality for women and increasing their ability to participate actively in society. These policies can be seen as part of the general scheme of redistribution and opportunity enhancement for the population as a whole. They range from the broadscale expansion of education and health programs, which have improved women's opportunities and allowed them to gain control over their fertility, to specific measures geared toward facilitating their participation in the work force and in community life. Among the latter are maternity leave, which provides for eighteen weeks of paid absence and job protection (which can be expanded to a year's unpaid leave), and leave to care for seriously ill relatives; child care centers; shopping plans designed to eliminate time-consuming standing in line for working women; boarding and semiboarding schools, for which children of working mothers have priority; and an increased supply of electric appliances to reduce women's burdens at home. Important pieces of legislation—Article 45 of the 1976 Constitution and Articles 24–28 of the 1975 Family Code—seek to guarantee women's equality in the economic, political, and familial spheres. These programs have been described as crucial in facilitating women's entry into the work force but not sufficient to create true equality in the home, the workplace, the community, or the political sphere.[29] Of particular concern here are those policies, programs, and services that help equalize the position of single mothers and their families in Cuban society and those that pose problems for these families and even tend to marginalize them. Economic provisions as well as educational and social programs will be discussed.

## The Social Wage and Rationing

Cuba has achieved significant redistribution of goods and services through the development of universally provided and equitably distributed free health and education programs and through subsidies for food, housing, clothing, and transportation. These programs serve not only to provide basic protections to the entire population but also to integrate sectors of the population that would otherwise remain marginalized and even destitute. Families headed by single mothers are especially assisted by these programs because they have a high probability of having fewer economic resources than other segments of the population.

The rationing of food deserves particular mention as a measure that assists single-parent households. In most industrialized countries (the United States is an exception), monetary grants called family allowances or children's allowances are paid to all families with children to assure the provision of basic necessities to this population. In Cuba, the rationing of basic food items serves a similar purpose and is considered to be a major factor in the country's virtual elimination of malnutrition.[30] Under the rationing system, all Cubans receive subsidization of basic foodstuffs and are thereby guaranteed a minimum healthful diet. Subsidies for housing similarly assist low-income earners. Rents—technically mortgage payments because housing units are now being sold by the state to their occupants—are set at 10 percent of the income of the head of household. Households with very low incomes pay nothing.[31] Again, these policies directly assist the single mother who, if she lives independently with her children, is likely to pay very little for housing. In addition to lessening the financial burden of poor families, these policies assure residential stability for them. Other subsidies that particularly help those with low incomes include medicines purchased at pharmacies, school uniforms, day care, and meals in worker cafeterias.

## Social Assistance

In industrialized countries, a primary source of income—either as a supplement for low wages or as the basic means of support for those who do not work—is a means-tested grant, often referred to as social assistance. Lessons from the industrialized world suggest that redistributive programs, including social assistance, for one-parent families are the single most significant factor in assuring economic well-being and in integrating these families into the fabric of society as a whole. Even in Sweden—where nearly all women work, salary differentials between men and women are substantially equalized, and women bear their first child at age 27 on the average—social assistance is heavily relied on to reduce the poverty of single mothers.

Cuba has apparently developed a rudimentary social assistance program, administered by the Department of Social Security, that supplements the wages of low earners (particularly those with large families) and families with no other means of support.[32] It is not known precisely, however, what proportion of families receives this assistance. One study conducted by law students in 1988, found that social assistance was aiding almost 90 percent of the population of single mothers in Havana.[33] In 1989 the *Granma Weekly Review* reported that 5,600 mothers received social assistance in 1988.[34] Countrywide, however, only a fraction of single mothers apparently received assistance (perhaps around 3 percent). Young mothers seem disproportionately represented among those who received assistance. In a study of recipients of social assistance conducted in Havana in 1989, approximately 21 percent were under the age of 20, and 63 percent were under 25. About 82 percent were under the age of 30.[35]

The Cuban Family Code requires that parents and children provide for each other economically. When extended families share living quarters, it is expected that the income from working members will be shared. Assistance, when it is given, is meager: One source estimated in a personal communication that the grant is 40 pesos per month for a mother with a child and another that it is 25 pesos per month per person. Such a level of assistance would condemn a recipient family to a subsistence existence, a situation that of itself creates marginalization.

## Child Support

The Cuban Family Code requires that both parents retain financial and social responsibility for any children resulting from their relationship, whether or not they were legally married. To facilitate this principle, Cuban law provides for deductions to be made from the salary of an absent parent if he does not cooperate voluntarily in paying child support. At a minimum, the father will have 30 pesos per month per child deducted from his pay, although the process is not automatic and requires that the child's mother petition the court. Recent evidence shows that child support provisions are not being carried out in practice. Many women have insufficient information about their children's fathers to locate them, or they are reluctant to pursue a court order; large numbers of fathers either abandon their children or inadequately support them.[36] There have been instances of collusion on the part of managers to help fathers avoid their support payments reported.[37] Fathers have been found to be irresponsible in their obligations to their children despite being otherwise identified with revolutionary ideals and activities such as involvement in their labor unions, CDRs, and political organizations. In one study, for instance, 4 percent of absent fathers were said by their former partners to be members of the Communist party.[38]

Mechanisms to enforce support collection are not strongly in place, and there are current proposals to increase control over support by creating a specialized family court or by centralizing reports of noncompliance with the Fiscal Office (presumably to transfer a portion of the man's wages to his former partner for the support of their children). Clearly, the absence of regularized child support enforcement procedures creates economic hardship for single-parent families.

## Education and Child Care

The rate of school dropout among young Cuban women, many of whom marry and give birth, is a significant concern to officials. Because of their resulting lack of preparation, these young women significantly lessen their opportunities to participate fully in the labor force. The situation is compounded by the apparent absence of schools that serve pregnant teens and the lack of day care services for school-aged mothers.[39] Thus, although the state is alarmed that a significant proportion of young women are failing to conform to the expectation that they become integrated into the worlds of work and productivity, it is failing to provide avenues for participation that would accommodate the needs of

women who may be conforming to traditional patterns of early reproductive activity. Indeed, researchers studying the children of single
mothers concluded that they are growing up in bad environments, are
intellectually deficient, and if they are girls, are likely to become single
mothers themselves.[40] A Cuban "culture of poverty" theory appears to
be in the making—one that ascribes non-normative behavior of single
mothers to personality and cultural deficiencies rather than looking to
structural causes of problematic behavior.

The recognition of the need for child care for children of working
mothers is a significant achievement of the revolution, and the quality
of care provided is high. However, the availability of child care has
consistently been far below the need. The recent rectification campaign,
constructing facilities through volunteer labor, dramatically increased the
numbers of day care centers, providing for the needs of 20,000 more
working women in Havana alone.[41] In 1990, 140,000 children (about 15
percent of the total) six years old and under could be accommodated
in over 1,000 day care centers.[42] Nonetheless, a severe shortage of places
continues. Priority is given to children of professional mothers over
those in service and office positions,[43] although single mothers are also
supposed to have priority for day care slots.[44]

Parents must pay for child care on a sliding scale up to 25 pesos
per month (much of the cost is subsidized); private arrangements can
cost up to three times as much as state-provided day care.[45] Thus, single
mothers, whose earnings are not likely to be substantial in any case,
confront obstacles and disincentives to work. This situation may ease
as their children get older because semiboarding schools that provide
all day care and meals for elementary school children and boarding
schools for junior high and secondary school children apparently accommodate a sizable proportion of all students. However, difficulties in
finding suitable child care arrangements have been cited as a reason
for turnover and work instability for women workers.[46]

## Conclusion

In Cuba, as elsewhere, there is growing attention to the existence of
a significant subgroup of families—ones headed by single mothers. Single
mothers face all the difficulties other women confront including work
segregation, generally lower salaries, job discrimination, and the double
burden of work and home and child care combined in Cuba with the
expectation that they contribute to voluntary labor as well as political
and community life. As difficult as all women may find it to cope with
these problems and juggle these burdens, most single mothers face even
harsher circumstances. Single mothers are likely to be young and

economically distressed. They are likely to be unskilled and therefore unable to find rewarding, well-paying work. They have limited educational opportunities and may have particular difficulty in getting child care. Finally, unless they have strong support from their families (and apparently many do), they must face their difficulties alone.

The nuclear family, with mutually supportive spouses who share in familial responsibilities, has emerged as the ideal in Cuban society.. The single-parent family does not conform to this ideal, yet demographic information discussed above indicates that significant numbers of women are likely to be single mothers for at least a portion of their lives. The data also raise questions about whether there really is a new crisis of teenage pregnancy in Cuba. What seems more likely is that a traditional pattern in which women bear children at a relatively young age is being followed. What has changed is the overall decline in fertility and the ability of partners to end unsatisfactory relationships. Teenage pregnancy and single parenthood, then, can be seen as examples of cultural lag in which norms and behavior have not quite caught up with the demands and expectations of the new society, which call for delayed reproduction and stable unions.

The situation of single mothers in Cuba is a difficult one, although far less so than in the United States. The disparities in income are relatively narrow, and the range of social support—including food and housing subsidies; universal, free health care; and an extensive, free system of education—provides the entire population with adequate basic support and relatively equalized and unrestricted opportunities. Nonetheless, there are clearly more and less advantaged populations in Cuban society, and single mothers and their children are among those with the greatest difficulties.

## Notes

1. See, for example, Timothy Smeeding, Barbara Boyle Torrey, and Martin Rein, "Patterns of Income and Poverty: The Economic Status of Children and the Elderly in Eight Countries," in John L. Palmer, Timothy Smeeding, and Barbara Boyle Torrey, eds., *The Vulnerable* (Washington, D.C.: The Urban Institute Press, 1988), and Gertrude S. Goldbery and Eleanor Kremen, "The Feminization of Poverty: Only in America?" *Social Policy*, vol. 17, no. 4 (Spring 1987), pp. 3–14.

2. Lourdes Casal, "Revolution and 'Conciencia': Women in Cuba," in Carol R. Berkin and Clara M. Lovett, eds., *Women, War and Revolution* (New York: Holmes & Meier, 1980), pp. 183–206.

3. See Carollee Bengelsdorf, "On the Problem of Studying Women in Cuba," in Andrew Zimbalist, ed., *Cuban Political Economy: Controversies in Cubanology* (Boulder, Colo.: Westview Press, 1988), and Lois M. Smith and Alfred Padula,

174   *Marguerite G. Rosenthal*

"Women Workers in Socialist Cuba, 1959–1988: Progress and Problems," *Ibero-Americana: Nordic Journal of Latin American Studies,* vol. 18, no. 2 (1988), pp. 33–56.

4. Smith and Padula, "Women Workers in Socialist Cuba," pp. 33–56.

5. Ibid.

6. Rita Liljestrom, Gunilla Furst Mellstrom, and Gunilla Liljestrom Svensson, *Roles in Transition: Report of an Investigation Made for the Advisory Council on Equality Between Men and Women* (Stockholm: Schmidts Boktryckeri A.B., 1978); Hilda Scott, "Women in Eastern Europe," in Jean Lipman-Blumen and Jessie Bernard, eds., *Sex Roles and Social Policy* (San Mateo, Cal.: Sage, 1979); Hilda Scott, *Sweden's 'Right to be Human': Sex-Role Equality: The Goal and the Reality* (Armonk, N.Y.: M. E. Sharpe, 1982).

7. Study cited in Muriel Nazzari, "The 'Woman Question' in Cuba: An Analysis of Material Constraints on the Solution," *Signs: Journal of Women in Culture and Society,* vol. 9, no. 2 (Winter 1983), pp. 246–263.

8. Comité Estatal de Estadísticas (CEE), *Anuario Estadístico de Cuba, 1988* (Havana: CEE, 1989), p. 190.

9. Federation of Cuban Women, *Statistics on Cuban Women* (Havana: Federation of Cuban Women, 1985), p. 22.

10. Reported in Sonia Catasus Cervera, et al., *Cuban Women: Changing Roles and Population Trends* (Geneva: International Labor Office, 1988), p. 31.

11. Comité Estatal de Estadísticas, *Anuario Estadístico de Cuba, 1986* (Havana: CEE, 1987), p. 190.

12. Claes Brundenius, *Revolutionary Cuba: The Challenge of Economic Growth and Equity* (Boulder, Colo.: Westview Press, 1984), p. 136.

13. *Granma Weekly Review,* March 23, 1989.

14. Lois M. Smith, "Teenage Pregnancy and Sex Education in Cuba," Paper presented at the Latin American Studies Association meetings, New Orleans, La., 1988.

15. Comité Estatal de Estadísticas (CEE), *Censo de población y viviendas, 1981,* vol. 16 (Havana: Comité Estatal de Estadísticas, n.d.), p. CLXIII.

16. Max Azicri, *Cuba: Politics, Economics and Society* (London: Pinter Publishers, 1987), p. 58.

17. Personal communication, Krause Peters, head of education program in Cuba, January 1989.

18. CEE, *Censo de población y viviendas, 1981,* p. CXLIV.

19. Cerrera, et al., *Cuban Women,* p. 40.

20. *Granma Weekly Review,* September 30, 1987.

21. Personal communications, Federation of Cuban Women officials and Peters, January 1989; Marta Rodríguez Calderón, "Madres solteras: Salto a la augustia," *Bohemia* (August 11, 1989); Smith, "Teenage Pregnancy."

22. Smith, "Teenage Pregnancy," p. 31.

23. Ibid., p. 20.

24. Ibid., p. 35.

25. Cerrera, et al., *Cuban Women,* chapter 6.

26. Smith, "Teenage Pregnancy," p. 35.

27. Reported in Cervera, et al., *Cuban Women*, p. 76.

28. CEE, *Censo de población y viviendas, 1981*, p. CXLII.

29. Nazzari, "The 'Woman Question' in Cuba"; Bengelsdorf, "On the Problem of Studying Women in Cuba," p. 46; Smith and Padula, "Women Workers in Socialist Cuba."

30. Joseph Collins and Medea Benjamin, "Cuba's Food Distribution System," in Sandor Halebsky and John M. Kirk, eds., *Cuba: Twenty-Five Years of Revolution, 1959–1984* (New York: Praeger, 1985), pp. 62–78.

31. Medea Benjamin, Joseph Collins, and Michael Scott, *No Free Lunch: Food and Revolution in Cuba Today* (San Francisco: Institute of Food and Development, 1984), p. 84.

32. Smith, "Teenage Pregnancy," pp. 21–22.

33. Rodríguez Calderón, "Madres solteras," p. 25.

34. *Granma Weekly Review*, March 23, 1989.

35. Rodríguez Calderón, "Madres solteras."

36. Smith, "Teenage Pregnancy"; Rodríguez Calderón, "Madres solteras," and "¿Por qué, papi, por qué?" *Bohemia* (February 23, 1990).

37. Rodríguez Calderón, "¿Por qué, papi, por qué?" p. 7.

38. Rodríguez Calderón, "Madres solteras," p. 26.

39. Smith, "Teenage Pregnancy," pp. 20, 22.

40. Ibid., p. 22; T. Reca Moneira, et al., *Caracterización de algunas tendencias de la formación de parejas y familias en la población joven* (Informe Resumen), Centro de Investigaciones Psicológicas y Sociológicas, Academia de Ciencias de Cuba, Universidad de La Habana (mimeographed).

41. Smith and Padula, "Women Workers in Socialist Cuba," p. 49.

42. *Granma Weekly Review*, April 8, 1990.

43. A Darling, J. Godoy, and D. Romero, "La lucha por la integración plena de la cubana: Male-Female Equality and the Socialization of Pre-school Children in Cuba," unpublished paper, Boston College Graduate School of Social Work, 1981.

44. Peters, personal communication.

45. Smith and Padula, "Women Workers in Socialist Cuba," p. 49.

46. Nazzari, "The 'Woman Question' in Cuba"; Smith and Padula, "Women Workers in Socialist Cuba."

# 9

# Sexuality and Socialism in Cuba

## *Lois M. Smith*

One of the most significant challenges to social stability faced by the Cuban revolution today comes not from the command posts of distant shores but from the mysterious and defiant forces at work in the Cuban bedroom. Sexuality has emerged as a subversive force in revolutionary society, leaving a trail of perplexing problems such as teenage pregnancy, abortion abuse, single motherhood, and early marriage and divorce in its wake. The Cuban revolution has undertaken to tame this force by establishing a coherent sexual policy capable of encouraging a code of "socialist sexual ethics." This policy has been essentially conservative in its objective—to establish stable heterosexual marriage as the final resolution of sexuality. It is a serious challenge, given its contrast with traditional sexual ideology and the price men would have to pay in order to conform to the new ideal.

In the past, theoretically, the rules of the game were well known to all. Women were to remain virgins until marriage. From that point on, appropriate sexuality ideally meant loyal submission to the husband. Good women earned social respect through sexual denial; fulfillment was the consolation prize of the shameful woman—the precocious and promiscuous, the prostitute, the mistress. Men's passion, on the other hand, was known to be universal, boundless, and virtually uncontrollable. Family honor depended on the chastity of its single women and the fidelity of its married ones, but accepted—indeed, expected—male behavior included frequent sexual conquests outside the family circle.[1] Adherence to the sexual ideal would, again theoretically, facilitate a certain patriarchal social stability. Men would be assured of clear patrilineage and control of property, and sinister female sexuality would be held in check.

Social reality was complicated by class, race, and location, among other factors, and Cuban society never conformed to the ideal set forth in its dominant sexual ideology. For instance, long-term unions without benefit of marriage have always been common, particularly in rural areas. And certain compromises were made between the male sexual impulse and social stability. The masculine value of proving virility through impregnating female companions outweighed the destabilizing presence of illegitimate offspring. Further, among the propertied, marriage and legitimate heirs protected one's belongings from the products of manly indiscretions.

The twentieth century brought increasing levels of industry, public education, commerce, and urbanization to Cuba. A schism emerged between cities—where women had better access to abortion (although it was illegal), contraception, education, and employment—and the countryside—where traditional values and patterns were less challenged by change. Yet even in urban areas the age-old dichotomy of good woman-bad woman and eternally roving man defined the sexual sphere. Even twentieth-century feminist reformers defined their demands in terms of the sexual ideal; few women sought to claim the male realm.[2]

## Changing Sexuality and Contemporary Dilemmas

The social changes introduced or at least accelerated by the Cuban revolution have complicated the perpetual struggle between reason and passion. Early mobilizational policies further undermined traditional views of femininity and masculinity. The symbol of the passive Virgin Mary receded as glorified images of women emerged—the heroic cane-cutter, the female construction laborer, the student-mother-worker-volunteer. These new *machista* Cuban women were surrounded by boyfriends, lovers, and spouses who did not adjust easily to this officially sanctioned female mobility. Although the philosophy of the revolutionary information machine was that women were being offered the chance to break the exploitive chains that had bound them for centuries, develop themselves fully as human beings, and contribute to the progress of the revolution, the message received by Cuba's *machista* men was much more direct and simple—namely, that they had lost sexual control.

They were right, but they were also wrong. Traditional sexual culture is not easily vanquished. Women's lives and responsibilities did encompass more than ever before. After the lack of access to contraception in the early 1960s wrought by the U.S. economic embargo, women did increasingly have access to a range of birth control options that forever jettisoned male certainty about female sexual behavior into uncertainty. Women did begin to explore this new sexual freedom with increasing enthusiasm until their statistics regarding frequency of sexual encounters and extramarital affairs came to rival men's.[3]

And yet tradition marked time with change. Old practices of male sexual dominance continued in the new Cuba. Home and family still played a primary role in the lives of Cuban women despite, or perhaps because of, their increased mobility. The greater mobility of women clearly increased conquest opportunities for men. Women's use—indeed, misuse—of contraception and abortion reflected a continuing concession to male prerogative and a profound social ambivalence about women's sexual lives. Women's seemingly increasing sexual activity was the result in part of new sociosexual pressures that emerged in modern Cuba.

Young women have more freedom to choose when to initiate sexual activity, but how to behave is less clear. The peer pressure to perform is greater than ever before, and traditional reluctance is met with derision. Some complain that sex has become "a false badge of feminine liberation";[4] that yielding to sexual pressure is to succumb to machismo.[5] Yet standing firm against male entreaties can result in loneliness and abandonment, especially when many willing partners are available. Ironically, however, research has shown that an overwhelming majority of teenage boys still want their brides to be virgins, but the vast majority of girls reject the idea that they should enter into matrimony without previous sexual experience.[6]

In short, the removal of procreative penalty from sexual activity has not produced a female population blindly seeking fulfillment. On the contrary, women often seem to be considering worthy issues of power, submission, progress, and tradition—indeed, everything but fleeting sexual pleasure.

One example of the complex interplay among mind, body, and society is the continued reliance of Cuban women on abortion as a means of birth control. Since the 1970s, Cubans have had easy access not only to abortion but also to birth control pills, diaphragms, intrauterine devices, condoms, spermicidal creams, and surgical sterilization (with certain limitations).[7] In the late 1980s, long-term hormonal injections became available to Cuban women, and work is underway on a chemical contraceptive for men. In spite of these advances, too many abortions occur. In 1979, for example, approximately 43 percent of all pregnancies ended in abortion,[8] and in 1988 there were eight abortions for every ten live births (approximately 44 percent of all pregnancies were terminated).[9] Furthermore, research has shown that two-thirds of all pregnancies occur within six months of the mother's first sexual experience, which suggests that most abortions occur among younger women.[10]

Why are women, and particularly the best-educated women, still resorting to abortion when so many other contraceptive means are available? Ignorance alone is not a sufficient explanation. It has been suggested that the widespread availability of abortion facilitates its abuse, particularly in a nation in which women had traditionally used abortion as a means of birth control due largely to male preference of abortion over contraception. In fact, only three out of one hundred women of all ages interviewed while seeking an abortion in 1989 were completely ignorant of birth control. Nevertheless, 80 percent had not used or asked their partner to use protection despite the fact that none wanted children at that time.[11] One young woman who had undergone nine previous abortions admitted to an interviewer that she had never used contraception because it wasn't "natural."[12]

Abortion abuse is just one of a number of disturbing trends. Irresponsible sexual behavior is also seen to be at the root of the rapidly increasing syphilis and gonorrhea rates that have plagued Cuba in recent years.[13]

Teenage pregnancy is a third phenomenon to be viewed with increasing concern by a government determined to provide universal education beyond the secondary level, steadily improving maternal health statistics, and the social stability that results from living according to rational choice and not biological determinism. Teenage pregnancy rates began to climb dramatically after 1959. The general postrevolution baby boom, which affected virtually every childbearing age group, peaked in 1965. Fecundity rates then declined among every group except those aged fifteen to nineteen.[14] In 1982, 35 percent of all births occurred to adolescent mothers; teenagers accounted for more than half of all births in seven provinces and the Isle of Youth.[15] This suggests that teenage pregnancy was most common in rural areas that have a long tradition of early marriage and motherhood.[16]

A 1983 study found that "a good portion" of pregnant teenage girls knew about contraception and had planned to use it eventually but did not think they would get pregnant "now."[17] A 1989 study of more than two hundred pregnant teenagers showed that despite the fact that none of those interviewed thought it was a good time for them to have a child, three-quarters had not used any contraception. More than half had never sought or received birth control information. One-fifth had undergone a previous abortion.[18]

The issue of teenage pregnancy is fraught with tensions between the old and the new. Girls complain that because much of the community still frowns on sexually active girls, they are reluctant to seek contraception or abortion. Many parents oppose abortion for pregnant teenagers—which is favored by the government—believing that a girl who is old enough to get pregnant is old enough to bear a child. Furthermore, teenage pregnancy often leads to early marriage, again to the dismay of the Cuban government. Nineteenth-century Cuban families demanded marriage to assuage family honor when a daughter was seduced, and contemporary Cuban parents also view matrimony as an appropriate solution for their pregnant daughters. A 1987 study of twenty-four pregnant teenagers revealed that all of the girls' mothers had pressured them to marry.[19] Overall, 32 percent of all women who married in 1984 were between the ages of twelve and nineteen, and 11 percent of all men who married were ages fourteen to nineteen.[20]

Cuban officials complain, on the other hand, that parents often feel no sense of responsibility when a girl becomes pregnant by their son.[21] There is increasing criticism of parents who urge their sons to indulge in numerous sexual liaisons as a sign of manhood.[22] The leader of Cuba's association of obstetricians and gynecologists stated in 1986 that "it is necessary to create in our young men feelings of responsibility for undesired pregnancy and the need for them to share in the use of contraceptives. . . . Boys ought to be punished by society when they display irresponsible attitudes towards sex."[23]

Male irresponsibility is perceived as a significant and growing problem in Cuban society. There is no punishment, however, for boys who display what has only in recent years been categorized as "irresponsible attitudes," and they can receive considerable rewards such as increased social status and individual gratification. Women are left with most of the responsibilities, perhaps even more than in the past. One in three marriages now ends in divorce. As of 1987 there were around two hundred thousand single mothers in Cuba.[24] There is concern that many single mothers forced by circumstance to abandon their educations become dependent on state welfare and thus perpetuate a culture of poverty within Cuba's socialist society. Where are the fathers going, and why do they not consider their duty to those they leave behind?

The Cuban government has been asking itself and the Cuban public these and other pressing questions for some time. It has gone beyond merely asking questions and undertaken to provide some answers to the dilemmas posed by modern society. Thus, the morass of sexual confusion has been confronted by psychologists, physicians, and sexologists in Cuba's new sexual industry—sex education.

Providing a coherent view of love and sexuality was not always a clearly defined goal of the Cuban revolution. Economic and political objectives took priority during the early years. There was no period of officially sanctioned sexual experimentation such as that which occurred during the decade following the Bolshevik revolution in Russia. In fact, there was little discussion of sexuality at all. Such discussion developed slowly, in part because traditional social trends such as teenage pregnancy came to be perceived as problems only as the revolution solidified its social goals.

By the early 1970s, the impact of "larger" social and political policies forced the revolution's leaders to begin formulating a coherent sexual program in response to specific social, demographic, and medical developments that emerged in the country. In 1974 basic sex education classes were introduced by the Ministry of Education in the primary, secondary, and pre-university grades. This limited, biology-oriented program was perceived as insufficient by many in both government and the public.

In 1975 preparations began for the implementation of an expanded national sex education program. The revolution was no longer content with merely disseminating specific biological information but attempted to instill in children a vision of sexuality that was consistent with socialist ethics. Moreover, in 1977 under the auspices of the Federation of Cuban Women, the National Working Group on Sex Education (GNTES) was established within the Permanent Commission on Infancy, Youth, and Women's Equality of the National Assembly. The immediate task of GNTES was to oversee the formulation and implementation of a massive sex education program aimed at all sectors of society with the goal of "establishing the individual's capacity for love, marriage and the family on the principle of equality between the sexes."[25]

GNTES began to disseminate information through the national press, printing articles on contraception, abortion, sexual ethics, and family relations that encouraged respect between the sexes, the need for responsibility and restraint, and an elimination of the sexual double standard, which encourages male and denies female sexuality. In 1979 GNTES began to revise and translate six East German books that would constitute the organization's basic sex library. The target readership ranged from three-year-old children to adults and health professionals. Tens of thousands of copies of each book were published and distributed to bookstores, schools, and pharmacies throughout the nation. Although some parents questioned teaching small children the basics of reproduction and childbirth, which many continued to view as indecent, the books were generally well received and demand far exceeded supply. By the end of 1986, approximately one million volumes were in circulation in Cuba.

Nevertheless, GNTES's efforts have been met with significant resistance—not only from parents but from health and educational officials as well. Although the Cuban public snapped up the sex education books sold in the bookstores, parents, teachers, and health workers disagreed with GNTES about what should be taught about sexuality and in what grades. Some parents did not want their children to receive any sex education at school.[26]

In 1987 GNTES director Dr. Alvarez Lajonchere complained that the level of distribution of contraceptive devices to adolescents remained insufficient. He and other officials charged that many sex education materials still in use in the schools were pre-GNTES and reinforced traditional views and bad practices.[27] School officials were caught between pressure from GNTES and parental resistance to sex education. Health professionals have criticized school administrators who avoid the problem. In 1987 one sex educator complained that "frequently we show up at a school and the students have all left. Why? Because no one took the time to tell them that this afternoon a psychologist would be coming to speak on sexuality. This subject is not part of the curriculum but of extra-scholastic activities, and the Ministry of Education simply doesn't support it!"[28]

In 1989 GNTES received an institutional promotion and a new name—the National Center for Sex Education—to indicate its permanent status and the government's commitment to the ongoing implementation of its programs. Despite a hesitant beginning and more than a generation of controversy, the Cuban revolution had firmly established its basic principles of love and sexuality.

## Socialist Sexuality

Cuba's sex education materials contain a number of clear messages about appropriate sexual behavior, the role of sex in a socialist society, and inherent differences between male and female sexuality. Certain enduring sexual myths have been challenged, whereas others have been reinforced. Cuban sexologists are promoting a more egalitarian vision of sexuality than that of Cuba's traditional sexual culture, but fundamental contradictions remain.

Cuban sex education materials portray heterosexuality as a natural and important part of a healthy human life. Gender is distinguished from sex as something that is taught to young children by parents who treat, dress, and play with boys and girls differently. Parents are told to be sensitive to subtle messages they send their children because patterns can be seen even before a child is born. Thus, by hoping for a boy during pregnancy, parents begin a process that devalues females. On the other hand, parents are warned against encouraging expressions and gestures that are "not in accordance with [the child's] sex" because this can cause children to be stigmatized "even if they have no tendency to homosexual conduct."[29]

Cuban sex education materials stress that acknowledging the differences in male and female sexuality will facilitate sexual self-discipline among young people. Because sexual maturity in boys is signaled by nocturnal emissions, they thus associate sex primarily with physical pleasure. Menstruation, on the other hand, elicits no such association: "For girls there is no experience similar to the intense sensation of pleasure in their sexual organs which occurs in boys during their first ejaculation. That is why boys are excited more quickly and have a more insistent and more physical sexual nature. The purely physical aspect of sex is not as important to girls. In its place develops a considerable sensoral receptivity, and a more general necessity for tenderness and caresses."[30]

The story of Sleeping Beauty is offered as a metaphor for girls' sexuality—it lies dormant; the girls scorn undesired suitors who pursue them until the one they love arrives to unlock their sensual awareness and receptivity. Thus, adolescent girls do not tend to separate sex from love; female sexual desire is often only awakened "with the caresses of a compañero."[31]

Adolescents learn that menstruation further complicates girls' sex lives by reminding them "of their future responsibilities as mothers," although it does not indicate readiness for maternity. Girls' sexual awakening is therefore tempered by practical concerns of the future, which are often reflected in "a spontaneous virginal aloofness" to boys' advances. Boys must understand this in order to treat girls with "sufficient care and tact."[32]

Parents are told not to discourage children from touching their genitals and that masturbation is a normal expression of children's developing sexuality that is generally no cause for concern. Nevertheless, Cubans learn that masturbation is much more prevalent among adolescent boys (approximately 90 percent engage in the activity) than girls (perhaps 50 percent so engage, and "mostly by accident").[33] Adolescent boys are told that although it is acceptable to masturbate with others of their own age, they should think of girls during the experience "to establish that important link with the other sex."[34]

In a major departure from tradition, Cuban sex education materials reject the veneration of female virginity as "unfounded and one-sided," one of the many unfortunate social legacies of religion. An end to the "obsession with virginity" is termed a "reasonable" development.[35] Yet although girls are to be less concerned about virginity in Cuba's new society, they are still expected to exercise sexual restraint and to be mindful of the more intense male sex drive. Because girls do not experience puberty sexually in the same way boys do, "They should learn the effects that their flirtations cause in boys and how to adequately interpret those effects." Girls are given a number of reasons why "it is good that [they] clearly set the limits."[36] First, although both men and women can enjoy sex without love, "this is rarer for women than men."[37] Second, adolescents are told that "women seem more stunted in their development than men" by engaging in sex as a diversion. Third, the breakup of a relationship is more difficult if the couple has engaged in sex, and "in this aspect girls suffer almost always more than boys."[38]

The Cuban revolution has substituted love for marriage as the appropriate prerequisite for sex. Sex education materials stress that sex can truly be satisfying only within a love relationship. Adolescents are told that premarital sex is acceptable "if all conditions exist for a mature relationship," including mutual respect, trust, and stability. Parents are reminded that "love and sexuality are not dangerous sicknesses from which we have to protect our children." Instead, children should be brought up properly to view love and sex as intimately linked human experiences and be given adequate information on biology and contraception to make informed decisions.

Although they do not explicitly condemn teenage sex, by emphasizing monogamy, love, and commitment as critical elements in sexual relationships, Cuban sex education materials discourage early intercourse. Nevertheless, given Cuba's high teenage pregnancy rate, the state is interested in ensuring that adolescents have easy access to information and to contraception. Condoms and spermicides are recommended as the best contraceptive option for young people, although it appears that birth control pills are the most popular choice. Teenagers are reminded that avoiding intercourse is the best means of avoiding pregnancy, but that "this doesn't necessarily mean practicing sexual abstinence."[39] They are told that "scientific research" has proven that people "with a higher cultural level" tend to begin having sex at an older age.

The manipulative games played by both boys and girls to maneuver a partner into having sex are outlined in the adolescent guide to sex and love. Boys tend to use promises, alcohol, sad stories designed to elicit sympathy, and the threat that "if you don't perform I'll find someone else who fills my needs." The guide points out that girls are particularly vulnerable to the latter threat, especially when boys raise the specter of "old maidhood." Girls' methods include wearing provocative clothing, questioning a boy's manhood, appealing to the boy's protective instinct, and making themselves indispensable to the boy by doing things for him. Adolescents are warned that a girl who is pressured into having sex may find it unpleasant and thus may lose any chance of a future rewarding conjugal life. No similar such predictions are made to reluctant boys, although all are told that "pleasure only occurs when there is mutual consent."[40]

Adolescents are advised to eschew telling dirty jokes, which are characterized as "remnants of the time of male social dominance that is disappearing." In portraying women as playthings, dirty jokes are said to reflect the deprecation of women that is unacceptable in contemporary Cuban society. Adolescents are also warned against pornography and are told that the United States was largely responsible for the proliferation of prostitution, a social by-product of capitalism, in prerevolutionary Cuba.

Homosexuality is addressed in the guide for adolescents in a chapter that includes topics such as exhibitionism, sado-masochism, incest, and rape. The author claims that research shows that prenatal factors play a role in some of "these problems." Teenagers are told that it is difficult to discern what is normal in sexual behavior and that behavior should not be considered abnormal simply because it is not practiced by the majority. The book explains that homosexuality occurs equally among women and men and that although homosexuals are able to function as competently as others at home, work, and play, "they really don't achieve the happiness that family brings." Furthermore, they "cannot develop complete sexual relations with reproductive ends." Adolescents are advised not to make young homosexuals the butt of jokes or teasing because this reflects misunderstanding and ignorance.[41]

When all factors point to the appropriateness of intercourse, adolescents are told to make sure that the "external conditions" are not overlooked. Thus, there should be no time limitations, and the couple should find a quiet and comfortable place—a definite challenge given Cuba's housing shortage. The manual advises against intimate encounters in cars because they are "not comfortable." Attention to these external conditions can help produce a rewarding intimate encounter and a positive lifelong attitude toward sex.

Information aimed at adults is similar to that for young Cubans; it is neither graphic nor explicit, and there is little attention to the specific details of sexual acts. The overwhelming emphasis is on the social aspects of sexuality and the critical social and personal importance of stable, loving, monogamous, heterosexual families. There is ongoing discussion of the inherent sexual differences between men and women, but considerable attention is paid to the need for sexual satisfaction in both partners.

Cuban literature on sex recognizes the importance of a moral code and argues for the establishment of a new socialist morality based on sexual equality. Although individuals should be free to choose their sexual partners, promiscuous behavior and extramarital affairs are strongly condemned. Sex education officials point out that according to Marxist sexual ethics, monogamy is best.[42] The Cuban public is assured that "some reformists who tried to abolish marriage could not offer better alternatives after analyzing all aspects of the problem."[43] Even single Cubans are urged to engage only in monogamous relationships. Most of the less conventional sexual practices that emerged in the West during the 1960s and 1970s such as group sex, wife swapping, and open marriage are condemned. "We are not enemies of pleasure and would not hesitate to recommend these practices if they really enriched human happiness," Cubans are told.[44] Women are said to suffer most when such alternatives are tried.

Pornography is also condemned as an exploitive business that stimulates "an excessive sexual life," moral degeneration, and criminal behavior. The airbrushed images of well-endowed and beautifully formed bodies engaged in various activities are said to produce destructive feelings of inferiority in the average person.

Homosexuality is presented as a sexual "variant" instead of a deviation, and any private behavior between consensual adults in which no one else is hurt is deemed acceptable. The author of the adult sex guide argues that although there is disagreement about its origins, it is clear that homosexuality is not simply a matter of the will of the individual. Thus, he states, "it would be unjust to disqualify a homosexual only for his homosexuality, and to always interpret it as a character disability which, unfortunately, is often done."[45] Furthermore, the guide advises that as long as homosexuals do not molest or seduce young people, they should be free to engage in sexual relations "according to their nature." What needs to be changed are the "social conflicts" that result from open homosexuality—that is, ridicule and discrimination.

One topic that receives a great deal of attention as a major impediment to achieving marital bliss is women's sexual reluctance. Men are encouraged to be more sensitive and considerate in their lovemaking and to create a romantic atmosphere conducive to women's sexual enjoyment. Women are warned repeatedly that losing interest in sex after the birth of a child can cause men to look elsewhere and ultimately lead to divorce. The adult sex guide refutes the idea that women's employment destroys their sex lives but acknowledges that the "double" day is a "major obstacle" to women's sexual fulfillment. Thus, by helping with domestic chores, men may improve their sex lives.[46]

Finally, Cuban sex information reassures men and women that sex is not merely for youth but is an important lifelong activity. Couples are urged to keep sexually active as long as their health permits. Women are reminded that menopause does not signal the end of female sexuality, and it can actually enhance sexual expression because postmenopausal women are free from the fear of pregnancy.

## Conclusion

Rapid social change, modernization, the availability of birth control, and the promotion of egalitarian ideals have undermined traditional sexual ideology and disrupted long-established modes of social control in Cuba. Although there are broader options for some restrictions on sexual behavior, certain old patterns of gender relations continue. To a degree, the proliferation of abortion and contraception has actually increased male sexual pressure on and control of women while at the same time facilitating male sexual irresponsibility. The resulting confusion has contributed to a host of social problems that clash with revolutionary goals.

In 1959 the Cuban revolution swept into power imbued with an overwhelming sense of moral prerogative. Although its immediate focus was the political and social realms, it inevitably turned to the most private spheres of individual life—prescribing not only codes of behavior but a fundamental vision of human motivation and redemption. In many ways, in fact, the Cuban revolution resembles that traditional watchdog of Cuban morality—the Catholic church. Intensely hierarchical, male dominated, ritualistic, and resonating with apocalyptic omens and visions of a euphoric future, the revolution has tenaciously pursued moral transgressions, such as prostitution, that the Catholic church could not or did not even attempt to eradicate. They share a number of fundamental positions on sexuality: a glorification of monogamous heterosexuality within the bounds of matrimony, a regard for reproduction as an essential component of sexuality, and a certain hostility toward homosexuality.

Yet there is also much divergence between the two. Cuban sex education materials have challenged the traditional veneration of female virginity and sought to teach both men and women that women can and should enjoy their sexuality. There has been an attempt to overcome a number of taboos such as those regarding menstruation and masturbation. Parents are encouraged to be more active and effective counselors to their children on sexual matters as long as they adhere to the principles of sexuality established by the revolution.

Although Cuban sex information continues to promote the notion that male sexuality is somewhat more sensation-oriented than female sexuality, men are now urged in effect to feminize their world by incorporating emotion and contemplation of familial stability into their sexual life. Men should consider the sexual needs of their partner, exercise self-restraint, and forego their traditional multiple conquest prerogative.

It will take some time to see whether the rather remote incentive of contributing to the establishment of a stable socialist society is effective in shaping sexual behavior.

## Notes

The author wishes to thank Carollee Bengelsdorf for her patience, encouragement, and valuable guidance in the preparation of this chapter. Muchas gracias a Nolverto Jiménez Ledezma por las lecciones importantes respecto al poder misterioso de machismo.

1. For further discussion, see Verena Martínez-Alier, *Marriage, Class and Colour in Nineteenth-Century Cuba* (London: Cambridge University Press, 1974), and Mirta Mulhare, "Sexual Ideology in Pre-Castro Cuba: A Cultural Analysis," Ph.D. dissertation, University of Pittsburgh, 1969.

2. See Mariblanca Sabás Alomá, *Feminismo: cuestiones sociales-crítica literaria* (Havana: Editorial Hermes, 1930), and Kathryn Lynn Stoner, "From the House to the Streets: Women's Movement for Legal Change in Cuba, 1898–1958," Ph.D. dissertation, University of Indiana, 1983.

3. Siegfried Schnabl, *En defensa del amor* (Havana: Editorial Científico-Técnica, 1985), p. 55.

4. See Heidi González, "¿Libertad o libertinaje?" *Muchacha*, January 1987, p. 29.

5. Aloyma Ravelo, "Hablemos francamente," *Muchacha*, November 1987, p. 52, and "Hablemos francamente," *Muchacha*, July 1987, p. 47. Also useful is Monika Krause, "¿Qué trae la golondrina?" *Muchacha*, July 1987, p. 61.

6. Monika Krause, interview in Havana, April 4, 1986, and Natividad Guerrero, *La educación sexual en la joven generación* (Havana: Editorial Política, 1985), p. 27.

7. Lois M. Smith, "Progress, Science and Myth: The Health Education of Cuban Women," *Cuban Studies*, vol. 19 (1989), pp. 182–183.

8. Data provided in Paula E. Hollerbach and Sergio Díaz-Briquets, *Fertility Determinants in Cuba* (Washington, D.C.: National Academy Press, 1983), p. 115.

9. Mirta Rodríguez Calderón, "¿Cuánto vale un aborto . . . ?" *Bohemia*, July 7, 1989, p. 14.

10. Ravelo, "Hablemos francamente," *Muchacha*, November 1987, p. 52.

11. Rodríguez Calderón, "¿Cuánto vale un aborto . . . ?" p. 15.

12. Mirta Rodríguez Calderón, "Con el índice en alto," *Bohemia*, September 8, 1989, p. 25.

13. Sarah M. Santana, "The Cuban Health Care System: Responsiveness to Changing Population Needs and Demands," *World Development*, no. 15 (1987), p. 116.

14. Luisa Alvarez Vázquez, *La fecundidad de Cuba* (Havana: Editorial Ciencias Sociales, 1985), pp. 26–28.

15. Monika Krause, *Algunos temas fundamentales sobre educación sexual* (Havana: Editorial Científico-Técnica, 1985), pp. 14, 22.

16. Fidel Castro, Speech to the Fourth Congress of the Federation of Cuban Women, *Granma*, March 11, 1985, p. 4.

17. José de la Osa, "Un aumento de los nacimientos ocurridos en 1982 corresponden a madres adolescentes," *Granma*, March 1, 1983, p. 3.

18. Rodríguez Calderón, "Con el índice en alto," p. 25.

19. Mirta Rodríguez Calderón, "Desconfía de sus padres en materia sexual la mayoría de las muchachas gestantes precoces," *Granma*, April 16, 1987, p. 2.

20. Comité Estatal de Estadísticas, *Anuario Estadístico de Cuba 1985* (Havana: Comité Estatal de Estadísticas, 1987), p. 76.

21. See Marta Matamoros and María de los Angeles Rodríguez, "Epidemia de alta frecuencia," *Bohemia*, June 26, 1987, p. 27.

22. Monika Krause, "Le contesta, la televisión y el sexo," *Bohemia*, July 24, 1987, p. 84.

23. Aloyma Ravelo, "El embarazo en la adolescente," *Muchacha*, April 11, 1986, p. 55.

24. Mirta Rodríguez Calderón, "Tenemos que ser ejemplo," *Granma*, September 30, 1987, p. 3.

25. Krause, *Algunos temas fundamentales sobre educación sexual*, p. 3.

26. Marie Withers Osmond, "Women and Work in Cuba: Objective Conditions and Subjective Perceptions," Paper presented at the Annual Meeting of the American Sociological Association, August 26–30, 1985, Washington, D.C., p. 26.

27. See Matamoros and de los Angeles Rodríguez, "Epidemia de alta frecuencia," p. 21 and "Educar a los educadores," *Bohemia*, July 7, 1987, pp. 25–26.

28. Mirta Rodríguez Calderón, "Implica desestabilización para toda la familia el embarazo de la adolescente," *Granma*, April 22, 1987, p. 4.

29. Heinrich Brückner, *¿Piensas ya en el amor?* (Havana: Editorial Gente Nueva, 1982), p. 86.

30. Ibid., p. 87.

31. Monika Krause, *Compilación de artículos sobre educación sexual para el médico de la familia*, Series 2 (Havana: Grupo Nacional de Trabajo sobre la Educación Sexual, 1987), p. 33.

32. Brückner, *¿Piensas ya en el amor?* p. 87.

33. Krause, *Compilación de artículos*, p. 33.

34. Brückner, *¿Piensas ya en el amor?* p. 57.

35. Schnabl, *En defensa del amor*, p. 18.

36. Brückner, *¿Piensas ya en el amor?* p. 122.

37. Schnabl, *En defensa del amor*, p. 9.

38. Brückner, *¿Piensas ya en el amor?* pp. 96, 122.

39. Ibid., p. 179.

40. Ibid., pp. 88–94.

41. Ibid., p. 210.

42. Guerrero, *La educación sexual en la joven generación*, p. 6.
43. Schnabl, *En defensa del amor*, p. 17.
44. Ibid., p. 11.
45. Ibid., pp. 65–66.
46. Ibid., p. 89.

# 10

# Race, Culture, and Social Change in Contemporary Cuba

*Gayle L. McGarrity*

Race relations have traditionally been conceptualized in the Western world according to a basic paradigm. Usually highlighted are the cases of South Africa and the United States, where race relations have become markedly polarized and where, through legal and sociocultural means, clear societal demarcations can be made between the black and white communities. Generalizations are usually made on the basis of these two extreme cases. Where race relations do not follow the South African or U.S. patterns, the tendency has been to minimize the importance of situationally specific patterns of prejudice and discrimination.

In societies such as Jamaica, the United States, Great Britain, and Ghana, black people developed a new sense of pride and promoted a more positive view of blackness during the 1960s. A paradox of socialist Cuba has been that although Afro-Cuban music, dance, and folklore are presented abroad as embodying the best of national culture, within Cuban society European cultural manifestations have been given far greater prestige. In the case of black Cuban women, the situation has been poignant. Many cling to European standards of physical beauty, desiring straighter hair, avoiding too much sun, and aspiring to marry or have children by lighter-skinned or white men so their children will be *adelantado*—advanced. This is despite the fact that the mulatto is projected symbolically on a national and international level as embodying the best of Cuban cultural and physical traits—the eroticism of the black woman combined with the elegance of the European.

Such phenomena have deep roots and do not negate the impressive advances the revolution has made in dismantling legal and institutional racial discrimination and segregation. The socialist revolution in Cuba is thus of particular interest because it gives us an opportunity to analyze the manner in which radical political and economic change has or has not affected attitudes and patterns of behavior resulting from centuries of ingrained racist ideology. The revolutionary government seems for many years to have considered the racial issue addressed because explicitly racist laws and structures were dismantled.[1] This attitude contrasted increasingly with the regime's attitude toward other issues of radical social change, such as workers' participation in management or the incorporation of women into the mainstream. Leaders felt that these changes would require many years of concentrated political action and consciousness-raising.[2]

The Cuban revolution took a monumental first step, unique in the Americas, by transforming the nation's economic structure. Other political regimes and social movements, which have emphasized the racial aspect of oppression to the minimization or exclusion of the class issue, may have succeeded in promoting the self-esteem, sense of pride, and dignity of peoples of African descent, who had been demoralized and humiliated by the slave and colonial experience. However, by not transforming the class structures and the exploitative apparatus of the societies concerned, or by failing even to recognize the role played by the indigenous bourgeoisie and local representatives of the capitalist system in perpetuating relentless economic exploitation, these movements did little—despite the crucial attainment of political independence—to end the economic victimization of the majority.

Those accustomed to the de facto racial segregation in the United States, the legalized apartheid of South Africa and Namibia, or the brutal economic exploitation elsewhere of peoples of African descent (which also occurs in many countries politically controlled by those of African descent) have to be impressed with the contemporary Cuban panorama. It may appear to those unfamiliar with Caribbean and Latin American patterns of race relations that there are no clearly delineated racial groups in Cuba because of the variety of physical phenotypes and the richness of ethnic diversity. However, a closer look at contemporary Cuba raises certain issues of importance to those concerned with theoretical issues of race, ethnicity, and culture as well as of class identification and struggle—especially in a process of socialist transformation. Ethnic jokes, anecdotes, proverbs, and patterns of social interaction all point to the pervasiveness of a racist ideology.

## The Race Variant in Cuba

When the revolutionary government of Cuba came to power in 1959, Western discourse surrounding race relations was markedly different from that of today. In the United States, the civil rights movement was characterized by an essentially pacifist, assimilationist stance in which the aim was to participate in the famous melting pot. In the Caribbean and Latin America, political discourse centered on issues of anticolonial and neocolonial struggle, occasionally accompanied by debates over the nature of class and caste but rarely racial oppression. Exceptions in the Caribbean were the conflict-ridden states of Guyana and Trinidad, where issues of a racial nature involved a power struggle between two almost numerically equal groups—East Indians and Africans. Those countries did not have populations that represented shades along a continuum, as was the case in Cuba.

The Iberian variant on race relations was markedly different from the Anglo-Saxon one. The somatic norm of the Spaniard was considerably darker than that of the Englishman or the Dane, which facilitated absorption of the mulatto into white society much more rapidly than occurred in the United States or Jamaica. This did not mean that slavery or racism was any less brutal, but it did lead to a demographic trend in the Hispanic Caribbean of the progressive whitening of the population. This was achieved to some extent through continuous Spanish peasant migration, but it also occurred through the process referred to popularly as *adelantándose*—approximating the aesthetic norm of the politically and economically dominant ethnic strain through producing lighter-skinned offspring. Being white did not automatically guarantee higher social status in Cuba because there were poor whites. However, although it was possible to be poor and white, it was less acceptable to be rich and black—particularly for the nineteenth-century slave society with its growing free-colored class.[3] This sense of white superiority was challenged to some extent by the late nineteenth-century struggle for independence from Spain, which ultimately consolidated the abolition of slavery, a development which did not occur in Cuba until 1886. But it was again powerfully demonstrated in the so-called Little War of 1912 when the country's only independent black political party was crushed; a mulatto middle class was never again a viable force in the Cuban sociopolitical scene.[4]

In contemporary Cuba in 1959 there was no strong, separate black movement for equal political representation or the promotion of such issues as a reinterpretation of Cuban history to compensate for years of the lack of African presence in bourgeois intellectual circles. Nor was there a call for an aesthetic revival akin to the "Black is Beautiful" movement in the United States or for self-pride movements, such as the black consciousness movement in South Africa. In the aftermath of the revolution, both nonwhite and white Cubans often denied the existence of racism or prejudice.[5]

Cuban President Fidel Castro articulated this problem shortly after assuming office when he proclaimed in a speech that there were two types of racial discrimination that had to be stopped. One was that which took place in recreational and cultural establishments; the other was discrimination in work centers. The reaction was extreme on the parts of the white petty bourgeoisie and the well-to-do mulattos whose social position was so precarious and vulnerable that they were often more racist than whites. Castro made a second speech several days later that again pinpointed the evils of racism but emphasized that no one would be forced to "dance" with anyone else (an attempt to assuage fears that innocent white maidens would be forced by law to dance in social clubs with "ignorant" blacks). It was another quarter of a century before race again was mentioned as a serious internal political issue in a major speech—this time in Castro's keynote address to the Third Congress of the Communist party of Cuba in 1986, which remained unpublished.

Well into the revolution it was noted that in the sphere of domestic and intimate relations and in the political and administrative apparatus, changes were much less apparent than in the public arena where blacks and whites work and study together.[6] Cuban people demonstrated a strong and genuine sense of national unity. Despite invidious color prejudices, they saw themselves overwhelmingly as Cuban first and only second as being a certain color. Thus, black Cubans abroad interacted less with blacks in other countries and more with other Cubans, although, for instance, among the relatively small Cuban community resident in Grenada in the early 1970s, there was a tendency to socialize along color lines. At home, blacks were active traditionally in trade unions and in other revolutionary mass organizations such as the Committees in Defense of the Revolution (CDRs), yet they were conspicuously absent from the higher levels of political and administrative power even after electoral government was introduced in the form of People's Power.

Power appeared to be concentrated in a small sector from which Castro himself had emerged and that had supported him both during and following the revolutionary struggle. This relatively privileged group was predominantly white, although the insurrectional ranks in the 1950s had included blacks. In its undeniably elitist style of administration, this group may have conducted itself in the people's—including black people's—interest, but it could not be said to be controlled by them. Research conducted among exiles who left through the Mariel exodus in the 1980s has shown that many were not antisocialist but longed simply to have more control over their own lives. Furthermore, many appeared to be somewhat marginal to the revolutionary process—possessing less education, living in deteriorated neighborhoods, and demonstrating characteristics of what has been loosely referred to as the "lumpen" social category. Many were also black.[7] The extent to which their racial background can be correlated with their low level of integration into contemporary socialist Cuba is a question worth asking.

In accordance with statements of the revolutionary leaders in the early years of the revolution (1959–1962), the emphasis regarding racial prejudice was placed on the public rather than the private sphere. There were to be no legally segregated residential areas or schools, and blacks and whites increasingly were to study and work together. Statistics on occupation, level of education, and income according to race are not available in Cuba; thus, it is not possible to make broad generalizations about the economic and social status of those of African descent. However, ethnographic studies undertaken in the late 1960s and early 1970s pointed to a stronger black presence in poorer neighborhoods.[8] Similar findings can be gleaned from other studies: An epidemiological research study conducted by a team of public health workers in a sector of Havana in the early 1980s revealed that although instances of squalid living conditions, rates of infant mortality, and incidence of infectious disease were lower than would be the case in working-class communities of most Latin American and Caribbean capitals, they were significantly elevated in those communities containing a markedly higher proportion of blacks.[9] The newer housing settlements of Alamar and East Havana appear to be fully integrated, but the most deteriorated older sectors of Havana are those with significant black populations.

When census information is available, it is not reliable when it comes to race, given the subjectivity of both census enumerators and enumeratees in "whitening" census responses. It is safe to assert that at least 60 percent of Cubans (compared to the 30 percent recorded in the last [1981] census) have a significant degree of African ancestry. The black issue in Cuba cannot be dismissed as a minority issue. Rather, the discussion raises the even more fundamental question of the extent to which the majority of Cuban people participate fully in decisions that affect their lives in the schools, the workplace, universities, the armed forces, and institutions of political power.

A degree of social separateness persists in Cuban recreational centers. Adjacent to the prestigious Tropicana nightclub—a favorite of foreign visitors—is the Mambi, named after the heroic Cubans who struggled against Spanish colonial rule. In terms of the ethnic composition of its guests, the Mambi is overwhelmingly black, excluding both whites and mulattos. Another striking example of racial separateness (unless one subscribes to the notion that blacks are inherently superior to other racial types in the area of sports) is that blacks continue to be as overrepresented in Cuban sports and entertainment as they are under-represented in other areas.

It might be argued that there are social and cultural reasons for such divisions. Those whose homes lack a literary or scholarly tradition can be expected to be at a distinct disadvantage in terms of progressing and excelling academically. The Cuban Ministry of Education's policy of placing children from homes with chronic social problems in state-run boarding schools has undoubtedly done much to bridge the gap for traditionally disadvantaged black youth. However, such policies do not adequately address the structural problems that place such youngsters at risk educationally. Blacks continue to live predominantly in run-down neighborhoods in which schools are less well equipped and the dropout rate tends to be markedly higher than in other areas. The results of interviews conducted in central and Old Havana and the more outlying Luyano and Lawton districts indicated that there was a problem in Cuban society similar, although by no means identical, to that encountered in many deteriorated U.S. urban communities in which nonwhites are the majority.[10]

Similarly, a particular form of prerevolutionary Cuban criminology had long quoted racial attributes in connection with predilection to crime, and there is still a tendency to equate being black with a predilection for violence.[11] When a foreign student who could be described ethnically as a mulatto reported an attempted rape to a police officer in Santa María, the latter inquired in reference to the assailant, "Era negro, ¿no?" ("He was black, right?"). The officer, himself a mulatto, explained his presumption by saying that a high proportion of delinquents and criminals was black. When a white policewoman in the station was asked her opinion as to why this is the case, she explained, "Es que estaban oprimidos y más controlados antes de la Revolución. Ahora que Fidel les ha dado su libertad, se aprovechan" ("They were oppressed and more controlled before the revolution. Since Fidel has liberated them, they take advantage [of the situation]"). Such arguments are more commonly made than ones of marginality, and they raise more complex sociocultural questions.

### Defining Cuban Culture

There is a lively debate from varying analytical standpoints in the literature as to what composes Cuban culture. Fernando Ortiz, Cuba's foremost white ethnographer who died in 1969, legitimized the study of black Cuba. In a major study, he indicated that he saw Cuban culture as an expression of two relatively distinct influences determined by different forms of production.[12] He contrasted tobacco—characterized by small-farm production carried out primarily by peasants of Spanish descent who owned their own parcels of land—with sugar—which was produced by intensive slave labor carried out by persons of African descent on large plantations. The two forms of production produced markedly different cultural worlds that together helped shape Cuban nationality.

Walterio Carbonell, a black Cuban writer, agreed with Ortiz in viewing the country's two relatively distinct racial and cultural entities. However, he attached primary, deterministic importance to the African presence—not only because those of African descent constituted the majority of the Cuban population but because sugar exerted an overwhelming influence on every aspect of the Cuban economy and society.[13] The white Cuban writer Roberto Fernández Retamar argued that we can no longer talk about separate racial groups or cultures on the island but of a revolutionary *mestizo* mixed culture.[14] To echo a popular saying of Castro's, "El que no viene del Congo viene del Carabalí" ("Anyone who is not descended from the Congo [nation] is descended from the Carabalí [nation]").

To go beyond the politico-cultural analysis, it is important to note that the noun *cultura* (culture) and the adjective *culto(a)* (cultured, or educated) have somewhat different meanings in the Cuban context than their literal translations imply. Constant reference is made to people of *poca cultura* (little culture), or *baja cultura* (low culture). The context, it is explained, is not culture but rather education, with the term applied in an objective (as opposed to a disparaging) manner to Cubans with less education. However, the phrase is often used to refer to Cubans of African descent in a context of low cultural, not only low educational, level.

Epidemiological studies carried out in the early 1980s identified as pathological behavior not only child and drug abuse, truancy, and juvenile delinquency but also participation in Afro-Cuban religious cults. One cannot excuse the designation of such practices as pathological as being symptomatic of a previous social order because the practice of regarding them as pathological reflected the official policy of the Ministry of Health. A decade later, however, the government position had changed significantly, and Afro-Cuban religious practices were looked upon favorably.

Although Cubans have generally acknowledged Afro-Cuban cultural elements as valid expressions of national culture, throughout the world the emphasis on science (which is assumed to be value-free and culturally independent) and on technology has led to a minimizing of the significance and value of the African past.[15] In Cuba as well, beyond the traditions, folklore, dance, and music, there was comparatively little rigorous analysis of, for example, the civilizations and social stratification that existed on the African continent or in Cuba's own history. Africa was valued for its pulsating rhythms and for the physical strength of the black male, but it was not considered a center of learning and innovation whose contribution to world civilization was worthy of more serious consideration. Africa today is viewed in world circles essentially as an impoverished continent in desperate need of assistance to allow to effectively catch up with the rest of the world.

The National Folklore Group is an important national dance company committed to the preservation and presentation of not only African but all expressions of Cuban national culture. It has less prestige, however, than the National Ballet, which represents a more classical, European tradition.

Despite the intense U.S. blockade—or perhaps partly as a result of it—Cuban young people have tended to look outside of the island and away from themselves for stimulation and diversion. The most adamant members of the Young Pioneers or Communist Youth are often obsessed with U.S. and, more generally, Western pop music, clothing (jeans, for example), and cultural values. This is not unique in the Third World, nor should Cuban youth remain insulated from world culture and only appreciate and participate in their own national culture. For many years, however, the combination of isolation and periods in which only national music curried official favor with the absence of a meaningful cultural movement concerned with the promotion of national values, customs, and institutions rendered Cuban youth particularly susceptible to foreign cultural penetration. A serious exploration of popular Cuban culture coincided with the 1980s *salsa* boom abroad; this began to reveal to young Cubans that their culture is not inferior but is rich in variation and diversity and is popular beyond their national boundaries. After years of disdaining Cuban music, young Cubans rediscovered the *rumba*, the *son*, and the *guaguanco*.

### Sexual Relationships

In 1982 a long-awaited film based on Cuba's classic nineteenth-century novel, *Cecilia Valdés*, premiered in Havana. The film, which tells the story of a beautiful mulatto woman in colonial times, touched on issues of racial oppression and identity. The film itself, audience reaction, and the level of discussion in the press were all revealing about attitudes on race and ethnicity. First, there was considerable consternation over the selection of the leading actress, who was not considered to be mulatta but white. All nudity in the film involved black people, mostly black women—significantly, even in the scene involving the rape of a white plantation owner's wife there were no glimpses of the victim's anatomy. The film as a whole was disliked in Cuba largely because it glossed over major elements in the book and was folkloric in its treatment of black Cuba. Explanations of why scenes of barbaric torture of black slaves were greeted with laughter centered on what was perceived as the ludicrous way in which the scenes were depicted, but they also hinged on the notion that slavery in Cuba had not been that brutal or sadistic. Clearly, the film touched on issues that are far from being resolved in Cuban society when the topic of race is broached as a serious political or ideological issue. Although references to race and color abound in everyday speech, they remain somewhat taboo at the level of serious intellectual discourse. In the colonial period, it was quite rational for Cecilia to aspire to be white and to win the love of a white man. However, the image of her begging the Yoruba gods to give her a white man to love her epitomized perhaps in some disturbing sense the contemporary dilemma of the Cuban mulatto or mulatta (that is, the Cuban majority). Tied to Africa (blackness) culturally and genetically, he or she remains emotionally and intellectually chained to Europe (whiteness).

When describing each other, Cubans depend considerably on physical and national characteristics. Common terms include but are not restricted to (1) *negro(a)* or *prieto(a)*—dark-skinned black; (2) *blanco(a)* or *rubio(a)*—the latter meaning literally blond, or fair, but like the former used for whites in general; (3) *mulato(a)*—mulatto (person of mixed African-European ancestry); (4) *moreno(a)*—olive-complexioned person (usually lighter than a *mulato*); (5) *jabao(a)*—light-skinned mulatto with negroid features; (6) *india(o)*—mulatto with fine features; (7) *chino(a)*—Chinese-looking; (8) *gallego(a)*—Spaniard. The tendency in Cuban society and culture to idealize the European to the detriment of the African phenotype is reflected in expressions such as *coge la sombra* ("stay in the shade") and *una mulata para salir* ("a mulatta [good enough] to take out [in public]"). This indicates that although overt racial tensions between groups are not apparent on the island, and persons of different colors mingle freely in many social settings, persons of like phenotypes tend to date and marry each other. That is, more intimate relationships tend to take place not according to broad racial categories such as white and black but according to more subtle distinctions, particularly in the more socially conservative provinces such as Cienfuegos and Holguín. Thus, couples composed of a *mulata* and a *jabao* or a *moreno* and a *blanca* are observed far more frequently than a *rubia* with a *prieto*. Moreover, although there is no evidence to suggest that the state or the Communist party approves of or promotes racial prejudice, publicly exposed cases have occurred of white Communist party members opposing their daughters dating black or mulatto men.[16]

In urban areas, the critical housing shortage may have militated against changing race relations. Many young couples have to live in their respective parents' homes; for extramarital relations, often the only alternative is the *posada* where rooms can be rented by the hour, but waiting in line for a room is very public. Thus, young people who may have gone far in shedding racial prejudice on an intellectual level (due to increased interaction with youth, workers, and students of all colors) might still have to live at home with parents and grandparents who may find the idea of racial equality appalling.

## Conclusion

Structural Marxism has pointed to the ways superstructures can become the dominant forces in a social system, imparting intentional, evolutionary rationality. Similarly, an ideology of race relations can exert an insidious multifaceted influence, even under conditions in which the socioeconomic structure does not positively reinforce such attitudes. In Cuba's multiracial society, a tacit agreement was made shortly after the revolutionary triumph to allow the racial question to resolve itself gradually with the consolidation of socialism. It was felt within the highest echelons of Cuban political power that broaching the topic openly—as became the case increasingly with the women's issue, for example—would open up a keg of dynamite. However, it might also be asserted that such a basic societal contradiction cannot be left to the course of time and that a different approach to combating racism is required. When, in the 1980s, a high-ranking member of the Communist party was not ashamed to say in my presence that "todo lo que ha hecho Fidel está bien conmigo. Pero eso de forzarme a vivir al lado de estos negros, vecinos míos, ya es el último" ("everything that Fidel has done is fine with me. But to force me to live next to those black neighbors of mine, that's the limit")[17] and a black woman says that her greatest wish is that a foreigner would bring her a blond wig to conceal her *pasas* (raisins—a derogatory metaphor for nappy, African hair), it is clear that a different approach is needed.

Comparative research conducted among Cuban exiles in Miami, New York, and Mexico has shown that the more insidious aspects of racism are far less apparent in contemporary Cuban society than among the exile communities. This undoubtedly had much to do with the fact that the more reactionary, economically privileged, and whiter sectors of Cuban society were the most inclined to emigrate, although 1970s and

1980s exiles included more mulattos and blacks. However, many attitudes about race and culture are still remarkably similar between exile communities and those on the island.[18] I contend that an ingrained sense of racial inferiority in Cubans with African blood combined with a not-so-subtle contempt on the part of Cubans of primarily European descent represent a formidable obstacle to social and cultural development on the island and the consolidation of the Cuban revolutionary process. Afro-Cubans need to recognize the psychological transformation that must occur and define for themselves the ideological features and manifestations of Cuban racism and then propose viable solutions. Until recently, it was considered counterrevolutionary to protest against discrimination. Yet why, for example, were the overwhelming majority of Cuban youths arrested under the *Ley de Peligrosidad* (Law of Dangerous Conduct) prior to the 1985 Debt Conference black? The challenging task of eliminating racism from the minds and hearts of the Cuban people must be tackled.

The ideologies of pan-Africanism, black cultural nationalism, and negritude need not be viewed as intrinsically antithetical to historical and dialectical materialism. The fact that some of the most important social experiments of the twentieth century have taken place in Africa and the Caribbean and involved a syncretism of Marxism and black consciousness provides vivid proof of this fact. The Cuban revolution has consistently expressed symbolic identification with and provided material and strategic support for liberation movements on the African continent. However, the internal aversion to black cultural movements has meant that many Afro-American exiles who went to Cuba, encouraged by Castro's antiracist political stance on an international level, were profoundly disillusioned by the insensitivity and hostility they encountered when they attempted to present their views on international black liberation to important figures within the Communist party. They had little if any trouble, however, relating to many of the black Cubans with whom they had daily contact.

The egalitarian ethos promoted by the revolution has created a climate in which true democracy and full participation are possibilities. The fact that many black Cubans feel a strong sense of identity with others throughout the black diaspora should not be viewed as a threat to national unity or to the integrity of the Cuban revolution. An egalitarian ethos and transformation of the material relations of production do not lead automatically to the emergence of a revolutionary superstructure. In order to effectively address the contradictions that emerge at different stages of the revolutionary struggle, we must courageously confront the objective reality, not attempt to conceal it. In the words of Fidel Castro himself, "If the roots and history of this country are not known, the political culture of the masses of our people will not be sufficiently developed. Because we could not even call ourselves Marxists, if we do not start by comprehending our own revolutionary process."[19]

## Notes

1. See José F. Carneado, "La discriminación racial en Cuba no volverá jamás," *Cuba Socialista*, vol. 2, no. 5 (1962), pp. 54–67; Juan Sánchez, "Aspectos de la discriminación racial: Un mal del pasado," *Bohemia*, no. 65 (May 25, 1973); and Terry Cannon and Johnetta Cole, *Free and Equal: The End of Racial Discrimination in Cuba* (New York: Venceremos Brigade, 1978).

2. Max Azicri, "Women's Development Through Revolutionary Mobilization: A Study of the Federation of Cuban Women," in Irving L. Horowitz, ed., *Cuban Communism*, 5th ed. (New Brunswick, N.J.: Transaction Press, 1984), pp. 360–385.

3. Regarding slave society, see Diane Iznaga, *La burguesía esclavista cubana* (Havana: Editorial de Ciencias Sociales, 1978), and Franklin W. Knight, *Slave Society in Cuba During the 19th Century* (Madison: University of Wisconsin Press, 1970). For an assessment of the growing free-colored class, see Verena Martínez-Alier, *Marriage, Class and Colour in 19th Century Cuba* (Cambridge: Cambridge University Press, 1974).

4. For a discussion of the 1912 war, see Rafael Fermoselle, *Política y color en Cuba: la guerrita de 1912* (Montevideo: Ediciones Gerninis, 1974), and Serafín Portuondo Linares, *Los independientes de color: Historia del Partido Independiente de Color* (Havana: Ministerio de Educación, 1950). See also Carlos Moore, *Castro, the Blacks and Africa* (Los Angeles, Cal.: Center for Afro-American Studies, UCLA, 1989).

5. See John Clytus and Jane Ricker, *Black Man in Red Cuba* (Coral Gables, Fla.: University of Miami Press, 1970).

6. See, for example, David Booth, "Cuba, Color and the Revolution," *Science and Society*, vol. 40, no. 2 (Summer 1976), pp. 129–172, and Jean Stubbs, *Cuba: The Test of Time* (London: Latin American Bureau, 1989).

7. Among the studies on the Mariel emigrants, see Robert L. Bach, et al., "The Flotilla 'Entrants': Latest and Most Controversial," *Cuban Studies*, vol. 11, no. 2/vol. 12, no. 1 (1981–1982), pp. 29–48; Gaston A. Fernández, "Comment: The Flotilla Entrants. Are They Different?" *Cuban Studies*, vol. 11, no. 2/vol. 12, no. 1, pp. 49–54; and Barry Sklar, "Cuban Exodus 1980: The Context," in Horowitz, ed., *Cuban Communism.*

8. One such study is Oscar Lewis, *Living the Revolution. Four Men and Four Women* (Urbana: University of Illinois Press, 1977).

9. Carlos Hernández, Gayle McGarrity, et al., *Perfil epidemiológico de un sector de salud de La Habana* (Havana: Instituto de Desarrollo de la Salud, 1982).

10. Douglas Butterworth, *The People of Buena Ventura: Relocation of Slum-Dwellers in Post-Revolutionary Cuba* (Urbana: University of Illinois Press, 1980).

11. See Luis P. Salas, "Juvenile Delinquency in Post-Revolutionary Cuba," in Horowitz, ed., *Cuban Communism.*

12. Fernando Ortiz, *Cuban Counterpoint: Tobacco and Sugar* (New York: Alfred A. Knopf, 1947).

13. See Walterio Carbonell, *Cómo surgió la cultura nacional* (Havana: Biblioteca Nacional, 1960). Also worthy of note is the classic three-volume study by Manuel Moreno Fraginals, *El ingenio: complejo económico social cubano del azúcar* (Havana: Editorial de Ciencias Sociales, 1978).

14. Roberto Fernández Retamar, *Calibán* (Montevideo: Aquí Testimonios, 1973).

15. See St. Clair Drake, "The Black Diaspora in Pan-African Perspective," *Black Scholar*, vol. 7, no. 1 (1975), pp. 2–13, and *Black Folk Here and There*. Vol. 2 (Los Angeles, Cal.: Center for African and Afro-American Studies, UCLA, 1989); and Ivan Van Sertime, *Blacks in Science* (New Brunswick, N.J.: Transaction Books, 1983), and *African Presence in Early Europe* (New Brunswick, N.J.: Transaction Books, 1985).

16. Selva Nebbia, "Interview with Rafael López Valdés: Cuban Anthropologist on Revolution's Progress in Eradicating Racism," *The Militant*, vol. 53, no. 13 (April 14, 1989).

17. Comment expressed to the author in personal conversation in Havana, spring 1982.

18. See Lourdes Alquelles, "Stratification in Miami Cuban Enclave," *Contemporary Marxism*, no. 5 (Summer 1982) pp. 27–43; Geoffry Fox, "Race and Class in Contemporary Cuba," in Horowitz, ed., *Cuban Communism*; and Eric Wagner, "The Cuban Identity in the Americas: Some Parallel Values in the Exile and Revolutionary Societies," *Caribbean Review*, vol. 9, no. 4 (Fall 1981).

19. Quoted in Iznaga, *La burguesía esclavista cubana*, p. 9.

# 11

# Cuban Political Culture: Between Betrayal and Death

*Nelson P. Valdés*

*The most elemental and important facts about a society are those that are seldom debated and generally regarded as settled.*
—Louis Wirth

For the last two hundred years, Cuban politics has followed an identical script. The contenders have changed and the issues shifted, but the content of the political imagination, the discourse, and the symbols have shown a remarkable continuity. Political adversaries often fought to the death over their differences, but despite intense polemics, the discussions seldom dealt with issues of democratic government, balance of power, the relative importance of the market, or whether property and stratification patterns should be restructured.

Other questions prevailed. The themes of personal duty, political morality, patriotism, and the historic mission of the nation engaged Cubans from all political perspectives. The political actors, in addition to sharing a similar problematic, had identical political codes, meanings and categories. The Cuban revolution did not alter the pattern: Cuban revolutionaries and exiles still conform to the same discourse. The importance, influence, and resilience of this political culture are the central concerns of this chapter.

## The Nature of Political Culture and Semiotics:
## The Principal Codes of Cuban Political Culture

Every political culture has its own sense of reality. Sidney Verba defines political culture as "the system of empirical beliefs, expressive symbols, and values which define the situation in which political action takes place. It provides the subjective orientation to politics."[1] A political culture is a unique historical product. Comprehension of a political culture on the basis of its subjective reality—that is—its implicit codes, signs, and meanings—is the province of semiotics. People who function within their own political culture usually take too many things for granted, assuming that their conceptual universe is just "common sense." A semiotic understanding requires an intimate acquaintance with the world that one studies as well as a separation from it.

This chapter describes and analyzes the principal codes that have prevailed in Cuban political culture. The reader will not get a sociological study of these codes or a thorough explanation of their structural origins. The objective is more modest: to outline the codes (or patterned categories), to stress some of their basic features, and to trace their interconnections.

Clarence Schettler tells us that "if anyone wants to know what we think; what we have thought; what our beliefs, traditions, social perceptions, and public opinions are, he can find his answers by studying our language."[2] Political language discloses codes—that is, recurring categories with culturally defined meanings. The codes express imbedded ideas that shape our perception of reality. They manifest shared assumptions, whereas other aspects of observed reality are excluded.[3]

The recurrence of codes in Cuba's political history has been noticed by numerous authors. In his incisive book, *Cuba: Between Reform and Revolution,* Louis A. Pérez, Jr., writes that the "basic issues shaping the course of Cuban history have remained fundamentally fixed and firm" over the years.[4] Noticing the same phenomenon, Luis Aguilar wrote that by 1940, all twelve political parties in Cuba shared a common terminology and rhetoric.[5] The commonality of political language, image, and categories is a rather extraordinary testimony to the power of a learned political culture.

There are four major conceptual components of Cuban political culture. These are now inseparable, although they did not originate simultaneously. The four codes are (1) the generational theme, (2) the moralism-idealism syndrome, (3) the theme of betrayal, and (4) the duty-death imperative. Each had been a strong feature of Cuban political discourse prior to the 1890s. Although each of these codes is dealt with separately, they are integral parts of the whole that we call Cuban political culture, and there are logical ties among them.

## Generations

*Youth is happy because it is blind; this blindness is its grandeur, and this inexperience its sublime confidence. How beautiful a generation is that of the young and active!*

—José Martí

*We are young, and if we do not do all that nature expects of us, we will be traitors.*

—José Marti

*While generations are not born politically, one from the other—as happens in biological terms—the lack of understanding of our own history will continue to be the dominant sign of each historical period.*

—Aureliano Sánchez Arango

Cuban emigré historian José Kesselman has noted that the majority of political figures from "moderates to the leftists, tend to interpret the last one hundred years of the history of Cuba as a result of conflicts created by the appearance of a new generation of activists."[6] This is true for academics and politicians and in daily political discussions. Generational language is hegemonic regardless of whether reality is so. Political statements, journalistic accounts, and historical works tend to use a generational frame.

When social, economic, cultural, or political events are analyzed, described, or explained on the basis of the age of the parties involved, we have a generational interpretation. Generational claims to historical mission are traceable to the 1820s, when nineteenth-century European works on the "rise and decline" of civilizations entered Cuban intellectual circles.[7] Their message was "regeneration" at the hands of youth. Literary circles had adopted the Comtean thesis that older people tended to have the "instinct of social conservation," whereas the young had the "instinct of innovation."[8] José Martí, political leader of the 1895 war of independence, borrowed the language and framework when he proclaimed that the renewed struggle for independence was led by *pinos nuevos* (young men).[9] His message was clear: The young of Cuba were fighting a decrepit and old Spanish colonial system.

Positivism and nationalism merged at the turn of the century. Prior to the U.S. intervention, the positivist message proclaimed that the struggle for independence represented modernity and progress: It was young Cuba against old Spain. When the United States seized Cuba from Spain, the archetypes could no longer be used because the United States was also a "new" country. In their confrontation with the U.S. power, Cuban positivists could not claim modernity and progress, which were associated with acceptance of the hegemonic power of the neighbor to the north. Hence, such associations implied a forfeiture of Cuban independence. Instead, the emphasis shifted away from modernization and toward authenticity. Cubans countered U.S. power and materialism with a philosophy of idealism and vitalism.

Positivism now defined youth's role as opposition to materialism. The society imposed by the United States was depicted as decaying. Positivism, as Antoni Kapcia asserts, "extended to historiography, anthropology, sociology and even economics."[10] The strongest exponent of the "decay" thesis and the historical role of youth was the conservative philosopher Enrique José Varona.[11]

The generational thesis gained further force through the writings of the Mexican José Ingenieros, who had complete faith in the redeeming qualities of the young. Uruguayan thinker José Enrique Rodó, who denounced U.S. materialism and proclaimed that the salvation of Latin America would depend on the young acting on the basis of duty, ideals, and disinterest, found a receptive audience in Cuba.[12] By the 1920s, the "renovating role of generations" had become an article of faith.[13] It was the Spanish philosopher José Ortega y Gasset, however, who had the most lasting impact on political culture by offering Cuban nationalists and others a "theory" of generations and of history.[14]

The generational theme found exponents throughout the country. In 1923, twenty-five years after the War of Independence, the Association of Veterans and Patriots remained loyal to the earlier generational code, calling for the "regeneration of Cuba."[15] In 1925 Gerardo Machado, the liberal presidential candidate later turned dictator, announced his own program of "regeneration."[16] Intellectuals and artists—left and right— issued generational manifestos, claiming the right to be the conscience of the society. Numerous academics and essayists wrote about generations making history. Antonio S. Bustamante applied the concept to literary interpretations; Félix Lizaso popularized it with a series of essays on cultural issues; and Jorge Mañach applied it to historical analysis.[17] The most thorough series on Cuban history, *Historia de la Nación Cubana*, interpreted the past on the basis of the generational code.[18]

The university student movement of the 1920s and 1930s adopted the generational mission. Every political leader and organization of the period followed its precepts (the Partido Revolucionario Cubano, ABC, ABC Radical, Ala Izquierda Estudiantil, Directorio Estudiantil, Partido del Pueblo Cubano, Movimiento Socialista, Revolucionario, Unión In-surreccional Revolucionaria, Joven Cuba, and others).

Roberto Agramonte, the leading Cuban sociologist of the 1940s and 1950s and the major intellectual voice of the Partido Ortodoxo, saw history as follows.

There is no other, literary genre as biography to fully comprehend the meaning of history. Biography . . . is the [basic] cell of any history. History is, in its internal structure, that: flux and contrast—of a generation that comes together around a principal personality: thus we get Caballero, Varela, José de la Luz, Martí, Varona. Each of these generations tends to have hegemony during a third of a century, more or less, until—as Dilthey shows—the new generation knocks on the door of the previous one, with a new intention. . . . In spite of the existence of common traits between the two contiguous generations, an ideological rift develops between them. In this way, each generation is the interpreter of history. Because of this, the history of philosophy—and the intimate life of philosophers—demonstrates the succession of positions of the human psyche, and the picture of the vigorous older generation in ascendancy, culmination, and then descent; which is manifested in their lives and ideas. And we see the same picture in the young generation, in the process of constructive negation, which is a transcendence of the old.[19]

The manichean nature of historical change posited by Agramonte, national leader of the most important political party in the 1950s, is an indication of the strength of the generational code. Another leader of the Ortodoxo movement, Max Lesnik Menéndez, wrote in 1956, "I share the view that the 1930 Generation was a fraud, did nothing while in power, but was also responsible to an extreme degree for the profound crisis which the nation is undergoing at the present moment in its history."[20]

Lesnik claimed, like many of his contemporaries, that youths command "respect by their courage, their boldness, their audacity and their clear program." The Ortodoxos and the Auténticos were relentless opponents, yet they used the same words, the same meanings, and the same codes. Revolutionary groups that fought against the Batista dictatorship defined themselves as part of a "new generation." This was the case of the Movimiento Nacionalista Revolucionario, the Directorio Revolucionario, and the 26th of July Movement (the latter became known as the *Generación del Centenario* in honor of José Martí).[21] After 1959, the reference to generations has continued and, significantly, at present one of Cuba's two leading newspapers is called *Juventud Rebelde*.

Recently, revolutionaries and counterrevolutionaries have invoked such language to discuss the future of the revolution. One side claims the revolution will be continued by the young, whereas its adversaries expect otherwise. The conclusions may be polar opposites, but the framework is the same.[22] An aging Fidel Castro has begun to somewhat revise his generational references. He now refers to those who seized power in 1959 as *antiguos* (precursors) rather than *viejos* (old). The introduction of a semantic variation is an explicit acknowledgment of the importance of the code in political discourse, yet whether the semantic innovation can radically alter two centuries of socialization is questionable.

Implicit in the generational code is a scheme that goes beyond the rhetorical and represents a historical teleology. Generational statements are descriptive, normative, and analytical in the Cuban context. This is what Michael Foucault refers to as the architecture of a concept, the real meaning of the code. First, the population is simply classified by age or cohort group. There are no subtle transitions: One is either young or old. Second, the biological determines the existential and hence the political.

A young person is supposed to have a high sense of duty, strength, pure ideals, vigor, and a sense of commitment. The young, by definition, have the best interests of the nation at heart and are willing to fight for them. An illustration of this is found in the statement issued by José Antonio Echeverría, leader of the University Students Federation, after the 1952 coup d'état: "We are, once again, the standard bearers of the national conscience. The dramatic circumstances that the fatherland confronts call upon us to fulfill difficult and risky duties."[23] The older generation, on the other hand, has lost biological and vital energies; moral conviction has dissipated, and ideals have disappeared. This generation is more willing to live a life of hedonism and self-interest. The older people, in other words, have degenerated. The Spanish writer Carlos Alonso Quejada puts it thus: "The purity of young ideals contrasts brutally with the accommodating pragmatism of adults, who accept the vulgar routine of existence."[24]

Youth, in the generational code, has positive attributes, but the old do not. This belief is based on a projecting definition and a value assessment because the qualities of neither have ever been empirically demonstrated. Moreover, the code confuses a possible description with its explanation. The claim is an ideological assertion, no more, but behind the normative inferences is a philosophy of history.

The generational code embraces genealogy to explain history. There is a strong intellectual tradition behind this movement in Latin America and Spain. José Ortega y Gasset once wrote that history was a sub-discipline of biology.[25] This outlook had much appeal in Latin America among conservatives, church officials and educators, and a bourgeoisie that feared interpretations rooted in class analysis. In Cuba the generational code managed to merge positivism (with its denunciation of "decadence"), Spanish liberal biologism, and a strong sense of vanguardism.

The vanguardist nature of the generational code precedes any Leninist principles in Cuban politics. Generations, we are told, make history;

but history is shaped by the "conscious minority" (*la minoría histórica*), led by the great hero—the leader who comes to represent the generation—which in turn leads the rest of society.[26] Enrique José Varona thought that one of the tasks of the university was to bring together the most capable and "well-prepared" youth in order to convert them into a "genuine moral body" that would be "recognized as members of a vast corporation, invested with great dignity." This elitist-generational vanguardism has meant that historical interpretations usually end up as mere biographies—an enterprise worthy of a Thomas Carlyle.

A further dimension of the generational code is subjectivism. The generational thesis ignores the relation between a political phenomenon and the surrounding material and social circumstances. François Mentre defined a generation as "a group of men belonging to different families, whose [cohesive] unity results from a particular mentality." A generation, in other words, "is a collective state of mind incarnate in a group of people." It is then defined only "on the basis of its beliefs and desires, in psychological and moral terms."[27] This emphasis on morality is the second code of Cuban popular political culture.

## Moralism, Idealism, and Voluntarism

*What a fortunate state is that possessing a moral, educated people.*
                                                              —Félix Varela

*In this world there has to be a certain amount of both decency and light. When we find many people without decency, there are always others who possess themselves as much dignity as many others. They are the ones who rebel with tensile force against those who rob nations of their liberty, which is to rob people of their decency.*                                           —José Martí

Marxism has never been central to the Cuban intellectual tradition. Even self-proclaimed Marxists tend to approach the country on the basis of categories Karl Marx dismissed. In 1984 Carlos Rafael Rodríguez stated that the intellectual and political debates within Marxist circles in the 1960s and 1970s had little if any impact on the island. He disclosed that Marx was studied in a superficial and mechanical fashion. He added, "I have no news that the polemic about the 'humanist' or 'scientific' aspects of Marx, which provoked so many debates in Europe just a few years ago, had much impact among Marxists in our country."[28]

"In the history of Cuba," writes Armando Chávez Antúnez, "morality has played a decisive role in the development of the events that have transformed the national life." He goes on to add that "moral motivation has guided the behavior of our revolutionary vanguards."[29] Moral stance has been the common feature of almost every political group that has tried to gain the support of the Cuban people.

The marriage of politics, nationalism, and morality was initiated by Félix Varela. A moral person, he wrote, was one who was useful to the fatherland. Varela merged the Catholic morality with utilitarianism and a commitment to national self-determination.[30] Early in the nineteenth century, others raised their voices to "elevate" the moral level of Cuban society as well. But again, it was José Martí who best synthesized the theme of morality and politics by secularizing morality. According to Cintio Vitier, "Martí established a revolutionary ethics that became the foundation of his social and political preachings."[31] The key feature of his ethics was his concept of "decorum" and dignity.[32] Decorum meant purity of ideals, honesty, and honor. Dignity was the ability to fulfill those aims as well as a strong sense of duty toward country. The Cuban historian Jorge Ibarra maintains that Martí wished to install a "moral republic" based on ethical values.[33]

After Martí's death, others continued his emphasis on morality. The most influential twentieth-century Cuban philosopher and university professor, Enrique José Varona, made "morals" the centerpiece of his teachings at the University of Havana and in his writings.[34] As the leading sociology professor in the only university on the island, he passed on to students and colleagues one basic thesis: The problems besieging Cuba resulted from the absence of moral men in power. Others repeated the theme. José A. Ramos wrote in *Manual del perfecto fulanista* (1916) about the absence of morality. Luis Felipe Rodríguez did likewise in *La conjura de la ciénaga* (1923). The best representative of the immorality thesis, however, was the anthropologist Fernando Ortiz, who asserted that Cuban social and political institutions were in disarray because of the "immorality" of the country's rulers and who called on the United States to impose a "moral intervention."[35]

Whatever the issue, politicians adhered to the morality script. All problems were the consequences of someone's moral flaw. Political parties have been established with the precise intent of defending that thesis. On June 17, 1949, Eduardo Chibás proclaimed that "the Partido del Pueblo Cubano has been created in order to fulfill the great historical objectives of the Cuban people by means of a moral revolution in public life."[36] His battle cry *"vergüenza contra dinero"* (a sense of shame rather than money) was similar to Varela's denunciations of profiteers who opposed patriotism. Chibás's entreaty is echoed today in the Cuban emphasis on building socialism through "moral incentives."

Cuban revolutionaries may define themselves as Marxists and rugged materialists, but below the surface declarations one finds utopian socialists consistently submitting to the logic of a moral code. As early as 1947,

Cuban Political Culture    215

Fidel Castro understood politics in the country to be "the sad results of selfishness and privilege."[37] Castro has frequently made his views on this matter known: "I have been inclined, always, to believe much more in moral factors, in the consciousness of men, because I have seen what man is able to accomplish, and I have had many lessons on this throughout our country's history."[38] Although the components of a secular morality have not been clearly outlined, the concept of morality has been invoked to counter corruption, the misappropriation of funds, and excessive individualism. Implicit in the message is the belief that a moral person is honest, willing to sacrifice personal interest for the common good, and indifferent to material possessions.

This belief has been a constant before and after the 1959 revolution. In August 1952, Castro wrote, "The Revolution opens the way to true merit, to those who have sincere courage and ideals, to those who risk their lives and take the battle standard in their hands."[39] The following year he asserted, "The centennial of Martí's birth is the culmination of a historical cycle marked by progression and regression in the political and moral realms of the Republic."[40] He summarized his political moralism as follows: "A decisive battle is being waged between those who have ideals and those who have vested interests."[41] Idealism versus materialism; Hegel against Marx.

This moralism, although secular, has an idealist metaphysics with a particular emphasis on duty. The moralism, moreover, presupposes individual autonomy from class interests and total freedom to make a choice. Neither social structure nor social conditions nor necessity dictates human behavior.

The insistence on moral autonomy and choice is closely attached to voluntarism. To succumb to material conditions or to social pressure is to exhibit weak moral character. Rapid economic growth, the revolutionaries expected, would be achieved on the basis of this framework. Moral resources would be mobilized to attain concrete economic goals. "Palabra de cubano, ¡los diez millones, van!" ("The word of a Cuban, the ten million will be achieved")—this was the message appearing in late 1969 and early 1970. The revolutionary leadership had announced that the country would produce 10 million tons of sugar, and although numerous analysts doubted that it could be done, the regime staked its honor on it. The goal was not achieved. Rather than revise the revolutionaries' perspectives, Castro concluded:

> Some people without morals and without a sense of their social duty today take the liberty of scorning their work, remain idle, let the weight of the productive effort fall on the shoulders of others, cheat, and do a million and other things. . . . Perhaps our greatest idealism lies in having

believed that a society that had barely begun to live in a world that for thousands of years had lived under the law of "an eye for an eye, and a tooth for a tooth," the law of the survival of the fittest, of egoism and deceit, the law of exploitation, could, all of a sudden, be turned into a society in which everybody behaved in an ethical, moral way.[42]

Transcendental voluntarism permeates Fidel Castro's speeches. This is not unique to him or to Cuban revolutionaries; it is a common characteristic shared by many others. Castro is just the best illustration of the pattern. In an interview, he recollected his school years with the Jesuits. They stressed willpower, discipline, self-sacrifice, total dedication, ethical norms, and a strong character. Castro, like the majority of Cuban political leaders, was shaped and influenced by these religious leaders. Even if the politicians did not accept the political content of the priests' ideology, they internalized the Catholic-Hispanic values. From these they learned discipline, hierarchical values, a language, a way of looking at reality, and even a sense of justice. It is hardly surprising that the Cuban revolutionary leader has noted that "all the qualities that make a priest are qualities needed in a good revolutionary."[43] In Cuba the idealist and moral traditions had a Hispanic-Catholic origin. The traditions were further maintained by a mass media and an intellectual milieu infused with a positivist ethic.

In the idealist outlook, faith and trust shape analysis. Michael Harrington once noted that the Cuban revolutionary approach perceived workers and peasants as more idealistic than the conditions of their life permited. He added that as long as the revolutionary regime acted on the basis of premises "in a situation where they did not apply, it was involved in practical, as well as philosophic, contradictions."[44]

The moralist, idealist, and voluntarist terminology reveals implicit concepts and assumptions about the important constituents of historical process. The content of the codes then imposes rule-making. No other way of assessing reality is even considered.[45] Whatever the issue, the challenge, the problem, or its source, it will be addressed as a test of moral convictions and willpower. Prescribed political action is transformed into a measure of honor. The moralist-idealist paradigm is, in the final analysis, an epistemology.[46]

The Cuban historian Manuel Moreno Fraginals once stated that it was difficult to find Marxist social scientists on the island.[47] In name there are people who proclaim themselves so, yet many of them succumb to idealist categories.[48] The tradition may even play a critical role in the future of the revolution itself.

## Permanent Betrayal

*In our [Latin] America there can be no Cains.*     —José Martí

*Our America is tired of traitors.*     —José Martí

*Treason is treason, whoever may commit it.*
    —Div. General Arnaldo Ochoa

*What they have done represents a betrayal of the officials and combatants of our heroic Revolutionary Armed Forces, and of the Ministry of the Interior [—] a betrayal of the honest compañeros who fell while fighting selflessly in Cuba and abroad, it is an outrage for our principles, and an insult to our fatherland.*
    —*Granma* editorial, June 22, 1989

In Cuba, interpretations of social and political reality are often dominated by the belief that one's opponent is treacherous. Political differences then turn into charges of betrayal. If a national or political aim is not attained, there is only possible reason: treason, or betrayal. A few samples illustrate the point.

The 1868–1878 war of independence ended in failure because the independence forces split; some of the forces felt betrayed by the truce arrived at with the Spanish colonial system. Those who signed the Zanjón Pact have been portrayed as "betraying" the struggle for self-determination and national sovereignty. The U.S. intervention in 1898, after the Cubans began a second independence war, led to similar divisions and a feeling that true nationhood had not yet been achieved. As Louis A. Pérez, Jr., has noted, expectations were unfulfilled, promises remained unkept, and "every substantive revolutionary promise" was defaulted on. Betrayal and "frustration" became the common descriptors of twentieth-century Cuban political reality.[49]

In the 1920s, numerous political and intellectual initiatives were allegedly undertaken to rescue the nationalist values "betrayed" when the United States intervened in Cuba in 1898. The theme of betrayal became particularly pronounced in the works of social, economic, and political commentators in the first half of the twenieth century in the writings of Alberto Lamar Schwyer, Jorge Mañach, and Fernando Ortiz, among others.[50]

The 1933 revolution against the dictatorship of Gerardo Machado was justified as a struggle against the betrayal committed by those who had exercised power from 1902 to 1933. Fulgencio Batista, then a sergeant, mobilized noncommissioned officers against the officer corps and managed to seize power. Those he ousted considered his actions to be a betrayal. He proceeded to hand over some degree of political power to civilians who also supported the political ideals put forth over thirty years earlier.

But within five months, Batista overthrew the civilians he had installed. The displaced revolutionaries considered Batista's action a betrayal as well. Ambrosio Fornet, for example, has written that "like 1895, the revolution of the 1920s was a sellout, a betrayal, a frustrated and interrupted revolution."[51]

It was not unusual for political manifestos or political commentaries to include a charge of betrayal. In 1937, for example, leading conservative and liberal intellectuals and political figures called for a constitutional convention. They began their manifesto by stating, "The Government, once again, has betrayed the responsibilities it has received."[52]

Despite their different respective targets, the political message of the Partido Revolucionario Cubano (Auténtico) in the 1930s and the Partido del Pueblo Cubano (Ortodoxo) in the 1940s was the same: Someone else had betrayed Cuba.[53] Fidel Castro's early political activity within the Ortodoxo party meant that he internalized the values of that party. At one point he accused the Auténtico party of "betraying the revolution it had proclaimed."[54] At another time, Castro similarly charged Batista. He wrote, "Aided by the night, by surprise and treachery" the coup succeeded. He went on to add that "the citizenry, completely unaware of the treason," awoke to the rumors and could not act.[55] Subsequently, Castro hurled the same charge at the Ortodoxos. On December 25, 1955, he published an article that read in part, "The nation is at the point of witnessing the great betrayal of the politicians."[56] In the early hours of January 1, 1959, the guerrilla high command issued a general strike proclamation. At one point the document states, "A coup d'état to betray the people cannot be permitted."[57]

Once overthrown, Batista produced a book in his own defense entitled *Cuba Betrayed.*[58] He, of course, was not describing his own political history as a series of betrayals; rather, he classified those who fought against him as having betrayed their own country. Conservatives who served in his last regime have accused Batista of betraying them.[59]

The radical nature of the Cuban revolution did not alter this pattern of accusing opponents of betrayal. Those who opposed the revolutionary course immediately invoked the concept. Liberals who wanted some ill-defined social revolution without communism also seized on the betrayal thesis. Rubén Darío Rumbaut, a leading Christian Democrat and member of the exile Frente Revolucionario Democrático, wrote *La revolución traicionada.*[60] Manuel Antonio de Varona, an Auténtico leader who also went into exile, wrote *El drama de Cuba o la revolución traicionada.*[61] Fermín Peinado, another exile, described "the case of Cuba, communized against the will of its people through the treason of a small group controlling the arms and the propaganda."[62]

Conservatives were not remiss in finding betrayals as well. Mario Lazo pointed an accusing finger at a betrayal by U.S. policymakers that "allowed" the revolution to take place.[63] A chapter in Paul Bethel's book *The Losers* is entitled "The Great Betrayal Begins." Even non-Cuban authors, once in contact with the exile community, repeat the same theme. (An example would be J. A. Acuña's book, *Cuba: revolución traicionada.*[64])

The charge of betrayal or treason was used by the revolutionaries as well—to combat either counterrevolutionaries or those who deviated from the dominant norms within their own ranks. Rolando Cubela, president of the Federation of University Students, purged student ranks in 1959–1960 on the grounds of removing "the traitors who conspired against the University."[65] "The Revolution," Fidel Castro claimed in early 1961, "was able to end treason" against revolutionary principles.[66]

The betrayal theme has continued to be a central feature of political discourse. During the June 1989 Ochoa case, in which a number of officers were charged with drug-trafficking, the betrayal-of-the-revolution thesis resonated within the Council of State. Pedro Miret captured the mood well when he said "history has once again summoned us at a decisive moment. Within our people, but behind our people's backs, the germ of corruption, disloyalty, and treason has once again surfaced."[67]

In June 1990, a former Moncada Barracks attack veteran, Gustavo Arcos Bergnes, who had been in prison for opposing the Communist turn of the revolution, issued a manifesto to all Cubans from Havana. In his declaration he urged a dialogue with the Castro government. Arcos claimed that Fidel Castro had betrayed the revolution's ideals; nonetheless, he still hoped a peaceful resolution could be found. The reaction of the exile media was predictable. Armando Valladares, who had served as U.S. special envoy to the U.N. Human Rights Commission in Geneva, declared, "The Arcos Committee's statements . . . are based on false assumptions, on alterations of Cuban reality to benefit the dictatorship of Fidel Castro, and constitute a betrayal of those who fought, died and still remain in prison for nearly 30 years."[68]

When the U.S. liberal establishment appropriated the betrayal thesis in the 1960s as a cover to oppose the revolution although claiming sympathy with the social aspirations of Latin Americans, they did not understand the long historical tradition behind such charges. The White Paper on Cuba issued during the Kennedy administration by the State Department, but written by Arthur Schlesinger, Jr., in April 1961, began with the heading "The Betrayal of the Cuban Revolution."[69]

U.S. writer Theodore Draper became famous with the thesis that "the revolution Castro promised was unquestionably betrayed."[70] None of the authors understood that although their concept of betrayal was social in nature, the Cubans were speaking of personal trust.[71] The word may have been the same, but it had two entirely different contexts. To U.S. politicians and writers, betrayal means a departure from a set of political promises or moving away from a given political program (behavior familiar to politicians everywhere). To Cubans, the term had an entirely different meaning. This is why Antonio de la Carrera, a Cuban social-democratic critic, wrote, "It is difficult for so many American scholars to believe that the decision to turn Cuba into a Communist country obeyed no social law but was the caprice of one individual, Fidel."[72] Carrera failed to explain why it was so easy for Cubans to accept the thesis.

Why the continual reference to betrayals? The right to competing and distinct political perspectives has not gained acceptance in Cuban politics. As with other social relations, politics appears to be based on total, complete, and absolute loyalty to an individual or a set of "morals." Politics, hence, requires unconditional loyalty, trust, and faith. These then become an index of political commitment. Within this framework, any wavering or deviation is treasonous and consequently constitutes betrayal. Betrayal is always defined by the "betrayed." The person who trusts is betrayed, freeing the person from any responsibility. Hugh Thomas has noted that "people who place faith in a 'hero and guide' are usually deceived."[73]

Loyalty and faith are related features in a political culture that adheres to an absolutist view of truth and reality. This culture is also grounded on reliance on the loyalty of others. This may be a highly esteemed quality, but in politics, to paraphrase Carlos Rafael Rodríguez, "trust is fine, but control is better."[74] Faith and intolerance are also connected. Translated to the political arena, they preclude the possibility of honest differences of opinion or compromise.

The roots and persistence of betrayal as a political theme may be found in the Spanish colonial system, which taught and encouraged respect of authority. The plantation economy fostered similar patterns of authority and obedience. Cuba before 1959 was a society filled with discord, with no fundamental community of interests, and it could not foster a culture of tolerance and diversity. The revolutionary experience after 1959 heightened the divergence and the polarization. The political categories of the nineteenth century continue to this day, in Cuba as well as in the exile community.[75]

The theme of betrayal discloses a political culture in which political relations, like other social relations in a traditional society, are highly personal and lack effective neutrality. Betrayal connotes a political culture that believes that group integration is sacred and should not be violated. The person is expected to be fully part of the group and to accept the group's demands as his or her own. In that sense, deviation from group identity implies choosing individualism over group demands. Deviation, then, is denial of selflessness and hence a "betrayal" of the group. One who deviates is by definition immoral. The antithesis of deviation and betrayal is heroic death.

## Politicization of Thanatos

*Man died on the cross on one particular day; but we have to learn to die on the cross every day.*
                                                            —José Martí

*Kill for ekwé, if it is necessary, and defend ekwé until our death.*
                                        —Second Abakuá Commandment

*Let death be welcome wherever it surprises us—as long as our war cry has reached a receptive ear, and others rush to intone the mournful song of death with the rattle of machine guns and new cries of war and victory.*
                                        —Ernesto Ché Guevara

Death permeates Cuba's historical and political imagination. The willingness to die for a political ideal or for the nation represents the highest form of patriotism and a true measure of altruism. People must be willing to sacrifice all, otherwise they cannot be taken seriously from a political standpoint.

In the nineteenth century, the forces fighting for independence did so under the banner of "Liberty or Death." This dichotomy was much more than a battle cry: It touched the deepest recesses of a shared definition of what politics is ultimately all about. The Cuban national anthem reminds every child that "to die for the fatherland is to live." The refrain has been repeated by people from completely dissimilar political perspectives. José Martí elaborated on the politicization of death throughout his writings. A patriot was the one who knew how to die and when to die. To be a Cuban, in a sense, was to be comfortable with the prospect of death. Martí proclaimed in one of his last statements, "for me the time has arrived" ("para mí ya es hora").

Offering one's life to Cuba has been a constant in politics. "¡Patria o Muerte, Venceremos!" ("Fatherland or Death, We Shall Overcome!") proclaims the revolutionary slogan. Indeed, Thanatos and politics are inseparable in Cuban political discourse. A political patriot is expected to die by his or her own hand to demonstrate purity and commitment. Young Cubans of all classes have been taught José Martí's philosophy in school, at home, and by the mass media: "Death is nothing, to die is to live, to die is to plant. The one who dies, if he dies where he ought to, serves."[76]

A willingness to die at the hand of any enemy may also require the capacity to end one's life to serve the common national good. (José Martí wrote a play, *Abdala*, that basically puts forth this view.) Under the proper circumstances, suicide is acceptable political behavior in Cuba. In a thoughtful essay, Cuban writer Guillermo Cabrera Infante concludes that "the practice of suicide is the only and, of course, definitive Cuban ideology. It is a rebel ideology—permanent rebellion by means of permanent suicide."[77]

Over the years, numerous political figures killed themselves to show that they had the best interests of the country in mind and that they held high patriotic and moral standards. Political norms expected suicide to demonstrate at times how strongly felt was one's commitment or patriotism. Among "justifiable" reasons for suicide, one could include the hopeless actions of political leaders who by their very initiative put themselves in situations that could only lead to their death. The following could be considered implicit suicides.

- José Martí, the leader of the war of independence, a civilian with no military experience, charging Spanish forces with his handful of bodyguards (1895)
- Antonio Guiteras leading a few men against Fulgencio Batista's military (1934)
- The Moncada Barracks attack in which inexperienced young men— with little knowledge of military tactics, few weapons, and no knowledge of the surrounding area—tried to seize the second-largest fortress on the island (1953)
- A similar attack against the Goicuria Barracks in which all the participants were massacred (1956)
- The attack on the presidential palace by people who had few weapons and even less knowledge of proper urban warfare (1957)
- Josué País challenging Batista's police to come out and fight in the streets of Santiago de Cuba (June 1957)

There are more explicit suicides in which the victims took their own lives, including Eduardo Chibás, leader of the Partido Ortodoxo, who killed himself as a way of "knocking at the conscience of the Cuban people" (1951); and Osvaldo Dorticós and Carlos Prío Socarrás, both former presidents (the latter died in exile, and the former died in Cuba). There are many other examples.

The politicization of death can be traced to a Hispanic-Catholic tradition in which the willingness to face death is an indication of fulfilling one's duty. The teaching of St. Augustine, "For once Christ died for our sins," was taken to heart. The ultimate sacrifice was to be willing to die. As

José Martí put it, "All great ideas have their Nazarene."[78] Martí, the man most closely identified with Cuba's ideology of nationhood and national self-determination, went on to proclaim that one should be willing to take one's life if doing so served the country's future. This prompted Félix Lizaso, in a major study on Martí, to call him a "mystic of duty" ("místico del deber").[79] Martí is hardly the exception. He drew on the Hispanic and Christian tradition in which sacrifice, particularly the ultimate sacrifice, was the highest expression of selflessness.

Implicit in the politicization of death is the view that personal interest should be sacrificed to the needs of the nation. The individual is not as important as the collectivity that will seemingly benefit from the sacrifice. This general value was elucidated by the nineteenth-century Cuban priest-philosopher Félix Varela who wrote that "when personal interest is not found in the common good of the fatherland, personal interest becomes depravity and infamy."[80]

Death, this ideology maintained, was preferable to a life of dishonor. The struggle for self-determination, even if it led to death, was more acceptable than a life without honor. In "History Will Absolve Me," Fidel Castro stated that from "heroic corpses there will rise the victorious specter of their ideals."[81] He then quoted from a poem by José Martí that he said spoke for him. The poem ended,

When one dies
In the arms of the grateful fatherland,
Death ends, prison is broken,
At last, with death, life begins!

Death has meaning if it serves a national purpose. Suicide in the Cuban context is neither anomic nor egotistical in Emile Durkheim's terms.[82] Political suicide is altruistic and is an expression of a political culture that has stressed renunciation and unquestioned abnegation. The phenomenon, Durkheim noted, could be found in societies with a high degree of social integration and solidarity. Voluntary dying as sacrifice was taught as an example by the Catholic church, although suicide was proscribed. José Martí taught otherwise. Nationalism, as the secular religion of a country struggling for independence, accepted suicide as long as it was done with a national purpose.[83]

## Conclusion

The four major components of political culture in Cuba have been fundamental operative premises in the country's intellectual tradition. The political codes had a special appeal that was not due to their powerful logic; rather, they were inseparable from the rest of the cultural milieu that prevailed among the educated. The frequency of use shows the extent to which these codes were entrenched in Cuban political culture. The regularity further demonstrates the degree to which the language and the implicit meanings had been uncritically accepted.

In using the political codes, Cubans apprehended social, economic, and political reality in dichotomous terms: old/young, corruption/purity, idealism/materialism, loyalty/betrayal, selfishness/duty. Such Manichaean thinking reflected and contributed to a polarized reality. The polarities were normative and compelled one to judge rather than to understand. Political polemics, diatribes, and manifestos readily relied on the codes. But our understanding of social reality did not benefit from them.

The search for nationhood influenced the appearance of the codes and their survival for over two centuries. The failure of U.S. policymakers to notice and penetrate the codes and their relationship to a national identity exacerbated a conflict that had deep roots elsewhere. In holding on to these codes, Cubans have shaped their concept of themselves, their relation to others, and the actions they have taken. Yet, they have done so with no self-conscious knowledge of what has transpired. They may even be condemned to act in the future on the basis of those beliefs as well.

Isaiah Berlin once noted that "the first step to understanding" is bringing to the consciousness of people the models that "dominate and penetrate their thought and action." But, he added, "like all attempts to make men aware of the categories in which they think, it is a difficult and sometimes painful activity, likely to produce disquieting results."[84] If the categories are disclosed, then the result cannot be disquieting at all.

## Notes

1. Sidney Verba, "Comparative Political Culture," in Lucian W. Pye and Sidney Verba, eds., *Political Culture and Political Development* (Princeton, N.J.: Princeton University Press, 1965), p. 513.

2. Clarence Schettler, *Public Opinion in American Society* (New York: Harper, 1960), p. 29.

3. Donald J. Devine, *The Political Culture of the United States: The Influence of Member Values on Regime Maintenance* (Boston: Little Brown and Co., 1972), p. 107.

4. Louis A. Pérez, Jr., *Cuba: Between Reform and Revolution* (New York: Oxford University Press, 1988), p. viii.

5. Luis Aguilar, *Cuba 1933: Prologue to Revolution* (Ithaca: Cornell University Press, 1972), p. 241.

6. Cited in José Kesselman, "La otra revolución cubana," *Areíto*, no. 2 (1975), p. 6.

7. In 1823 students at the San Carlos seminary issued a manifesto that mentioned the theme. See Larry R. Jensen, *Children of Colonial Despotism: Press, Politics, and Culture in Cuba, 1790-1840* (Tampa: University of South Florida Press, 1988), pp. 102–103.

8. Auguste Comte, *Cours de philosophie positive*, vol. 4 (Paris: Bachelier, Imprimour Libraire, 1939), pp. 635–639.

9. José Martí, *Antología* (Madrid: Editora Nacional, 1975), p. 331.

10. Antoni Kapcia, "Cuban Populism and the Birth of the Myth of Martí," in Christopher Abel and Nisa Torrents, eds., *José Martí, Revolutionary Democrat* (London: The Athlone Press, 1986), p. 37.

11. Enrique José Varona, *Con el eslabón* (San José, Costa Rica: n.p., 1918).

12. Jean Franco, *The Modern Culture of Latin America: Society and the Artist* (New York: Praeger, 1967), p. 51.

13. Antoni Kapcia, "Language and the Popularization of Revolutionary Ideology in Cuba," Paper presented to the conference Thirty Years of the Cuban Revolution: An Assessment, Halifax, Nova Scotia, Canada, 1989, p. 13.

14. Julián Marías, *Generations, A Historical Method* (University: University of Alabama Press, 1967), chapter 3.

15. Pérez, *Cuba*, p. 247.

16. Aguilar, *Cuba 1933*, p. 57.

17. Antonio S. Bustamante, *Las generaciones literarias* (La Habana: Imprenta Molina, 1937); Félix Lizaso, *Ensayos contemporáneos* (La Habana: Editorial Trópico, 1938); Jorge Mañach, *Pasado vigente* (La Habana: Editorial Trópico, 1939).

18. Francisco Ichaso, "Ideas y aspiraciones de la primera generación republicana," in *Historia de la Nación Cubana*, vol. 8 (La Habana: Editorial Historia de la Nación Cubana, 1952).

19. Roberto Agramonte, *José Agustín Caballero y los orígenes de la conciencia cubana* (La Habana: Universidad de la Habana, 1952), p. 2.

20. *Bohemia* (Havana), June 24, 1956, pp. 61, 96.

21. Nelson P. Valdés, "Análisis generacional: realidad, premisas y método," *Areíto*, vol. 3, no. 4 (1977), pp. 19–26.

22. On the thesis that the "new" generation remains revolutionary, see José R. Vidal Valdés, "Youth in the Cuban Society Today," Havana, unpublished manuscript, April 1990, p. 2. On the opposite point of view, see Rhoda Rabkin, "Cuba: The Aging of a Revolution," in Sergio G. Roca, ed., *Socialist Cuba: Past Interpretations and Future Challenges* (Boulder, Colo.: Westview Press, 1988), pp. 33–58.

23. Julio A. García Olivares, *José Antonio Echeverría, la lucha estudiantil contra Batista* (La Habana: Editora Política, 1979), p. 46.

24. Carlos Alonso Quejada, "Las generaciones, drama de vida y de fatalidad," *Indice*, May–June 1975, pp. 65–68.

25. Ciriaco Morón Arroyo, *El sistema de Ortega y Gasset* (Madrid: Ediciones Alcalá, 1986), pp. 286–287.

26. José A. Portuondo has written that every generation has its leader "who guides it and understands the ideal that the generation aspires to or personifies

the ideal." See "Períodos y generaciones en la historiografía literaria hispano-americana," *Cuadernos Americanos*, vol. 39, no. 3 (May–August 1948), p. 241. For a critical view, see Ricardo Jorge Machado, "Generaciones y revolución," in Francisco Fernández and José Martínez, eds., *Cuba, una revolución en marcha* (Paris: Ruedo Ibérico, 1970).

27. Julián Marías, *Obras* (Madrid: Revista de Occidente, 1951), pp. 86–87.

28. Carlos Rafael Rodríguez, *Palabras en los setenta* (La Habana: Editorial de Ciencias Sociales, 1984), pp. 151–152.

29. Armando Chávez Antúnez, "Consideraciones acerca del pensamiento ético de Félix Varela," *Universidad de la Habana*, no. 235 (1989), p. 73.

30. Félix Varela, *Lecciones de Filosofías*, vol. 1 (La Habana: Universidad de La Habana, 1961), p. 244. See also Sheldon Liss, *Roots of Revolution, Radical Thought in Cuba* (Lincoln: University of Nebraska Press, 1987), pp. 10–15.

31. Cintio Vitier, *Ese sol del mundo moral, para una eticidad cubana* (Mexico: Siglo XXI, 1975), p. 86.

32. Roberto I. Hernández Biosca, "La Edad de Oro, un contemporáneo," *Unversidad de la Habana*, no. 235 (1989), p. 109.

33. Jorge Ibarra, *José Martí, dirigente político e ideológico revolucionario* (La Habana: Editorial Ciencias Sociales, 1980), p. 216. See also José Martí, *Obras completas*, vol. 1 (La Habana: Editorial Nacional, 1963–1966), p. 101.

34. Enrique José Varona, *Conferencias filosóficas, Tercera Serie: Moral* (La Habana: O'Reilly, 1988), pp. 178–195.

35. Pérez, *Cuba*, p. 259.

36. Cited in Luis Conte Aguero, *Eduardo Chibás, el Adalid* (Mexico City: Editorial Jus, 1954), p. 629.

37. Fidel Castro, "Against the Reelection of Ramón Grau San Martín," in Rolando E. Bonachea and Nelson P. Valdés, eds., *Revolutionary Struggle, Selected Works of Fidel Castro* (Cambridge, Mass.: MIT Press, 1972), p. 132.

38. Ibid., p. 181.

39. Fidel Castro, "Critical Assessment of the Ortodoxo Party," in Bonachea and Valdés, *Revolutionary Struggle*, p. 153.

40. Fidel Castro, "The Cuban Revolution," in ibid., p. 158.

41. Fidel Castro, "Grau Will Suffer a Shameful Defeat," in ibid., p. 133.

42. *Granma*, September 20, 1970, p. 3.

43. Cited in John M. Kirk, *Between God and the Party, Religion and Politics in Revolutionary Cuba* (Tampa: University of South Florida Press, 1989), p. 122.

44. Michael Harrington, *The Twilight of Capitalism* (New York: Simon and Schuster, 1976), p. 177.

45. This is an example of a dominant paradigm in politics. On paradigms, see Robert W. Friedrichs, *A Sociology of Sociology* (New York: Free Press, 1970).

46. Clifford Geertz, *Local Knowledge, Further Essays in Interpretive Anthropology* (New York: Basic Books, 1983), p. 58.

47. Nelson P. Valdés, "Entrevista al historiador cubano Manuel Moreno Fraginals," *Boletín Reunión*, no. 158 (August 1984), pp. 2–5.

48. See as an example of this the work by Jorge Ibarra, *Un análisis psicosocial del cubano: 1895–1925* (La Habana: Editorial de Ciencias Sociales, 1985). This is, nonetheless, a sensitive and creative contribution to a cultural analysis of Cuba.

49. Louis A. Pérez, Jr., *Cuba Between Empires, 1878–1902* (Pittsburgh: University of Pittsburgh Press, 1983), p. 385.

50. See Alberto Lamar Schwyer, *La crisis del patriotismo* (La Habana: Editorial Martí, 1929), Jorge Mañach, *Indagación del choteo* (La Habana: Editorial Lex, 1936), and Fernando Ortiz, *La decadencia cubana* (La Habana: La Universal, 1924).

51. Ambrosio Fornet, "Nota a la primera edición," in Raúl Roa, *La revolución del 30 se fue a bolina* (La Habana: Editorial de Ciencias Sociales, 1976), p. 9.

52. "Manifesto al País," in Hortensia Pichardo, ed., *Documentos para la Historia de Cuba*, vol. 4 (La Habana: Editorial de Ciencias Sociales, 1980), p. 220.

53. Conte Aguero, *Eduardo Chibás*, and Enrique Vignier and Guillermo Alonso, *La corrupción administrativa en Cuba, 1944–1952* (La Habana: Instituto del Libro, 1963).

54. Fidel Castro, "I Accuse," in Bonachea and Valdés, *Revolutionary Struggle*, p. 143.

55. Fidel Castro, "Brief to the Court of Appeals," in ibid., p. 149.

56. Fidel Castro, "Against Everyone!" in ibid., p. 300.

57. Fidel Castro, "General Strike Proclamation," in ibid., p. 449.

58. Fulgencio Batista, *Cuba Betrayed* (New York: Vantage Press, 1962).

59. José Suárez Núñez, *El gran culpable* (Caracas: n.p., 1963).

60. Rubén Darío Rumbaut, *La revolución traicionada* (Miami: Frente Democrático Revolucionario, 1962).

61. Manuel Antonio de Varona, *El drama de Cuba o la revolución traicionada* (Buenos Aires: Editorial Marymar, 1960).

62. Fermín Peinado, *Beware Yankee: The Revolution in Cuba* (Miami: n.p., 1961), and Mario Llerena, who wrote, "Castro's betrayal became manifest from 1960 on," in his *The Unsuspected Revolution, the Birth and Rise of Castroism* (Ithaca, N.Y.: Cornell University Press, 1978), p. 44.

63. Mario Lazo, *Dagger in the Heart, American Policy Failures in Cuba* (New York: Funk and Wagnalls, 1968).

64. J. A. Acuña, *Cuba: revolución traicionada* (Montevideo, 1962).

65. Jaime Suchlicki, *University Students and Revolution in Cuba* (Miami: University of Miami Press, 1969), p. 96.

66. Fidel Castro, "Discurso del 2 de Enero," *Revolución*, January 3, 1961, p. 2.

67. Pedro Miret, *Causa 1/89, Fin de la conexión cubana* (La Habana: Editorial José Martí, 1989), pp. 405–407.

68. Cited in Liz Balmaseda, "The Ironic Diplomacy of Armando Valladares," *Miami Herald*, October 7, 1990, p. H1.

69. U.S. State Department, *Cuba*, Inter-American Series, no. 66 (Washington, D.C., 1961).

70. Theodore Draper, *Castro's Revolution: Myths and Realities* (New York: Praeger, 1965), p. 20. See also Draper's "Castro's Cuba: A Revolution Betrayed?" *Encounter*, March 1961, pp. 6–23.

71. A methodological challenge of the thesis can be found in Samuel Farber, *Revolution and Reaction in Cuba, 1933–1960, A Political Sociology from Machado to Castro* (Middletown, Conn.: Wesleyan University Press, 1976), p. 15.

72. Antonio de la Carrera, "Castro's Counter-Revolution," *New Politics*, vol. 2, no. 1 (Fall 1962), p. 87.

73. Hugh Thomas, "Middle Class Politics and the Cuban Revolution," in Claudio Véliz, ed., *The Politics of Conformity in Latin America* (Oxford: Oxford University Press, 1967), p. 277.

74. Carlos Rafael Rodríguez, "Sobre la contribución del Ché al desarrollo de la economía cubana," *Cuba Socialista*, vol. 8, no. 3 (May–June 1988), p. 10.

75. Jorge Más Canosa, the most powerful exiled political leader in Miami, recently faced his brother in court over business matters. Each brother accused the other of "treason." See Pedro Sevcec, "Más Canosa se enfrenta a su hermano en corte," *Nuevo Herald*, October 24, 1990, pp. 1a, 5a.

76. Cited in Vitier, *Ese sol del mundo moral*, p. 86.

77. Guillermo Cabrera Infante, "Entre la historia y la nada (Notas sobre una ideología del suicidio)," *Escandalar*, vol. 5, no. 1–2 (January–June 1982), p. 83.

78. Cited in Vitier, *Ese sol del mundo moral*, p. 122.

79. Félix Lizaso, *Martí: Martyr of Cuban Independence* (Westport, Conn.: Greenwood Press, 1974).

80. Chávez Antúnez, "Consideraciones acerca del pensamiento ético de Félix Varela," pp. 73–93.

81. Fidel Castro, "History Will Absolve Me," in Bonachea and Valdés, *Revolutionary Struggle*, p. 205.

82. Cabrera Infante suggests that political suicides in Cuba are of the "egotistic" type. Ibarra, on the other hand, asserts that they are anomic. On each type, see Emile Durkheim, *Suicide* (Glencoe, Ill.: Free Press, 1951).

83. Florence W. Kaslow, "Suicide—Causation, Indicators and Interventions," *Journal of Sociology and Social Welfare*, vol. 3, part 1 (1975), pp. 60–81.

84. Isaiah Berlin, "Does Political Theory Still Exist?" in Peter Laslett and W. G. Runciman, eds., *Philosophy, Politics and Society* (Oxford: Basil Blackwell, 1962), p. 19.

# About the Book

Cuba is experiencing the most difficult dilemma of its revolutionary period: Although the leaders increasingly recognize the need for reform, they remain dedicated to the revolution's goals and ideals. Yet, with the fall of the former socialist bloc, the disintegration of the Soviet Union, and the introduction of a mixed economy in China, Cuba's ability to pursue its socialist path has become increasingly precarious and the future of its revolution uncertain.

This book addresses the crisis facing Cuba's political system, its economy, and its society. In the first section, the contributors provide a detailed analysis of the nature of participatory democracy in a revolutionary context. In the second section, the contributors examine Cuba's economic prospects in a rapidly changing international environment. The book concludes with a series of studies of the texture of life for average Cubans, emphasizing issues of class and gender. Together these contributions provide a thoughtful and critical analysis of the problems and potential of the western hemisphere's only socialist nation.

# About the Editors
# and Contributors

**Max Azicri** is professor of political science at Edinboro University of Pennsylvania. He has written extensively on Cuban society and its politics, legal system, and international relations. His most recent study is *Cuba: Politics, Economics, and Society* (1988).

**Carollee Bengelsdorf** is professor of politics and feminist studies at Hampshire College, Amherst, Massachusetts. She has published works on women in Cuba as well as on questions of state and society relationships in socialist society. Her forthcoming *Between Vision and Reality: Marxism and the Problem of Democracy in Cuba* (1991) reflects her broader interest in problems of democracy and socialism in both the Marxist theoretical legacy and in socialist societies. Currently she is engaged in a collaborative study of the Cuban family.

**Sandor Halebsky** is professor of sociology at Saint Mary's University in Halifax, Nova Scotia, Canada. He has published studies on issues of political conflict and on urban society. Most recently he coedited *Cuba: Twenty-Five Years of Revolution, 1959–1984* (1985) and *Transformation and Struggle: Cuba Faces the 1990s* (1990).

**Richard L. Harris** is a coordinating editor of the journal *Latin American Perspectives*. He has written widely on Latin America, including his coedited *Nicaragua: A Revolution under Siege* (1985) and his *Marxism, Socialism, and Democracy in Latin America* (1992). His current and long-term research interests have been on questions of revolutionary political change, democratization, and debureaucratization in the Third World.

**Gareth Jenkins** is an economic consultant based in London. He has worked on problems of East-West trade since the late 1970s, including preparing many studies for Cuban foreign trade enterprises. Since 1987 he has published the newsletter *Cuba Business*. His contribution to this volume is part of a longer forthcoming study to be published by the Center for Caribbean Studies, University of Warwick, U.K., at which he is a visiting fellow.

**John M. Kirk** is professor of Spanish and Latin American studies at Dalhousie University in Halifax, Nova Scotia, Canada. He has written on Latin American literature and culture, the church in Cuba, and José Martí. His work includes coedited volumes such as *Cuba: Twenty-Five Years of Revolution, 1959–1984* (1985), *Transformation and Struggle: Cuba Faces the 1990s* (1990), and *Cuban Foreign Policy Confronts the New International Order* (1991). He wrote *José Martí, Mentor of the Cuban Nation* (1983) and *Between God and the Party: Religion and Politics in Revolutionary Cuba* (1989).

**Sheryl L. Lutjens** is assistant professor of political science at Northern Arizona University. She is interested in questions of power, participation, and democratization, especially under conditions of socialist transition. She is currently studying the Cuban educational system and has coedited *Cuba: 1953–1978: A Bibliographic Guide to the Literature* (1986).

**Gayle L. McGarrity** was born in Chicago of native American and mixed West Indian descent. She is currently completing her doctoral dissertation in anthropology at the University of California, Berkeley. In the early 1980s she was a graduate student at the Institute of Public Health in Havana. Her research interests include issues of race, class, and ethnicity in Latin America and medical anthropology. Her contribution to the present volume is part of a larger research study.

**Morris H. Morley** is a lecturer in politics at Macquarie University in Sydney, Australia. He has written extensively on U.S. activities and policies in regard to Latin America. He is author of *Imperial State: The United States and Revolution and Cuba, 1952–1986* (1987), editor of *Crisis and Confrontation: Ronald Reagan's Foreign Policy* (1988), and coauthor of *United States Hegemony Under Siege: Class Politics and Development in Latin America* (1990).

**James F. Petras** is professor of sociology at the State University of New York at Binghamton. He has published extensively on Latin America, especially on issues of development, class, the state, and U.S. policies. He is author of *Latin America: Bankers, Generals, and the Struggle for Social Justice* (1986) and co-author of *United States Hegemony Under Siege: Class Politics and Development in Latin America* (1990).

**Archibald R.M. Ritter** is professor of economics in the Norman Paterson School of International Affairs at Carleton University, Ottawa, Canada, and a former president of the Canadian Association of Latin American and Caribbean Studies. He has written on the Cuban economy for many years, including *The Economic Development of Revolutionary Cuba: Strategy and Performance* (1974). His most recent research has analyzed Cuban economic performance and prospects.

**Sergio G. Roca** is professor of economics at Adelphi University, Garden City, New York. His articles on Cuban economic issues have appeared in various professional journals. He recently edited the volume *Socialist Cuba: Past Interpretations and Future Challenges* (1988).

**Marguerite G. Rosenthal** is currently director of the School of Social Work at Salem State College in Massachusetts. Her research interests include social welfare history, comparative social welfare, and policies affecting women and children. Her contribution to the present volume is part of a larger research study on social welfare policies and women.

**Lois M. Smith** is a writer and researcher on Latin America whose interests center on gender, culture, and sexuality. Her articles and reviews have appeared in various professional journals. She recently completed a coauthored book-length study, *Women in Revolutionary Cuba.*

**Jean Stubbs** is coordinator of the Joint Caribbean Studies Program of the Latin America Institute of Commonwealth Studies and Latin American Studies at the University of London. A British historian who has lived in Cuba for over twenty years, her recent publications include *Tobacco on the Periphery: A Case Study in Cuban Labor History, 1860–1958* (1985) and *Cuba: The Test of Time* (1989). She is currently organizing, with a number of colleagues, a research project on pan-Caribbean alternate development strategies for the 1990s.

**Nelson P. Valdés** is professor of sociology at the University of New Mexico. He is also director of the Latin America Data Base at that university. A long-time student of Cuban affairs, he has published works on health, women, and bureaucracy in Cuba. He coedited *Revolutionary Struggle, 1947–1958, Selected Writings of Fidel Castro* (1972) and *Cuba in Revolution* (1973). He is currently writing a book on Santería and political culture in Cuba.

**Andrew Zimbalist** is professor of economics at Smith College. He has written extensively on the Cuban economy and comparative economic systems. He has published a number of books, and is coeditor of *Cuba's Socialist Economy Toward the 1990s* (1987) and editor of *Cuba's Political Economy: Controversies in Cubanology* (1988) and is coauthor of *The Cuban Economy: Measurement and Analysis of Socialist Performance* (1989).

# Index

235